WOMEN AND PROFESSIONAL DEVELOPMENT IN INDIA

WOMEN AND PROFESSIONAL DEVELOPMENT IN INDIA

Rajiv Sagar

CYBER TECH PUBLICATIONS
4264/3, Ansari Road, Daryaganj, New Delhi-110002 (India)
Ph.: 011-23244078, 011-43559448 Fax: 011-23280028
E-Mail: cyberpublicationsdelhi@yahoo.com
Website: www.cybertechpublications.com

WOMEN AND PROFESSIONAL DEVELOPMENT IN INDIA

Rajiv Sagar

First Edition 2010

Asian Offset Printer

Published by :

G.S. Rawat for **Cyber Tech Publications**
4264/3, Ansari Road, Daryaganj, New Delhi-110002 (India)
Ph.: 011-23244078, 011-43559448 Fax: 011-23280028
E-Mail: cyberpublicationsdelhi@yahoo.com
Website: www.cybertechpublications.com

Preface

Women should have more facilities for education, applied sciences, professional courses and training and more career prospects and avenues of employment. Women have now certainly got a status in society. Although women have joined almost every profession in our country and most of them are doing excellent work. But everything does not stop there. She has to fight hard to retain her position and make people realise the worth of her skills.

Economic independence is essential for the personality development of woman and for providing economic support to her family. It gives her confidence, liberty, identity, security, a status and a feeling of sharing the economic needs of the household. Much work is needed on the social front for the harmonious development of the position of women in our society.

Social evils like girl abuse, women abuse, dowry deaths, sati, gender discrimination etc are painful realities of our society. We have to deal with these problems seriously and sincerely. The dominant nature of the male in our society is one of the major factors to be sublimated to the spirit of equality. Girls should not be considered an unwanted burden, liability and problem. They need equal attention and loving treatment for the mental and physical development of their personality.

We need more opportunities for the development of women entrepreneurship in the socio-economic, industrial and commercial spheres so that women can play a definite role in the economic development of the country and contribute significantly in the task of nation building.

—Author

CONTENTS

1

Introduction

Developmental policies and programmes that do not address gender disparities miss critical developmental opportunities. Education of girls is vital not only on grounds of social justice but also because it accelerates social transformation. Promotion of gender equality in education is essential for human resource development. By educating a woman you educate the whole family. Given that a woman has the responsibility of the whole family on herself, an educated woman is better capable of taking care of the health, nutrition and education of her children and more so be an active agent in the social and economic development of the country. It is evident that economic success everywhere is based on educational success. Literacy is the basic building block of education. It is a basic component of social cohesion and national identity. It leads to an improvement in the depth and quality of public opinion, as well as to more active participation of the marginalized in the democratic process. No society has ever liberated itself economically, politically, or socially without a sound base of educated women. Education has a direct impact on women empowerment as it creates in them awareness about their rights, their capabilities and the choices and opportunities available to them. Studies have indicated that there is a strong correlation between female education and several developmental indicators such as increased economic productivity, improvement in health, delayed age at marriage, lower fertility, increased political participation, and effective investments in the next generation

The progress of women's education since the introduction of planned development in the country. After India became independent the first governmental act to organise the education system in the light of independence was the setting up of the University Education Commission, headed by Prof. S. Radhakrishnan to 'suggest improvements and extensions that may be desirable to suit the requirements of the country'. The Commission covered the problems of admission, length and contact of courses, the relation between teaching and research, examination, student discipline, teachers' service conditions etc. Widely acclaimed, the report of the Commission on the issue of women's education referred that: "Women's present education is entirely irrelevant to the life they have to lead. It is not only a waste but often a definite disability". "The present system of women's education, based as it is upon men's needs, does not in any way make them fit for coping with the problems of daily life". "The modern educated Indian women is neither happy nor contented nor socially useful. She is a misfit in life. She is highly suppressed, and needs opportunities for self- expression. The new education must provide this opportiinity".

POLICIES AND PROGRAMMES IN INDIA

In India, providing education to all the citizens is a constitutional commitment. The principal of gender equality is enshrined in the Indian constitution, in its Preamble, Fundamental Rights, Fundamental Duties and Directive Principals. The Constitution not only guarantees equality to women, but also empowers the State to adopt measures of positive discrimination in favour of women. Just after Independence, in 1951, literacy levels were very iow (25% for men and 9% for women), In the next ten years there was not much progress in the literacy levels. It is only after the recommendations of the Indian education commission (1964) and the National policy of education (1968) that the education of girls was seen as a means of accelerating social transformation. The policy placed special emphasis on initiating programmes to give equal educational opportunities to all the groups and both sexes. The constitution also gave primary responsibility for elementary education to the state governments, while the central government was given responsibility for technical and higher education. This situation changed in 1976 after the 42nd Amendment to the constitution was passed, making all education the joint responsibility of the central and state governments. One of the consequences of this was that the foreign assistance, so far restricted to technical and higher education, now began to flow into primary education as well. Between the mid-1960 and the early 1980s, the proportion of resources going into elementary education showed a steady increase. National Policy on Education (NPE), 1986 and its Programme of Action (POA) gave high priority to gender equality and committed the entire educational system to work for Women Development in Information.... The National Perspective Plan 1988-2000 reiterates this point of view and states that women themselves must overcome their handicaps. Thus, there has been a careful articulation of education for equality for women, which is reflected in the educational policy discourse.

Central and State governments attached lot of significance to actually operationalising the NPE's Programme of Action and in a series of regional meetings with the State Governments, a special review of gender issues in education was undertaken. At the same time it was emphasized to the States, that gender concerns must be built into all educational processes. Monitoring committees for women's/girls' education at the Ministry of Human Resource Development level and also state level were formed to monitor the indicators of gender concerns in all policies and projects. Emphasis was laid on enrolment and retention of the girl child in formal and non formal schooling; recruitment of rural women teachers and removal of gender bias in the curriculum.

Mass literacy campaigns in different parts of India were launched which brought out volunteers from all sections of society as instructors, master trainers and organizers. Adult Education Programmes, Total Literacy Campaigns, Post Literacy Programmes, and continuing Education Programmes were also started. Nation wide gender sensitization programmes were undertaken to cover a large number of educational personnel to include educational administrators, teachers and teacher educators. Complementary to this strategy, media campaigns and parental awareness programmes for generating a positive climate for girls' education were also started. Mobilization of women's groups and projects like Mahila Samakhya (Education for Women's Equality) with focus on the constraints that had so far prevented women and girls from accessing educational inputs were launched. The purpose of these groups was to address issues of self image and self confidence of women and alter societal perception about them. Its overall goal was to create circumstances to enable women to better understand their predicament, to move from a state of abject disempowerment towards a situation in which they could determine their own lives and influence their environment, and simultaneously create for themselves and their family an educational opportunity which enhanced the process of development.

The Constitution introduced in 1950 included a number of important provisions which had direct and indirect bearing on education.

After two years the country entered into a new era of planned development through the Five Year Plans. The First Five Year Plan visualised education as the vehicle for the successful achievement of planned development. Deriving lessons from the University Education Commission's recommendations on women's education the Ist Plan stated that "everyone realises the significance of the problem of women's education in the special circumstances of our country today and the need for adopting social measures for solving it. The general purpose and objective of women's education can not of course be different from the purpose and objective of men's education. There are, however, vital differences in the way in which this purpose has to be realized."

The commencement of Ist Plan coincided with the appointment of Secondary Education Commission headed by A. Mudaliar. Mention may be made here, that the government constituted special commissions for university education and secondary education to go into the details of problems and hurdles and suggest ways and means to remove them but till now no special Commission has been constituted to enquire the problems of elementary education which is the most important stage for the educational development in terms of both quality and quantity.

The secondary education commission on the issue of girls education stated interalia "in a democratic society where all citizens have to discharge their civic and social obligations, differences which may lead to variations in the standard of intellectual development achieved by boys and girls can not be envisaged".

A National Committee on Women's Education was appointed by the Government in 1958 to go into the difficulties that hindered the progress of girl's education and to make recommendations in order to bring girls' educational par with the boys. The Committee had recommended several measures which were generally accepted by the Government. In essence these measures were: top priority for the expansion of girls education at the elementary stage; campaign against the traditional prejudices against girls education; appointment of women teachers; on demand separate schools for girls at higher secondary stage; incentives, special central assistance to all states till 80 per cant of girls in the age group 6-11 are enrolled; parity between boys and girls be reached as soon as possible; earmarking special fund by UGC for higher education of women; and establishment of National Council for Women's Education. The Government appointed another Committee on differentiation of curricula for boys and girls in 1963.

The Committee proposed common curricula for both boys and girls up to primary stage. The Committee also recommended a core curricula of home-science for both sexes at the middle stage and inclusion of crafts or handiwork or productive labour on the general courses at the secondary level.

A year later the Bhaktavaslam Committee was appointed to look into the causes for the lack of public support particularly in rural areas for girl's education and to enlist public cooperation. The Committee after going into details of the causes suggested interalia "the strategy for the development of the education of girls and women will have to take two forms. The first is to emphasise the special, programmes recommended by the National Committee on Women's Education and the second is to give attention to the education of girls at all stages and in all sectors as an integral part of the general programmes for the expansion and improvement of education".

The Education Commission (1964-66) which discussed at great length almost all aspects of education, on the issue of women's education endorsed all recommendations made by the previous Committees on girls education. In addition the Commission recommended that "education of women should be regarded as a major programmes for some years to come and bold and determined effort should be made to face difficulties involved and to close the existing gap between the education of men and women in as short a time as possible......".

Based on the broad recommendations of the Education Commission the Government declared a National Policy on Education in 1968 whose aim was to achieve "economic and cultural development of the country for national integration and for realising the ideal of a socialistic pattern of society".

The policy committed for a continuous effort for the expansion and equalization of educational opportunity, sustained effort to raise quality, emphasis on development of science and technology and cultivation of moral and social values. Regarding girls education the policy stated "the education of girls should receive emphasis not only on grounds of social justice but also because it accelerates social transformation".

Despite these efforts the Committee on the Status of women in India in 1975 identified that in 1971, about 68 per cent of the total number of women in the age group 15-25 years and nearly 87 per cent in the age group of 25 years and above were illiterate. The significant point to be noted according to the Committee report was that although the enrollment has increased at a faster rate but the rate of increase in literacy is rather slow. On the basic issues of non-enrolment wastage, drop-out and non-retention the Committee observed that in classes I to V one girl out of every three in the age group 6-11 years is out of school and one girl out of every five in the age group 11-14 years is in the school. The drop-out rate among girls is very high. Of every 100 girls enrolled in class I only about 30 reach class V. The problem of non-retention, wastage and stagnation are therefore found to be much higher among girls. The Committee was of the view Report of Committee to look into the causes for lack of public support, particularly in rural areas for Girls Education and to enlist Public Support and Cooperation, Government of India, 1965.

The year 1975 must be regarded as a watershed when rethinking on women's issues started when United Nationals declared 1975-85 as women's decade. The year coincided with the publication of the report of the Committee on the status of women in India, the findings of this report provided shock to many people. Most of the recommendations made by the Committee were accepted by the Empowered Commttee and thus were incorporated into the National Plan of Action for women.

The post '75 phase saw more official concern towards improving women's access to

education. The draft sixth Five Year Plan (1978-83) prepared by the Janata Government took a very critical view of the education structure existing so far. The plan mentioned that the benefits from the education system failed to reach majority of population due to "inadequate principle of national education policy". The plan envisaged to change in the priorities in order to bring everyone into the fold of education system. Eradication of illiteracy and promotion of adult education programmes and more emphasis on universalization were given priority on the educational front. In fact these were the issues mostly affecting girls and women. When the Government at the Centre changed in a span of 30 months the new Government incorporated most of these issues on priority basis in the Sixth Plan Document.

Thus the Sixth Five Year Plan (1980-85) emphasized eradication of illiteracy, universal primary education and introduction of job-orientation. The plan for the first time include a chapter on "Women and Development" which deals with the issues of education, health and employment of women. On the issues of education, efforts were directed towards higher enrollment and retention of girls in schools, income generating work for girls outside the school hours to supplement the family income, increase in the number of women teachers specially in the rural areas, construction of residential quarters for women teachers, strengthening science teaching in girls" schools and colleges, streaming the admission policy to promote greater enrollment of women in professional courses like engineering, electronics, agriculture, veterinary science, pisciculture and forestry, expansion of functional literacy programmes specially in areas having low female literacy, special non-formal educational programme for girls in the age groups 15-20 years who could not complete formal schooling earlier, construction of more hostels for women belonging to backward classes and "instead of increasing separate women's polytechnics for imparting training in arts, crafts etc. co-educational institutions would encouraged as far as possible".

The Seventh Plan 1986-90 by and large envisages similar measures. Resume of the Recommendations of the Committee on the Status of Women in India and views of the Empowered Committee Thereon, Government of India. Ministry of Education and Social Welfare, 1976.

Female literacy rate has improved from 7.95 per cent to 24.82 per cent between 1951 to 1981. The decadal growth rates and changes in the sex ratio among literates at the national level during this period is indicated in the table give below. The table indicates that while the decadal growth rate in female literacy is higher as compared to males, the trend shows a steep decline for both sexes:

More than three decades of planned development, in addition to several committees and commissions recommendation, the data on education indicates widening gender gap in access to knowledge. The number of female illiterates show a faster rate of increase from 161.9 million in 1951 to 185-2 million in 1961, to 215.3 million in 1971 and 241.6 million in 1981 (figures are inclusive of 0-4 age group). During this period the number illiterate males increased from 137 million to 198 million. What is more disturbing is that this gender gap in literacy instead of narrowing in increasing at a faster rate although this was minimal during the colonial period. Till 1931 for every 1000 illiterate men there were 1058 illiterate women which jumped to 1138 in 1951, to 1250 in 1961, to 1248 in 1971 and to 1322 in 1981 (figures inclusive of 0-4 age group).

"An analysis of illiteracy data is an important indicator of changes in women's access to the educational process and the reduction of the gender gap because it helps to prevent any attitude of complacency and identifies a new problem of widening gender gap amongst the illiterate population.

Recognition of this widening gap has resulted in some special efforts to increase the enrollment of women in adult education centres during the last few years. According to the Monitoring Report of the Directorate of Adult Education Centre in the first quarter of 1983 shows a marked improvement over the situation reviewed in 1980 when women constituted only 35.7 per cent of the total number enrolled in such centres. The position has improved further and by the end of December, 1984, the percentage coverage of adult women in these centres was 52.23 of the total coverage."

Significantly, the table indicates that the states where female literacy is high the gender gap in access to literacy is also high. Kerala where female literacy is highest followed by Tamil Nadu, Maharashtra are some of such examples in contrast to the states where female literacy is very low. The sex ratio of illiterates is also relatively low. Enrollment

The enrollment figures indicate that the gulf between boys and girls continue at a high proportion. The table give below indicates that nearly 30 per cent girls of 6-ll years age group and nearly 62 per cent girls of 11-14 years age group were not enrolled till the end of 1984-84. The figures for boys, for the same year here a cent per cent enrollment in the 6-11 age group and nearly 34 per cent non-enrolled in 11-14 age group, What is more intriguing is the fact that the rate of girls enrollment is increasing at much slower rate than that of boys. It is important to note here that the Planning

Commission targets by themselves provide for a big gap between boys and girls enrollment at the elementary stage. An official document indicates that by the end of 1984-85, the proportion of girls out of schools in the age group 6-11 years is nearly 50 per cent in Uttar Pradesh and Rajasthan, nearly 40 per cent in Bihar, 36 per cent in Jammu & Kashmir, in the age group 11-14 years only in the states of Himachal Pradesh, Kerala, Manipur, Punjab, Tamil Nadu Tripura and West Bengal more than 50 per cent girls are enrolled in schools. All other states have less than 50 per cent in the schools.

WOMEN IN MODERN INDIA

Modern India wittnessed improvements in the Status of Women There were many women reformers who worked for the betterment and upliftment of their other female counterparts.The begum of Bhopal discarded the purdah and fought in the revolt of 1857.

Many reformers like Ishwarchandra Vidyasagar, Jyotiba Phule with his wife Savitribai Phule undertook various measures to eradicate social stigmas from the society. Sir Sayyed Ahmad Khan established the Aligarh Muslim University for the spread of education among the Muslims. He also abolished the purdah system among muslim women. Many Acts were passed for the upliftment of women among those Widow Remarraige Act of 1856 was important.

In the modern times, Indian women were given liberties and rights such as freedom of expression and equality, as well as right to get education. But still today, we are fighting for crisis such as dowry, female infanticide, sex selective abortions, health, domestic violence, etc.

Women today are educated but illiterate in terms of knowing their rights properly.Another harmful practise is the Dowry system where gift of money or valuables given by the bride's family to the groom's at the time of their marriage. This is the new harrasment in the name of wedding gift. Women are killed if they bring less dowry after marriage. The term Bride Burning is criticized within India itself.

India has a low sex ratio, the chief reason being that many child die before reaching adulthood.They are aboted in the womb itself as many people do not want a girl child because they cannot pay dowry.

This is a vicious circle which is linked to one another.It is somewhere a criticism that highest female ratio lies in Kerala and Tribal societies in India knowing the fact that tribal communities have far lower levels of income, literacy and health facilities.Female infanticide (killing of girl infants) is still prevalent in some rural areas. Dowry has been one of the main reasons for female infanticides in India.

The level of Domestic violence is also high in India.Husbands beat their wifes in a drunken state to get rid of their frustration. Domestic violence is also prevalent because of 'dowry'. Trafficking is also a big reason for female abuse.

Trafficking means girls are sold to big people for satisfying their sexual needs or kidnapped to make them prostitutes. In many rural families, girls and women face nutritional discrimination within the family, and are anaemic and malnourished.

The maternal mortality in India is the second highest in the world. Only a few percentage of births in the country are supervised by doctors. Most women deliver with the help of traditional nurses in the village who often lack the skills and resources to save the mother's life if it is in danger. Women suffer many health problems because of abuse and other mal-nourishments.

The average Indian woman has little control over her own fertility and reproductive health. So women today in short are suffering from various other problems but still thanks to the reformer's like Jyotiba Phule, Dayanand Saraswati, Swami Vivekanand that they still can live to an extent on their own & fight for their Rights

The persistence of hunger and abject poverty in India and other parts of the world is due in large measure to the subjugation, marginalization and disempowerment of women. Women suffer from hunger and poverty in greater numbers and to a great degree then men. At the same time, it is women who bear the primary responsibility for actions needed to end hunger: education, nutrition, health and family income.

Looking through the lens of hunger and poverty, there are seven major areas of discrimination against women in India:

- *Malnutrition*: India has exceptionally high rates of child malnutrition, because tradition in India requires that women eat last and least throughout their lives, even when pregnant and lactating. Malnourished women give birth to malnourished children, perpetuating the cycle.
- *Poor Health*: Females receive less health care than males. Many women die in childbirth of easily prevented complications. Working conditions and environmental pollution further impairs women's health.
- *Lack of education*: Families are far less likely to educate girls than boys, and far more likely to pull them out of school, either to help out at home or from fear of violence.
- *Overwork*: Women work longer hours and their work is more arduous than men's, yet their work is unrecognized. Men report that "women, like children, eat and do nothing." Technological progress in agriculture has had a negative impact on women.
- *Unskilled*: In women's primary employment sector-agriculture-extension services overlook women.
- *Mistreatment*: In recent years, there has been an alarming rise in atrocities against women in India, in terms of rapes, assaults and dowry-related murders. Fear of violence suppresses the aspirations of all women. Female infanticide and sex-selective abortions are additional forms of violence that reflect the devaluing of females in Indian society.

- *Powerlessness*: While women are guaranteed equality under the constitution, legal protection has little effect in the face of prevailing patriarchal traditions. Women lack power to decide who they will marry, and are often married off as children. Legal loopholes are used to deny women inheritance rights.

India has a long history of activism for women's welfare and rights, which has increasingly focused on women's economic rights. A range of government programs have been launched to increase economic opportunity for women, although there appear to be no existing programs to address the cultural and traditional discrimination against women that leads to her abject conditions.

It is said that women enjoyed equal status with men in all fields of life in ancient India. In the early Vedic period women were educated. We can see this in the works of Grammarians such as 'Patanjali' & 'Katyayana'. Women got married at a mature age and were also free to select their husbands. Scriptures such as Rig Veda and Upanishads mention many women sages and seers, notably Gargi and Maitreyi.

There are some kingdoms in ancient India, which had customs such as 'nagarvadhu' i.e. the bride of the city. According to this custom women competed to win the prestigious title of 'nagarvadhu'. Amrapali is the most famous example of a 'nagarvadhu'. Women in fact had superior position than their male counterparts. It is truly in this period that women were really treated as Durga and Parvati.

There was a special thread ceremony in which girls were tied threads of honour based on merit. Later this ceremony was replaced by 'child-marriage'. Child-Marriage by this time was started on a large scale because of many holy books. Girls were married when they were infants.

They were send to their husbands house when they attained puberty. Girls were not permitted to gain education. Although many Jain institutions admitted girls but it was of no use as only few number of girls attended these institutes.

WOMEN IN MEDIEVAL INDIA

The condition of Women in society was deteriorated more during the medieval period. At this point of time child-marriage, sati, female infanticide was practiced largely. The Muslim seclusion in India introduced the 'purdah' system by and large on Muslim women. These women were also forced to practice 'zenana'.

The Rajput women of Rajasthan who are known to place a high premium on honour practiced 'jauhar'. Jauhar refers to the practice of the voluntary immolation of all the wives and daughters of defeated warriors, in order to avoid capture and consequent molestation by the enemy. Polygamy i.e. husband marrying more than once was practised by most Hindu Kshatriyas. At the same time many women excelled in arts, literature, music. Women were also rulers in the medival period. Some of the great women rulers were Razia Sultan, the only women monarch to rule the throne of Delhi.

The Gond queen Durgavati ruled for fifteen long years, before she lost the battle to mughal emperor Akbar's general Asaf Ali. Chand Bibi also fought the mughals in 1590's. Nur Jehan the only mughal women ruler is still today considered the most effective ruler.

Inspite of all these successful women the condition of a poor Indian women was the same. At this time, girls were married at an early age say 5-6 years. Sati was also practised where women were forced to jump in the burning funeral of their dead husband.

Purdah was practised among muslim women i.e. to cover their heads fully with a 'veil'. Devdasi was prevalent in south India where girls were married to deity or trees. This practise had destoyed the lives of many girls as they were physically molested and sexually exploited by many pundits.

THE INEXTRICABLE LINK

The greatest tragedy facing humanity today is the persistence of chronic hunger-an intolerable phenomenon that takes the lives of 24,000 of us every day. For fully one-fifth of humanity, life is a daily struggle to survive in conditions of relentless poverty. Day after day, the lives of one billion individuals are cut short or terribly diminished by chronic, persistent hunger. Day after day, one billion people are denied the opportunities they need to lead healthy and productive lives.

People living with chronic hunger exist in conditions of severe poverty. What they lack is the chance to change their situation, to develop their own self-sufficiency. The most potent confirmation of this fact can be seen in the lives of women. They, along with their children, are the main victims of hunger, and they are also most lacking in opportunities to end their own and their families' hunger.

The Hunger Project has come to the recognition that the persistence of hunger in India-and elsewhere in the world where hunger is still an overriding social issue-is, to a large degree, due to the subjugation, marginalization and disempowerment of women. Furthermore, women's suppression is rooted in the very fabric of Indian society-in traditions, in religious doctrine and practices, within the educational and legal systems, and within families.

Ironically, much of the essential work of ending hunger rests in women's hands.

Traditionally, women bear primary responsibility for the well-being of their families. Yet they are systematically denied access to the resources they need to fulfill their responsibility, which includes education, health care services, job training, and access and freedom to use family planning services.

In order to gain a shared understanding of the condition of the status of women in India and its impact on the persistence of hunger, this document surveys papers done by leading scholars in Indian development issues.

It is organized in a framework of seven issues that characterize the plight of resource-poor women, with a focus on rural women, in India: malnutrition, poor health, lack of education, overwork, lack of skills, mistreatment and powerlessness.

The link between these issues and the persistence of hunger in India was underscored in a 1996 study: The Asian Enigma, by Vulimiri Ramalingaswami:

> *In short, the poor care that is afforded to girls and women by their husbands and by elders is the first major reason for levels of child malnutrition that are markedly higher in South Asia than anywhere else in the world.*

AN OVERVIEW

India, with a population of 989 million, is the world's second most populous country. Of that number, 120 million are women who live in poverty.

India has 16 percent of the world's population, but only 2.4 percent of its land, resulting in great pressures on its natural resources.

Over 70 percent of India's population currently derive their livelihood from land resources, which includes 84 percent of the economically-active women.

India is one of the few countries where males significantly outnumber females, and this imbalance has increased over time. India's maternal mortality rates in rural areas are among the world's highest. From a global perspective, Indian accounts for 19 percent of all lives births and 27 percent of all maternal deaths.

"There seems to be a consensus that higher female mortality between ages one and five and high maternal mortality rates result in a deficit of females in the population. Chatterjee (1990) estimates that deaths of young girls in India exceed those of young boys by over 300,000 each year, and every sixth infant death is specifically due to gender discrimination." Of the 15 million baby girls born in India each year, nearly 25 percent will not live to see their 15th birthday.

> *"Although India was the first country to announce an official family planning program in 1952, its population*

grew from 361 million in 1951 to 844 million in 1991. India's total fertility rate of 3.8 births per woman can be considered moderate by world standards, but the sheer magnitude of population increase has resulted in such a feeling of urgency that containment of population growth is listed as one of the six most important objectives in the Eighth Five-Year Plan."

Since 1970, the use of modern contraceptive methods has risen from 10 percent to 40 percent, with great variance between northern and southern India. The most striking aspect of contraceptive use in India is the predominance of sterilization, which accounts for more than 85 percent of total modern contraception use, with female sterilization accounting for 90 percent of all sterilizations.

The Indian constitution grants women equal rights with men, but strong patriarchal traditions persist, with women's lives shaped by customs that are centuries old. In most Indian families, a daughter is viewed as a liability, and she is conditioned to believe that she is inferior and subordinate to men. Sons are idolized and celebrated. May you be the mother of a hundred sons is a common Hindu wedding blessing.

The origin of the Indian idea of appropriate female behavior can be traced to the rules laid down by Manu in 200 B.C.: "by a young girl, by a young woman, or even by an aged one, nothing must be done independently, even in her own house". "In childhood a female must be subject to her father, in youth to her husband, when her lord is dead to her sons; a woman must never be independent."

A study of women in the Swayam Shikshan Prayog (SSP), based in 20 villages in four districts in Maharashtra state was introduced in this way:

The primary issue all women in the SSP were struggling with was that of everyday survival. Insufficient incomes and the lack of employment were reported to be their most pressing concerns. Survival is a constant preoccupation and at its most basic, survival means food (Chambers 1983). The most common problems were the lack of basic amenities such as food, water, fuel, fodder and health facilities.

In addition, the deterioration of the natural environment and the fact that many of their traditional occupations were no longer viable were conditions that were making it increasingly hard for women to continue sustaining their families, as they had done in the past.

SSP is a loose, informal network of women's collectives, voluntary organizations, action groups and unions.

WOMEN ARE MALNOURISHED

The exceptionally high rates of malnutrition in South Asia are rooted deeply in the soil of inequality between men and women.

> *"...the poor care that is afforded to girls and women by their husbands and by elders is the first major reason for levels of child malnutrition that are markedly higher in South Asia than anywhere else in the world."*

This point is made in the article, The Asian Enigma, published by UNICEF in the 1996 Progress of Nations, in which the rates of childhood malnutrition in South Asia are compared with those in Africa. We learn that malnutrition is far worse in South Asia, directly due to the fact that women in South Asia have less voice and freedom of movement than in Africa. "Judgement and self-expression and independence largely denied, millions of women in South Asia have neither the knowledge nor the means nor the freedom to act in their own and their children's best interests."

> *"Gender disparities in nutrition are evident from infancy to adulthood. In fact, gender has been the most statistically significant determinant of malnutrition among young children and malnutrition is a frequent direct or underlying cause of death among girls below age 5. Girls are breast-fed less frequently and for shorter durations in infancy; in childhood and adulthood, males*

are fed first and better. Adult women consume approximately 1,000 fewer calories per day than men according to one estimate from Punjab. Comparison of household dietary intake studies in different parts of the country shows that nutritional equity between males and females is lower in northern than in southern states."

Nutritional deprivation has two major consequences for women: they never reach their full growth potential and anaemia. Both are risk factors in pregnancy, with anaemia ranging from 40-50 percent in urban areas to 50-70 percent in rural areas. This condition complicates childbearing and result in maternal and infant deaths, and low birth weight infants.

One study found anaemia in over 95 percent of girls ages 6-14 in Calcutta, around 67 percent in the Hyderabad area, 73 percent in the New Delhi area, and about 18 percent in the Madras area. This study states, "The prevalence of anaemia among women ages 15-24 and 25-44 years follows similar patterns and levels. Besides posing risks during pregnancy, anaemia increases women's susceptibility to diseases such as tuberculosis and reduces the energy women have available for daily activities such as household chores, child care, and agricultural labor. Any severely anaemic individual is taxed by most physical activities, including walking at an ordinary pace.

WOMEN ARE IN POOR HEALTH

Surviving through a normal life cycle is a resource-poor woman's greatest challenge.

"The practice of breast-feeding female children for shorter periods of time reflects the strong desire for sons. If women are particularly anxious to have a male child, they may deliberately try to become pregnant again as soon as possible after a female is born. Conversely, women may consciously seek to avoid another pregnancy after the birth of a male child in order to give maximum attention to the new son."

A primary way that parents discriminate against their girl children is through neglect during illness. When sick, little girls are not taken to the doctor as frequently as are their brothers. A study in Punjab shows that medical expenditures for boys are 2.3 times higher than for girls.

As adults, women get less health care than men. They tend to be less likely to admit that they are sick and they'll wait until their sickness has progressed before they seek help or help is sought for them. Studies on attendance at rural primary health centers reveal that more males than females are treated in almost all parts of the country, with differences greater in northern hospitals than southern ones, pointing to regional differences in the value placed on women. Women's socialization to tolerate suffering and their reluctance to be examined by male personnel are additional constraints in their getting adequate health care.

CONTRACEPTION USE

Women's health is harmed by lack of access to and the poor quality of reproductive services.

> *"About 24.6 million couples, representing roughly 18 percent of all married women, want no more children but are not using contraception. (Operations Research Group, 1990). The causes of this unmet need remain poorly understood, but a qualitative study in Tamil Nadu suggests that women's lack of decision-making power in the family, opportunity costs involved in seeking contraception, fear of child death, and poor quality of contraceptive service all play an important role." (Ravindran 1993).*

Some estimates suggest that some 5 million abortions are performed annually in India, with the large majority being illegal. As a result, abortion-related mortality is high. Although abortion has been legal since 1972 in India, "studies suggest that although official policy seeks to make pregnancy-termination services widely available, in practice guidelines on abortion limit access to services, particularly in rural areas. In 1981, of the 6,200 physicians trained to perform abortions, only 1,600 were working in rural areas."

JOB IMPACT ON MATERNAL HEALTH

Working conditions result in premature and stillbirths.

The tasks performed by women are usually those that require them to be in one position for long periods of time, which can adversely affect their reproductive health. A study in a rice-growing belt of coastal Maharashtra found that 40 percent of all infant deaths occurred in the months of July to October. The study also found that a majority of births were either premature or stillbirths. The study attributed this to the squatting position that had to be assumed during July and August, the rice transplanting months.

IMPACT OF POLLUTION ON WOMEN

Women's health is further harmed by air and water pollution and lack of sanitation.

The impact of pollution and industrial wastes on health is considerable. In Environment, Development and the Gender Gap, Sandhya Venkateswaran asserts that "the high incidence of malnutrition present amongst women and their low metabolism and other health problems affect their capacity to deal with chemical stress. The smoke from household biomass (made up of wood, dung and crop residues) stoves within a three-hour period is equivalent to smoking 20 packs of cigarettes. For women who spend at least three hours per day cooking, often in a poorly ventilated area, the impact includes eye problems, respiratory problems, chronic bronchitis and lung cancer. One study quoted by WHO in 1991 found that pregnant women cooking over open biomass stoves had almost a 50 percent higher chance of stillbirth.

Anaemia makes a person more susceptible to carbon monoxide toxicity, which is one of the main pollutants in the biomass smoke.

Given the number of Indian women who are anaemic-25 to 30 percent in the reproductive age group and almost 50 percent in the third trimester-this adds to their vulnerability to carbon monoxide toxicity.

Additionally, with an increasing population, diseases caused by waste disposal, such as hookworm, are rampant. People who work barefooted are particularly susceptible, and it has been found that hookworm is directly responsible for the high percentage of anaemia among rural women.

MATERNAL MORTALITY

India's maternal mortality rates in rural areas are among the highest in the world.

A factor that contributes to India's high maternal mortality rate is the reluctance to seek medical care for pregnancy-it is viewed as a temporary condition that will disappear. The estimates nationwide are that only 40-50 percent of women receive any antenatal care. Evidence from the states of Bihar, Rajasthan, Orissa, Uttar Pradesh, Maharashtra and Gujarat find registration for maternal and child health services to be as low as 5-22 percent in rural areas and 21-51 percent in urban areas.

Even a woman who has had difficulties with previous pregnancies is usually treated with home remedies only for three reasons: the decision that a pregnant woman seek help rests with the mother-in-law and husband; financial considerations; and fear that the treatment may be more harmful than the malady.

It is estimated that pregnancy-related deaths account for one-quarter of all fatalities among women aged 15 to 29, with well over two-thirds of them considered preventable. For every maternal death in India, an estimated 20 more women suffer from impaired health. One village-level study of rural women in Maharashtra determined on the basis of physical examinations that some 92 percent suffered from one or more gynecological disorder.

WOMEN ARE UNEDUCATED

Women and girls receive far less education than men, due both to social norms and fears of violence. India has the largest population of non-school-going working girls.

India's constitution guarantees free primary school education for both boys and girls up to age 14. This goal has been repeatedly reconfirmed, but primary education in India is not universal. Overall, the literacy rate for women is 39 percent versus 64 percent for men. The rate for women in the four large northern states-Bihar, Uttar Pradesh, Rajasthan and Madhya Pradesh-is lower than the national average: it was 25 percent in 1991. Attendance rates from the 1981 census suggest that no more than 1/3 of all girls (and a lower proportion of rural girls) aged 5-14 are attending school.

Although substantial progress has been achieved since India won its independence in 1947, when less than 8 percent of females were literate, the gains have not been rapid enough to keep pace with population growth: there were 16 million more illiterate females in 1991 than in 1981.

Sonalde Desai in Gender Inequalities and Demographic Behavior asserts that "parents' reluctance to educate daughters has its roots in the situation of women. Parents have several incentives for not educating their daughters. Foremost is the view that education of girls brings no returns to parents and that their future roles, being mainly reproductive and perhaps including agricultural labor, require no formal education. As more and more boys are engaged in education, there is a growing reliance on the labor of girls. Girls are increasingly replacing their brothers on the farm while carrying on their usual responsibilities in housework. A large proportion of the roughly 40 million "nonworking" girls who are not in school are kept at home because of responsibilities in housework."

The role of parents is to deliver a chaste daughter to her husband's family. Sonalde Desai goes on to point out that "another disincentive for sending daughters to school is a concern for the protection of their virginity. When schools are located at a distance, when teachers are male, and when girls are expected to study along with boys, parents are often unwilling to expose their daughters to the potential assault on their virginity."

There is little response to counter these obstacles: school hours remain inflexible to the labor demands of girls; many villages do not have a school; and fewer than 1/3 of India's primary and middle-school teachers are women.

According to Mapping Progress, "educational funds were cut by 801.3 million rupees in the 1991-92 budget. Funds for the mass literacy movement, in which women participate enthusiastically, have been reduced by 5 percent from the previous year. Budgetary provisions for non-formal education have been cut by 17 percent, leading to closure of many night schools and adult education programs in which working-class women participate. Reduction in government expenditures on higher education and encouragement to private colleges will reduce women's opportunities for higher education since privatization in education promotes only male-dominated professional and technical courses, as they are lucrative."

WOMEN ARE OVERWORKED AND WORKED HOURS

Women work roughly twice as many as many hours as men. Women's contribution to agriculture-whether it be subsistence farming or commercial agriculture-when measured in terms of the number of tasks performed and time spent, is greater than men. "The extent of women's contribution is aptly highlighted by a micro study conducted in the Indian Himalayas which found that on a one-hectare farm, a pair of bullocks works 1,064 hours, a man 1,212 hours and a woman 3,485 hours in a year." Women work longer hours and their work is more arduous than men's. Still, men report that "women, like children, eat and do nothing."

In Andhra Pradesh, (Mies 1986) found that the work day of an woman agricultural labourer during the agricultural season lasts for 15 hours, from 4 am to 8 pm, with an hour's rest in between. Her male counterpart works for seven to eight hours, from 5 am to 10 am or 11 am and from 3 pm to 5 pm.

Another study on time and energy spent by men and women on agricultural work (Batliwala 1982) found that 53 percent of the total human hours per household are contributed by women as compared to 31 percent by men. The remaining contribution comes from children.

The linking of agricultural activities to male dominance is described by Roy Burman (in Menon 1991):

> *The anxiety of man to monopolize his skill in plough culture is reflected in the taboo that is observed almost all over India, against the women's handling the plough. In many societies, she is not even allowed to touch it.*

Mies further observed that "whereas operations performed by men were those that entailed the use of machinery and draught animals, thereby using animal, hydraulic, mechanical or electrical energy, women almost always relied on manual labour, using only their own energy." Rice transplantations, the most arduous and labour intensive task in rice cultivation, is carried out entirely by women without the help of any tools.

> *"Girls learn to assist their mothers in almost all tasks, and from the age of 10 years participate fully in the agricultural work done by women. Mies cites the case of Laxmi, a three-year-old infant who, along with her mother, pulled seedlings for transplanting. Boys on the other hand were seldom seen transplanting or weeding though they did help out in ploughing or watering the fields."*

"Not only do women perform more tasks, their work is also more arduous than that undertaken by men. Both transplantation and weeding require women to spend the whole day and work in muddy soil with their hands. Moreover, they work the entire day under the intensely hot sun while men's work, such as ploughing and watering the fields, is invariably carried out early in the morning before the sun gets too hot. Mies argues that because women's work, unlike men's, does not involve implements and is based largely on human energy, it is considered unskilled and hence less productive. On this basis, women are invariably paid lower wages, despite the fact that they work harder and for longer hours than do men."

In contrast, a study in Uttar Pradesh reports that men "only reluctantly conceded that their womenfolk really work. The researchers in this area were repeatedly told that women, like children, simply eat food and do nothing."

THE INVISIBILITY OF WOMEN'S WORK

Women's work is rarely recognized.

Many maintain that women's economic dependence on men impacts their power within the family. With increased participation in income-earning activities, not only will there be more income for the family, but gender inequality should be reduced. This issue is particularly salient in India because studies show a very low level of female participation in the labor force. This under-reporting is attributed to the frequently held view that women's work is not economically productive.

In a report of the National Commission on Self-Employed Women and Women in the Informal Sector, the director of social welfare in one state said, "There are no women in any unorganized sector in our state." When the Commission probed and asked, "Are there any women who go to the forest to collect firewood? Do any of the women in rural areas have cattle?" the director responded with, "Of course, there are many women doing that type of work." Working women are invisible to most of the population.

If all activities-including maintenance of kitchen gardens and poultry, grinding food grains, collecting water and firewood, etc.-are taken into account, then 88 percent of rural housewives and 66 percent of urban housewives can be considered as economically productive.

Women's employment in family farms or businesses is rarely recognized as economically productive, either by men or women. And, any income generated from this work is generally controlled by the men. Such work is unlikely to increase women's participation in allocating family finances. In a 1992 study of family-based texile workers, male children who helped in a home-based handloom mill were given pocket money, but the adult women and girls were not.

THE IMPACT OF TECHNOLOGY ON WOMEN

The shift from subsistence to a market economy has a dramatic negative impact on women. According to Sandhya Venkateswaran, citing Shiva, the Green Revolution, which focused on increasing yields of rice and wheat, entailed a shift in inputs from human to technical. Women's participation, knowledge and inputs were marginalized, and their role shift from being "primary producers to subsidiary workers."

Where technology has been introduced in areas where women worked, women labourers have often been displaced by men. Threshing of grain was almost exclusively a female task, and with the introduction of automatic grain threshers-which are only operated by men-women have lost an important source of income. Combine harvesters leave virtually no residue. This means that this source of fodder is no longer available to women, which has a dramatic impact on women's workload. So too, as cattle dung is being used as fertilizer, there is less available for fuel for cooking.

> *"Commercialization and the consequent focus on cash crops has led to a situation where food is lifted straight from the farm to the market. The income accrued is controlled by men. Earlier, most of the produce was brought home and stored, and the women exchanged it for other commodities. Such a system vested more control with the women."*

Women are Unskilled

Women have unequal access to resources. Extension services tend to reach only men, which perpetuates the existing division of labour in the agricultural sector, with women continuing to perform unskilled tasks. A World Bank study in 1991 reveals that the assumption made by extension workers is that information within a family will be transmitted to the women by the men, which in actual practice seldom happens. "The male dominated extension system tends to overlook women's role in agriculture and proves ineffective in providing technical information to women farmers."

Mapping Progress, states, "in the farm sector, the process of mechanization of agricultural activities has brought in tendencies for gender discrimination by replacing men for a number of activities performed by women and also by displacing the labor of women from subsistence and marginal households. Women are employed only when there is absolute shortage of labor and for specific operations like cotton-picking.

> *"To supply food-processing industries being set up with foreign collaboration, there has already been a major shift from subsistence farming method of rice, millet, corn and wheat to cash-crop production of fruit, mushrooms, flowers and vegetables. This shift has led to women being the first to lose jobs."*

A number of factors perpetuate women's limited job skills: if training women for economic activities requires them to leave their village, this is usually a problem for them. Unequal access to education restricts women's abilities to learn skills that require even functional levels of literacy. In terms of skill development, women are impeded by their lack of mobility, low literacy levels and prejudiced attitudes toward women. When women negotiate with banks and government officials, they are often ostracized by other men and women in their community for being 'too forward.' Government and bank officials have preconceived ideas of what women are capable of, and stereotypes of what is considered women's work.

Women are Mistreated

Violence against women and girls is the most pervasive human rights violation in the world today.

Opening the door on the subject of violence against the world's females is like standing at the threshold of an immense dark chamber vibrating with collective anguish, but with the sounds of protest throttled back to a murmur. Where there should be outrage aimed at an intolerable status quo there is instead denial, and the largely passive acceptance of 'the way things are.'

Male violence against women is a worldwide phenomenon. Although not every woman has experienced it, and many expect not to, fear of violence is an important factor in the lives of most women. It determines what they do, when they do it, where they do it, and with whom. Fear of violence is a cause of women's lack of participation in activities beyond the home, as well as inside it. Within the home, women and girls may be subjected to physical and sexual abuse as punishment or as culturally justified assaults. These acts shape their attitude to life, and their expectations of themselves.

The insecurity outside the household is today the greatest obstacle in the path of women. Conscious that, compared to the atrocities outside the house, atrocities within the house are endurable, women not only continued to accept their inferiority in the house and society, but even called it sweet.

In recent years, there has been an alarming rise in atrocities against women in India. Every 26 minutes a woman is molested. Every 34 minutes a rape takes place. Every 42 minutes a sexual harassment incident occurs. Every 43 minutes a woman is kidnapped. And every 93 minutes a woman is burnt to death over dowry. One-quarter of the reported rapes involve girls under the age of 16 but the vast majority are never reported. Although the penalty is severe, convictions are rare.

Selective Abortions

The most extreme expression of the preference for sons is female infanticide and sex-selective abortion. A study of amniocentesis in a Bombay hospital found that 96 percent of female fetuses were aborted, compared with only a small percentage of male fetuses.

"Government officials event suspect that the disproportionate abortion of female fetuses may be a major underlying cause of the recent decline in the nation's sex ratio. In 1971 there were 930 females for every 1,000 males. A decade later this figure had increased to 934, but by 1991, instead of continuing to rise, the ratio dropped to 927, lower than the 1971 figure. This sex ratio is one of the lowest in the world."

Sonalda Desai reports that there are posters in Bombay advertising sex-determination tests that read, "It is better to pay 500 Rs. now than 50,000 Rs. (in dowry) later."

Government has passed legislation to curb the misuse of amniocentesis for sex selection and abortion of female fetuses. Women activists have been critical of this act because of its provision that calls for punishing the women who seek the procedure. These women may be under pressure to bear a male child.

Women are Powerless

Legal protection of women's rights have little effect in the face of prevailing patriarchal traditions.

Marriage: Women are subordinate in most marriages.

Exposure to and interactions with the outside world are instrumental in determining the possibilities available to women in their daily lives. The situation of women is affected by the degree of their autonomy or capacity to make decisions both inside and outside their own household.

"The position of women in northern India is notably poor. Traditional Hindu society in northern rural areas is hierarchical and dominated by men, as evidenced by marriage customs. North Indian Hindus are expected to marry within prescribed boundaries: the bride and groom must not be related, they have no say in the matter, and the man must live outside the woman's natal village."

"Wife givers" are socially and ritually inferior to "wife takers", thus necessitating the provision of a dowry. After marriage, the bride moves in with her husband's family. Such a bride is "a stranger in a strange place."

They are controlled by the older females in the household, and their behavior reflects on the honor of their husbands. Because emotional ties between spouses are considered a potential threat to the solidarity of the patrilineal group, the northern system tends to segregate the sexes and limit communication between spouses-a circumstance that has direct consequences for family planning and similar "modern" behaviors that affect health.

A young Indian bride is brought up to believe that her own wishes and interests are subordinate to those of her husband and his family. The primary duty of a newly married young woman, and virtually her only means of improving her position in the hierarchy of her husband's household, is to bear sons."

Sonalde Desai points out that the perception that sons are the major source of economic security in old age is so strong in the north that "many parents, while visiting their married daughters, do not accept food or other hospitality from them. However, given women's low independent incomes and lack of control over their earnings, few can provide economic support to their parents even if parents were willing to accept it."

In the south, in contrast, a daughter traditionally marries her mother's brother or her mother's brother's son (her first cousin). Such an arrangement has a dramatic impact on women. "In southern India, men are likely to marry women to whom they are related, so that the strict distinction found in the north between patrilineal and marital relatives is absent. Women are likely to be married into family households near their natal homes, and are more likely to retain close relationships with their natal kin."

"Over the past several decades, however, marriage patterns have changed markedly. Social, economic, and demographic developments have made marriages between close relatives less common, and the bride price has given way to a dowry system akin to that in the north. Nevertheless, as long as the underlying ethic of marriage in the south remains the reinforcement of existing kinship ties, the relatively favorable situation of southern Indian women is unlikely to be threatened."

CHILD MARRIAGES

Child marriages keep women subjugated.

A 1976 amendment to the Child Marriage Restraint Act raised the minimum legal age for marriage from 15 to 18 for young women and from 18 to 21 for young men. However, in many rural communities, illegal child marriages are still common. In some rural areas, nearly half the girls between 10 and 14 are married. Because there is pressure on women to prove their fertility by conceiving as soon as possible after marriage, adolescent marriage is synonymous with adolescent childbearing: roughly 10-15 percent of all births take place to women in their teens.

A May 1998 article in the New York Times states: Child marriages contribute to virtually every social malaise that keeps India behind in women's rights. The problems include soaring birth rates, grinding poverty and malnutrition, high illiteracy and infant mortality and low life expectancy, especially among rural women. The article cites a 1993 survey of more than 5,000 women in Rajasthan, which showed that 56 percent of them had married before they were 15. Barely 18 percent of them were literate and only 3 percent used any form of birth control other than sterilization. Sixty-three percent of the children under age 4 of these women were severely undernourished.

"Each year, formal warnings are posted outside state government offices stating that child marriages are illegal, but they have little impact."

One man interviewed for the article has seven daughters. He borrowed some 60,000 rupees to pay for the dowries for six of his daughters, ranging in age from 4-14. He reported that "the weddings mean that he can now look forward to growing old without being trapped in the penury by the need to support his daughters." (NYT)

Dowries: Women are kept subordinate, and are even murdered, by the practice of dowry.

In India, 6,000 dowry murders are committed each year. This reality exists even though the Dowry Prohibition Act has been in existence for 33 years, and there are virtually no arrests under the Act. Since those giving as well as those accepting dowry are punishable under the existing law, no one is willing to complain.

It is only after a "dowry death" that the complaints become public. It is estimated that the average dowry today is equivalent to five times the family's annual income and that the high cost of weddings and dowries is a major cause of indebtedness among India's poor.

A December 1997 article in India Today, entitled, Victims of Sudden Affluence states, "A woman on fire has made dowry deaths the most vicious of social crimes; it is an evil endemic to the subcontinent but despite every attempt at justice the numbers have continued to climb. With get-rich-quick becoming the new mantra, dowry became the perfect instrument for upward material mobility."

A study done by a policy think-tank, the Institute of Development and Communication, states, "the quantum of dowry exchange may still be greater among the upper classes, but 80 percent of dowry deaths and 80 percent of dowry harassment occurs in the middle and lower stratas." The article goes on to state, "So complete is the discrimination among women that the gender bias is extended even toward the guilty. In a bizarre trend, the onus of murder is often put on the women to protect the men. Sometimes it is by consent. Often, old mothers-in-law embrace all the blame to bail out their sons and husbands."

Despite every stigma, dowry continues to be the signature of marriage. Says Rainuka Dagar, "It is taken as a normative custom and dowry harassment as a part of family life."

Divorce: Divorce is not a viable option.

Divorce is rare-it is a considered a shameful admission of a woman's failure as a wife and daughter-in-law. In 1990, divorced women made up a miniscule 0.08 percent of the total female population.

Maintenance rights of women in the case of divorce are weak. Although both Hindu and Muslim law recognize the rights of women and children to maintenance, in practice, maintenance is rarely set at a sufficient amount and is frequently violated.

Both Hindu and Muslim personal laws fail to recognize matrimonial property. Upon divorce, women have no rights to their home or to other property accumulated during marriage; in effect, their contributions to the maintenance of the family and accumulation of family assets go unrecognized and unrewarded.

RIGHT TO INHERITANCE

Women's rights to inheritance are limited and frequently violated. In the mid-1950s the Hindu personal laws, which apply to all Hindus, Buddhists, Sikhs and Jains, were overhauled, banning polygamy and giving women rights to inheritance, adoption and divorce. The Muslim personal laws differ considerably from that of the Hindus, and permit polygamy. Despite various laws protecting women's rights, traditional patriarchal attitudes still prevail and are strengthened and perpetuated in the home.

Under Hindu law, sons have an independent share in the ancestral property. However, daughters' shares are based on the share received by their father. Hence, a father can effectively disinherit a daughter by renouncing his share of the ancestral property, but the son will continue to have a share in his own right. Additionally, married daughters, even those facing marital harassment, have no residential rights in the ancestral home.

Even the weak laws protecting women have not been adequately enforced. As a result, in practice, women continue to have little access to land and property, a major source of income and long-term economic security. Under the pretext of preventing fragmentation of agricultural holdings, several states have successfully excluded widows and daughters from inheriting agricultural land.

Economic, social and physical factors are the compelling reasons. Several studies have identified that poverty and involvement of girls in activities necessary for the survival of their families are the primary reasons. Such activities include domestic work - a large component of which is looking after younger siblings, and in rural areas engaged in fetching water, fuel and fodder for the family. The enrollment data of the 3rd and 4th Educational Surveys (1973 and 1978) have been used to calculate group out and wastage rate among children enrolled in schools during this period. Results are presented in the table given below.

The table indicates that 67.73 per cent of girls and 58.61 per cent of boys did not reach the middle schools stage and 61.77 per cent and 51.01 per cent of boys did not reach the secondary stage. At the all India level there has been a marignal reduction in drop-out/wastage rate for both boys and girls. It appears that the states of Andhra Pradesh, Bihar Karnataka, Madhya Pradesh, Orissa, Uttar Pradesh and West Bengal have not only a high drop-out rate for girls but also present a high gender differentiation.

There is a distinct change in the patter of faculty-wise enrollment during this period. Thus while there have been marginal increase in share of enrollment in most of the faculties there has been a sharp drop in share of arts and humanities with a comparative rise in share of commerce. While most of the other faculties have recorded a slight improvement there is a decline in share of enrollment in medical faculty.

Thus while in 1950-51 the share in enrollment in medical faculty stood at 51.78 per cent it come down to 4.52 per cent in 1960-61 and declined further 3.39 per cent in 1970-71. In 1983-84 it showed only a marginal improvement to 3.52 per cent. It is important to note here that this decline has took taken place in spite of reservation of seats for women in medical, institutions.

Entry of women to higher education has been gaining ground since 1950-51. This is indicated by the rising share of women's enrollment in total enrollment in different faculties. Thus in the arts and humanities the share rose from 16 per cent to 42 per cent, in commerce from 0.6 per cent to 15.3 per cent, in medical from 16.3 per cent to 24.3 per cent, in engineering and technology from 0.2 per cent to 4.1 per cent, in law from 2 per cent to 7.7 per cent and in veterinary science from 0.5 per cent to 5.3 per cent.

Despite constitutional guarantee for equal opportunity of education for both the sexes women's education continues to be plagued with bias. There has been persistent ambivalence between the traditional view who support women's education to equip them to become better wives and mothers and modern attitude who visualise education as an instrument for women's equality and development.

These two views opposite to each other has been influencing those who are responsible for the promotion of education in the country. While Radhakrishan Commission finds women's education based upon 'men's needs' which does not make them 'fit for coping with the problems of daily life', it fails to counter the traditional view on women's education rather strengthens this view in its recommendation.

It says: "Women's and men's education should have many elements in common but should not in general be identical in all respects, as in usually the case today. A woman should learn something of problems that are certain to come up in all marriages and in the relations of parents and children, and how they may be met.

Her education should make her familiar with problems of home management and skill in meeting them, so that she may take her place in a home with the same interest and the same sense of competence that a well trained man has in working at his celling".

Persistence of this ambivalence between traditional and modern attitudes of which, the overriding influence of the traditional attitudes towards women's education, was observed by the Committee on the Status of Women in India.

The Committee mentioned that for a proper examination the progress of women's education an understanding of this ambivalence is prerequisite because 'it has an impact on academic planning, allocation of resources and development of values in society for both men and women'.

The subsequent official and non- official documents have been critically highlighting this ambivalence and recommending measures to remove them.

2

Women's Empowerment in Rural India

INTRODUCTION

Since the 1990's women have been identified as key agents of sustainable development and women's equality and empowerment are seen as central to a more holistic approach towards establishing new patterns and processes of development that are sustainable. The World Bank has suggested that empowerment of women should be a key aspect of all social development programs (World Bank, 2001). Although a considerable debate on what constitutes empowerment exists, in this paper we find it useful to rely on Kabeer's (2001) definition: "The expansion in people's ability to make strategic life choices in a context where this ability was previously denied to them." For women in India, this suggests empowerment in several realms: personal, familial, economic and political. Since the 1980's the Government of India has shown increasing concern for women's issues through a variety of legislation promoting the education and political participation of women (Collier, 1998).

International organizations like the World Bank and United Nations have focused on women's issues especially the empowerment of poor women in rural areas. In the late 1980s and early 1990s, non-governmental organizations (NGOs) have also taken on an increased role in the area of women's empowerment (Sadik, 1988). NGO's, previously catering to women's health and educational needs, have moved beyond this traditional focus to addressing the underlying causes of deprivations through promoting the economic and social empowerment of women. (McNamara: 2003). There are many challenges that face NGOs who make it their goal to empower women (Narayan: 2002; Mayoux: 2000; Malhotra and Mather: 1997). This paper addresses one specific challenge that is faced by NGOs located in rural areas that wish to promote women's empowerment. These NGOs have little or no access to skilled social workers. They must often depend on the local population for their employees, employees who may be vulnerable to the similar social pressures and are often equally marginalized as their clients.

For rural NGOs to be successful they must attract employees who must at some level be relatively more empowered than the clients. They must have certain credibility to be able to effectively persuade their marginalized clients to alter their ways of thinking on many long-standing traditional issues, such as dowries, child labor, and patriarchal subjugation. The literature of behavior change in the health field suggests that self-efficacy is one of the four most commonly cited constructs for behavioral change Although stated for different purposes and from different perspectives, the literature on self-efficacy can be brought to bear on issues of empowerment. Self-efficacy determines when an individual will undertake new behaviors such as self-empowerment. Low self-efficacy beliefs of women in rural India often stem from the limited and disadvantaged positions women have in society.

Women confront many obstacles to better lives. Women need change in many areas simultaneously. Thus the agenda for policies to give women more opportunities must be broad. In addition to assuring women's ability to control their own fertility, important elements.

THE SOCIAL AND ECONOMIC CONDITIONS THAT SUBJUGATE WOMEN

The social and economic conditions that subjugate women are expressed and reinforced by the institution of dowry. To secure a husband for their daughter, a girl's parents must pay up to five times their annual income in dowry "gifts" to the husband's family. As a result, having a girl is a great burden, while having a boy is a great asset. Although dowry has been illegal since 1961, its practice is flourishing and on the rise, cutting across all classes and castes. For most women, there is no way out. Subjugation and submission are a pervasive pattern, enforced by violence and the threat of violence throughout their lives.

- *Unwanted before Birth.* Often, a baby girl in India is born into a family that had wished and prayed for a boy. Increasingly, girls are not born at all. Modern science allows parents to determine the sex of their child before birth-and abort it if it is a girl. In some areas, midwives or relatives simply murder the girl child-often considering it a "mercy killing". As a result, India now has a population ratio of 900 females (and in some areas as low as 600 females) to1,000 males.
- *Deprived as a Baby Girl.* Girls may be breast-fed for a shorter time than boys-in the hope that the mother can soon become pregnant with a boy. They are fed less food, and lower quality food. When girls become ill, they are less likely to receive medical care than boys-resulting in under-five mortality rates 43 per cent higher for girls than boys.
- *A Childhood of Drudgery.* By age five, girls carry adult responsibilities both inside and outside the home. At home, a girl cares for her younger siblings, and for her sick or pregnant mother. She fetches water, firewood and fodder, and makes dung cakes for fuel. Outside, she works in agriculture and wage labour. Thirty per cent of women's work burden in India is carried by girls between 6 and 11 years old. Education and play are nearly unthinkable.
- *Adolescence: Health Crisis and Sexual Violation.* Girls who reach puberty face a new set of harrowing and untreated problems of physical and mental health. At the very time her body needs more nutrition, she receives less. Adolescent girls suffer high rates of anaemia, vitamin deficiencies, tuberculosis,

gynaecological problems, urinary tract infections and irregular menstruation. As almost everything in her life tells her she is worthless, her mental health deteriorates. Adolescent girls run high risks of sexual assault.

- *Marriage*: a new cycle of subjugation. She is married young, to an older man she has never met, and into a family and a village where she is a stranger. Early and frequent pregnancies about which she has little choice-and during which she rarely receives medical care-put her health at risk. She is isolated-often not permitted to leave the household, and thus unable to be assisted, supported or protected by other women.
- *Adulthood*: overworked and undernourished. A woman in India may work twice as many hours as her husband. Her triple burden-child-rearing, unpaid household work and wage labour outside the home-goes unrecognised and unsupported. She is often malnourished throughout her life.
- *Outcast in Widowhood*. When her husband dies, a woman may be socially, economically and emotionally outcast, stripped of her only place in society. A widow in India is often forced to shave her head, eat only one meal per day and sleep on the floor.

ISSUES OF THE ADOLESCENTS

Adolescents comprise about a fifth of India's population, but they have so far not been recognized as a target of any strategy for development in the country. They are important human resource material, which can be effectively moulded and channelised for nation building. A bulk of population in this age group, particularly in the rural areas, are drop outs from schools and are vulnerable to exploitation of various sorts. The adolescent girls particularly are at high risk of anemia and mental and behavioral disorder. A three-fold strategy must be adopted for helping adolescents in the country. First, efforts should be made to retain them in the education system by progressively reducing the rate of dropouts from schools and colleges through improvement in educational facilities.

Secondly, vocational training and skill development for the drop outs should be organized in various traditional and non traditional trades, depending on their aptitudes and job opportunities, to prepare them to become self sufficient economically and responsible citizens of the country. Thirdly, the nutritional requirement of the adolescents, particularly of the adolescent girls, should be a matter of special concern, since they are the potential mothers and any investment in their health and nutrition shall not only empower them to be better women, but also be an insurance against the underweight and under nourished children of the future.

Improvement of health of the adolescent girl is a definite way of breaking the inter generational cycle of malnutrition in the population. The adolescent girls need also to be protected from unwanted pregnancies and sexually transmitted diseases. Reproductive health services for adolescent boys and girls is particularly needed in rural areas where adolescent marriages and pregnancies are widely prevalent.

STRATEGIES FOR INTERVENTION

The intervention strategy for empowering women to have informed and effective choices on their health and nutrition and for the development of children and adolescents has to be multi-pronged.

Convergence of Service Delivery at Village Levels

There are two main programmes in the Department of Women and Child Development, which aim at convergence of services delivery at the village level, namely, Integrated Child Development Scheme (ICDS) and Integrated Women.'s Empowennent Programme (IWEP).

The ICDS network through Anganwadi Centres reaches 85% of the villages and hamlets in the country. The IWEP (erstwhile Indira Mahila Yojana) which extends to 650 blocks operates through the self help groups of women. Both these programmes can be effective vehicles for the implementation of the National Population Policy. It is therefore critical that both the schemes are universalized.

Nutrition

The Supplementary Nutrition provided under the ICDS Scheme is one of the most vital components under Basic Minimum Service Programme aimed at eradication of the menace of malnutrition of children and women. The success of the programme however depends largely on adequate provision of funds to the States and UTs. An Action plan needs to be drawn up for taking up nutrition in a mission mode to cover infants, adolescent girls, pregnant and lactating mothers-the three critical links in the inter-generational cycle of malnutrition. One intervention that has successfully worked in improving nutrition levels as well as impacting favourably on retention of children in schools is the mid-day meal scheme. This has shown positive results in programmes like TINP and needs to be replicated widely.

Formation of Self-Help Groups

The formation of self-help groups as a basis for the social and economic empowerment of deprived and disadvantaged women has been found to be a successful mechanism for the organization, mobilization and self development of women. This has been tested through the IMY and Swa Shakti projects of the Department of Women and Child Development and is being replicated in a number of programmes of other Departments.

These groups can facilitate the process of economic empowerment through thrift and savings, training and skill upgradation and access to credit and other productive resources. They can also be instruments of social empowerment through awareness generation and convergence of delivery of schemes. With the feeling of ownership and management of their own resources and savings, poor women have been able to choose their priorities and have even been found to cover the cost of additional nutrition and health gaps. The success of this approach has resulted in universalization of this mode of organization in all the southern States. There is a need to replicate this mode throughout the country.

Access to Resources

The issue of improved health and nutrition is intimately linked to access to and control over local, social, and economic structures. For women to be empowered we need to ensure

(a) equitable access and distribution of resources like land, credit etc.

(b) access to education.

(c) access to health/nutrition

(d) access to water and sanitation

This implies that resources should flow into these areas to bridge the gender gap and that systems be developed to plan, implement and monitor the 'bridging' of the gap. Various studies have shown that ownership of land tends to reduce fertility by providing an alternate means of security. Similarly education has its own impact on reproductive behaviour of both men and women. Improving the access of women/households in rural areas and urban slums to safe sources of drinking water will free them from the drudgery of fetching water and in decreasing the morbidity resulting from water-borne diseases such as diarrhoea and cholera. This will impact positively on the health and energy levels of women. Access to technologies which can reduce the drudgery of women on the various works performed by them both within and outside the household is also a very useful intervention for empowering the women.

Women's Component Plan

While the Planning Commission has already incorporated the concept of Women's Component Plan in the 9th Five Year Plan whereby 30% of funds/benefit on every women related sector actually flow to women, it is important that guidelines are finalized early so that this could be implemented effectively.

Development of Gender Disaggregated Data System

One of the constraints in the preparation, implementation and monitoring of plans for the development of women is the absence of gender segregated data on various indices of development at the State, district and sub district levels. This lacunae in our statistical system should be addressed on a priority basis.

Legislation

Laws should be gender sensitive and ensure equal provision and access to resources for men and women. Also there needs to be a much broader focus on implementation issues. Many of the existing statutes such as Indecent Representation of Women's Act, Minimum Wages Act, Equal Remuneration Act, and Pre-natal Diagnostic Act, Maternity Benefit Act, etc., are implemented more in their violation. A number of these Acts are under review in order to strengthen their provisions. The Maternity Benefit Act needs to be strictly implemented and expanded to cover women in the informal sector, along with provision of paid leave for a longer period.

Freedom from Violence

Women and girls face violence in various forms at various stages of their life cycle. This takes the form of female foeticide and infanticide, rape, dowry death and more indirect forms such as desertion or abandonment of older women. This calls for a multipronged strategy of implementation of laws, awareness, community sanctions etc.

Participation in Political Life

For empowerment, women need to have a voice in decision making and planning through adequate representation. Reservation of women in the rural and urban local bodies had enabled representation of nearly a million women at the grassroots who play a very important catalytic role in transforming the society. Similar representation in State Legislature and Parliament would further strengthen the process of empowerment of women.

Sustained Media Campaign

One of the most effective interventions that can take place to address the issues of attitude and mind sets of men and women, of the community and also of the functionaries of the government-the bureaucracy, police and judiciary is media campaigns. A sustained campaign through the print, electronic and folk media is necessary on various issues related to empowerment of women, health and nutrition, laws, value of the girl child, violence against women etc.

As the Sub Group was deliberating on the issue of empowerment of women, the National Policy for Empowerment of Women (NPEW) was approved by the Government. The Policy makes a series of prescriptions for the economic and social empowerment of women and for mainstreaming the gender perspective in the development process. The policy has also enjoined upon all Central and State Ministries to draw up time bound Action Plan for translating the Policy into a set of concrete actions and measurable goals to be achieved by 2010.

The Policy has also talked about identification and commitment of resources and responsibilities for implementation of the action plans and of development of suitable structures and mechanisms to ensure efficient monitoring, review and gender impact assessment of plans and policies.

NATIONAL SOCIO ECONOMIC GOALS

The objectives of National Population Policy have been conceptualised into three stages:

(a) *Immediate*-to address the unmet needs for contraception, health care infrastructure, and health personnel, and to provide integrated service delivery for basic reproductive and child health care.

(b) *Medium-term*-to bring the TFR to replacement levels by 2010, through vigorous implementation of inter-sectoral operational strategies.

(c) *Long-term*-to achieve a stable population by 2045, at a level consistent with the requirements of sustainable economic growth, social development, and environmental protection.

In pursuance of these objectives, the NPP has fixed a set of fourteen National Socio Demographic Goals to be achieved in each case by 2010. The NPEW has also urged that measurable goals to be achieved by 2010 have to be fixed in the Action Plan although these goals have not been stated in the Policy itself. Both the Action Plans of NPEW and of the medium term objectives of the NPP have taken the year 2010 as their time frame. There is urgent need therefore for operationalisation of the convergence of the two Policies through the Action Plans of the Governments at the national and State levels. In other words, the fourteen National Socio Demographic Goals should inform the preparation of the Action Plans under NPEW and to that extent guidelines should be issued by the Department of Women and Child Development to all the State Governments and Union Territories. These fourteen National Socio Demographic Goals of NPP are:

(a) Address the unmet needs for basic reproductive and child health services, supplies and infrastructure.

(b) Make school education up to age 14 free and compulsory, and reduce drop outs at primary and secondary school levels to below 20 percent for both boys and girls.

(c) Reduce infant mortality rate to below 30 per 1000 live births.

(d) Reduce maternal mortality ratio to below 100 per 100,000 live births.

(e) Achieve universal immunization of children against all vaccine preventable diseases.

(f) Promote delayed marriage for girls, not earlier than age 18 and preferably after 20 years of age.

(g) Achieve 80 percent institutional deliveries and 100 percent deliveries by trained persons.

(h) Achieve universal access to information/counseling, and services for fertility regulation and contraception with a wide basket of choices.

(i) Achieve 100 per cent registration of births, deaths, marriage and pregnancy.

(j) Contain the spread of Acquired Immunodeficiency Syndrome (AIDS), and promote greater integration between the management of reproductive tract infections (RTI) and sexually transmitted infections (STI) and the National AIDS Control Organisation.

(k) Prevent and control communicable diseases.

(l) Integrate Indian Systems of Medicine (ISM) in the provision of reproductive and child health services, and in reaching out to households.

(m) Promote vigorously the small family norm to achieve replacement levels of TFR.

(n) Bring about convergence in implementation of related social sector programs so that family welfare becomes a people centred programme.

It may be seen that out of these fourteen goals the first seven relate directly to the women and children and the remaining seven concern them indirectly, although vitally. The Sub Group deliberated on each of these goals. Judging by the pace of progress achieved in the social sectors in the last fifty years, the Sub group felt that implementation of these goals during the course of a decade may become extremely difficult and challenging unless there is commitment of adequate resources by the Central and State Governments on the social sector, particularly in the fields of health, education and nutrition and unless there is strong and effective convergence of services at the grassroot level involving all the stakeholders and the functionaries of all the related Government agencies.

Reduction of IMR to below 30 per 1000 and of MMR to below 100 per 100,000 live births from 72 and 408 at present would require identification of the blocks (i) where IMR has already reached below 30 level, (ii) where it has reached a threshold level, (iii) where it would reach the mark during the decade given the normal rate of progress already achieved, (iv) where it would need additional input and (v) where it would require substantially additional input of both child and maternal care services. At present no scientific system of continuous grading and monitoring of ICDS services, according to the level of achievements of IMR and MMR, exists at the national level. Uniform guidelines and criteria are applied to all the ICDS blocks throughout the country, irrespective of the levels of achievement. This must be replaced by a block specific flexible approach with additional anganwadi centers and additional supplementary nutrition wherever required. This should be put in place immediately in consultation with the State Governments and other stakeholders.

Although there are marked differences in the level of IMR/MMR between ICDS and non-ICDS blocks, such differences are very marginal in many blocks. In Uttar Pradesh, for example, average IMR in ICDS blocks is 86 per 1000 live births against 86.5 in non-ICDS blocks. This strongly suggests that the programme has not been properly implemented in certain States of the country. There is an urgent need for analyzing the causes of poor performance in some blocks and to take effective remedial steps for improving the level of performance in a time bound manner.

It is unfortunate that in the division of responsibilities between the Central and State Governments, Government of India have chosen the 'easy to manage' task of providing the cost administrative services and of medicines and learning materials, while entrusting the job of funding and arranging the nutrition items to the State Governments. Given the critical resource position of most of the State Governments, nutrition always remains a neglected priority for them. There are reports that the supplementary feeding programme in the States was not taken up for months together. Even the Additional Plan Assistance under Prime Minister's Gramodaya Yojana (PMGY) was not utilized for supplementary nutrition in many States.

It is unfortunate that when the country is facing the problem of storage of surplus food grains procured by the Food Corporation of India, there are large number of infants and mothers who die every year due to lack of nutrition.

The country's achievement in food security must be converted into nutritional security by effectively distributing the surplus food grains at least to infants and mothers through the network of ICDS centers. This should be taken up in a mission mode, if the targets of IMR/MMR are to be achieved within the given time frame.

It is also unfortunate that the most backward areas of Bihar, Jharkhand and Uttar Pradesh, which have the highest incidence of infant and maternal mortality, have not yet been covered under the ICDS. These 450 blocks, which should have been the first charge on the programme, have been kept last in the priorities of the Government. The ICDS must immediately be extended to all the remaining blocks of the country and the unusual time lag between the sanctioning of the projects and the actual operationalisation must be reduced to a minimum. It is seen that the time lag is sometimes as high as two years, which cannot be justified by any means whatsoever.

The ICDS programme must also be effectively converged with the grassroot level programmes and infrastructure of Health and Family Welfare Departments, if the desired goals of IMR/MMR and of universal immunization of children against all vaccine preventable diseases are to be achieved. The States like Orissa and Gujrat, where such convergence has taken place, have done remarkably well, in a relatively short period of time.

In most of the States the programmes suffer due to the lack of effective co ordination between the Department of Women and Child development and the Department of Health and Family Welfare. The village Panchayats and the community should also be involved more effectively with the functioning of the ICDS centers.

It is a matter of national shame that despite the Constitutional directive to the State to endeavour to provide within a period of ten years from the commencement of the Constitution, free and compulsory education for all children until they complete the age of fourteen years, more than 100 million Indian children either do not get admitted to schools or drop out.

It is high time that the Directive Principle is converted into justifiable Fundamental Right of citizens and a comprehensive package of incentives and disincentives are built into our national education system to make it a reality. The Balika Samriddhi Yojana, which links payment of scholarship to girls to duration of school attendance should be implemented more vigorously and provided with adequate funds.

The average age of marriage at the national level has already reached 19.5 years and therefore achieving the target of 20 years by 2010 would seem to be an easily achievable task. But the average conceals significant regional differences. Child marriage is still a practice in many States.

About 20.3% percent of girls in the rural areas are married before 18 years. 8.3% percent of fertility in India is contributed by mothers below 19 years of age and this is closely linked with pregnancy wastages ranging form pre-mature death, stillbirth, neonatal deaths, low birth weight and maternal morbidity. Therefore, region specific strategies and action plans need to be worked out to achieve this national goal.

OPERATIONAL STRATEGIES

The Action Plan under NPP 2000 has outlined operational strategies for (i) empowering women for health and nutrition, (ii) child health and survival and (iii) adolescents. The Sub Group considered these strategies, but while broadly agreeing with them felt that the overwhelming emphasis placed on maternity and childcare services can not be taken as 'stand alone strategies'. Rather these should be effectively integrated with the overall perspectives, strategies and programmes for empowerment of women and of development of children and adolescents, as outlined in this report.

Recommendations

The Sub Group makes the following recommendations for the consideration of the National Commission on Population: The task of stabilization of population is not simply a question of birth control or contraceptives. It is intrinsically connected with the larger issues of alleviation of poverty, empowerment of women, changing mind set of men, women and community and of creation of opportunities and enabling environment of all round development of women, children and adolescents. There is a tendency to marginalize these 'strategic' issues in the belief that 'practical' needs are in some sense more immediate, urgent and easier to manage.

Unless these practical needs of women are conceived within a long run and 'strategic' framework, there is a danger of losing sight of the essential inter connections between the two. In principle a long-run goal may well be achieved through a series of co-ordinated short-term strategies, but in practice these may turn out to be stand-alone pieces, which could be symptoms of a long run structural malaise. Defining 'short term' goals simply in terms of combating such symptoms would be tantamount to treating the symptom of the disease rather than treating the disease itself. Therefore, it is extremely important to design strategies for empowerment of women and for development of children and adolescents, keeping this disease in mind.

The long awaited approval of National Policy for Empowerment of Women which has closely followed the National Population Policy is a welcome development. It is understood that a new National Policy on Health and a National Policy on Youth are under consideration. The Government is also seized with the idea of declaring basic education as a Fundamental Right of citizens and formulating a Charter of Rights of Children. All these efforts should be integrated and the National and State Action Plans to be framed under each of these Policies should be effectively converged for the effective delivery of services at the grassroot level. The broad National Socio Economic Goals of NPP should inform the process of preparation of the Action Plans under NPEW.

The Planning Commission should make a commitment of adequate resources for the effective implementation of Plans to achieve the National Socio Economic Goals. At present less than 10% of the Annual Budget is spent on the social sector. There is a strong need and justification to substantially step up allocation to all these sectors, such as health, education, women and child development, rural development, social welfare etc.

Both the programmes on Integrated Child Development Services (ICDS) and Integrated Women Development in Information... Programme (IWEP) should be universalized covering all the development blocks of the country, but the design, content and guidelines of the projects under both the programmes should be flexible enough to meet the specific requirement of the blocks so that they are in a position to achieve the National Socio Economic Goals within the time frame prescribed in the NPP.

Larger number of creches/day care centers should be opened to encourage female participation in the economy and also to create a positive impact on enrolment and drop out rates of girl children.

The Kishori Shakti Yojana as a component of ICDS, which has been taken up in 2000 blocks needs to be reworked and restructured to have a developmental approach rather sectoral approach. It should have a gender centred adolescent nutrition and development programme and should aim at a high level of adolescent participation. It should meet the requirements of nutrition, training and education of the adolescent girls so that they can gain the knowledge and self-confidence to be informed and capable members of society. The restructured programme should be universalized to cover all the blocks in the country.

A strong focus on the adolescents should be built in various programmes and schemes to address their concerns related to health, nutrition, sexual activity and behivour, vulnerability to HIV/AIDS etc. Sex education is an area which needs to be specifically addressed.

The gains made by the country in food security should be converted into nutritional security of children and the mothers below the poverty line to completely eliminate nutrition related deaths within a given time frame. Here again block specific strategies need to be worked out in consultation with all the stakeholders.

The constitutionally mandated country wide Panchayat Raj Institutions with one third of its Members and Chairpersons from among the women, has the potential to co-ordinate various programmes of the government on women and children according to the needs and requirements of the micro level realities and to monitor the services to the community. If properly constituted and adequately empowered, they have the potential to ensure the highest degree of transparency and accountability at the grassroot level. Panchayats can also be used for initiating popular movements, as has been done in the context of the National Literacy Mission in a number of States. A nation wide movement on informed fertility control through the Panchayats can very well be initiated under the auspices of the National Commission on Population. Village Panchayats can become regular forums for discussions on village health issues, including issues of reproductive health and fertility control.

Capacity of elected representatives at the grass roots should be developed so that they will be in a position to design projects on health and related areas as appropriate to the needs and requirements of local areas.

Given the size and heterogeneity of our population and the power structure within the Panchayats, even the Gram Panchayats may still be far away from the community. Some NGOs have found it expedient to create intermediate structures between the Panchatyats and the village communities for more efficient processes of information and dissemination and better service delivery. But these local elected bodies are by and large the best instruments for implementing community programmes.

The self help groups of women have been found very effective in organizing and sensitizing women to various issues and empowering them socially and economically. The collaboration of Panchayats,

NGOs and Self Help Groups at the grassroots level could become very effective for implementation of grassroot level initiatives in the social sectors. Depending on the strength of the stakeholders at the field level, different models of collaboration can be worked out for effective synergy of these initiatives, to transform the situation at the ground level.

The districts and blocks should be graded according to the level of achievements in the social sectors and block specific action plans should be framed for achieving the National Socio Economic Goals within the given time frame. Instead of uniform allocation of resources to blocks as is currently the practice in almost all the programmes, a more flexible and need-based approach should be taken. The segment of population and areas which have lagged behind in national development efforts, should be positively discriminated, so that they can be helped as quickly as possible to reach the minimum desired levels of standards and goals. But care should be taken to ensure that those blocks which have shown results do not feel discriminated against.

In order that district or block specific plans and projects can be prepared, implemented and monitored it is necessary to develop a system of gender segregated data on various indices of development at the district and sub district level at regular intervals. The absence of such data constraints the preparation of sound Women Development Plans at the field level.

The Medium Term perspective of 10 years should be adopted for the empowerment of women and development of children and adolescents. To that extent the National Socio Economic Goals of NPP should be accepted in the Action Plans for the Empowerment of Women and Development of Children and Adolescents. The achievement of these goals should be monitored on a quarterly basis and appraised on a bi-annual basis.

Involving the male is equally important for the empowerment of women and for stabilization of population. Reproductive decisions are typically taken within the family and hence promoting gender equality within the family has to be based on partnership and not on relationship of domination or subordination within the family. To achieve better understanding, every effort must be made to involve men in the promotion of reproductive rights. This is vital in order to change the societal perceptions about the contribution of women. This can happen only when women are seen by men-and by society-not as 'better halves' but as 'equal halves'.

There is a large unmet need for contraceptives and comprehensive information regarding their efficacy and usage. There has to be greater focus on male contraceptives as they are safer and easier to use. New contraceptives for women need to be carefully introduced with the fully informed participation of women.

A system of incentives/disincentive for the functionaries as also the beneficiaries of various programmes should be developed to convey clear messages about the priorities of the Government regarding population stabilization of the country. However, in order to ensure that disincentives do not become a tool for harassing the disadvantaged, it is necessary to create an environment enabling the women to have self-determination in terms of their reproductive life.

The target of achieving 80% institutional deliveries by 2010 is a tall order, considering that more than half of the deliveries still take place at home at present. The idea of maternity hut in each village to be used as the village delivery room, with storage space for supplies and medicine, and equipped adequately with kits for midwifery, antenatal care and delivery and basic medicines, contraceptives and drugs and medicines for common ailments, is conceptually very sound but may be difficult to implement within the given time frame. A more realistic and practical alternative is to train and equip the village midwives to ensure 100% safe deliveries. This must be taken up immediately as a time bound national programme, to upgrade their skills.

In view of the shortage of trained medical personnel at the PHCs and dispensaries, it should be made mandatory for medical students in both Government and private medical colleges to go to designated rural areas for service for a period of 12 months after they complete one year of residency but before their final degree is awarded. Posting to rural areas for a minimum period of two years at a time should be legally binding for medical officers. Similar arrangements should also be made mandatory for nurses, pharmacists and other paramedical staff.

A Core Group of Women Functionaries at the village level such as ANM, AWW, lady school teacher and elected women Panchayat members could co-ordinate the various programmes on women and children at the village or hamlet level. They should meet once in a fortnight at a fixed place and date to discuss among themselves the progress of the implementation of the programmes and to sort out the problems and difficulties at the purely local level. Coordinating and an integrated approach rather than competition among the local functionaries is essential to ensure positive results. Common training and parity in salaries could ensure this.

Training and capacity building of field level functionaries, NGOs, SHG workers and PRI members are extremely important if they are to perform their desired roles for the achievement of National Socio Economic Goals. Role of Angan Wadi Workers (AWW) is very crucial for the success of the various grassroot level initiatives of the Government. Today the contribution of AWW is not limited to the ICDS only. Her services are required in other programmes also. But she is paid very little-even less than the minimum wage prescribed by the Government itself. Therefore, the honorarium of the AWWs should be enhanced suitably with incentives for results shown. But the AWW must be a local person who stays in the villages.

In view of unacceptable high neonatal and perinatal mortality a comprehensive package needs to be developed at block level concentrating on improving home based care through trained personnel, with adequate referral linkages.

Every infant and maternal death must be compulsorily audited, to have better understanding of the underlying factors for such deaths. Simultaneously, a system of accountability of every functionary must be put in place to fix responsibility for every action or inaction for causing or precipitating such deaths.

Certain clinical and medical interventions can result in immediate and significant improvement in the maternal mortality. Such interventions can also be very cost effective. For example, Tetanus Toxoid injections can prevent a significant percentage of maternal deaths. Such interventions can be taken as a campaign on fixed dates throughout the country, for which nation wide publicity can be given. The same occasion can also be utilized for the health check up of pregnant mothers.

The provisions of Pre-natal Diagnostic Act is not at all be effective in checking the practice of female foeticide, which have become rampant in many States. The requirement of prior permission of 'competent authority' before a case for violation of the provisions of the Act can be challaned before the court, has been found to be a hindrance for booking the offenders, since most of the States have designated the Director of Health Services as the competent authority and they have been found to be reluctant to take action against their colleague doctors. The Act needs to be reviewed thoroughly. More than that a concerted public opinion involving religious leaders and opinion makers from every field should be built up against this highly undesirable social practice.

A sustained, systematic, concerted and pervasive campaign in the print, electronic and folk media should be built up in support of the National Socio Economic Goals of NPP and on various issues related to empowerment of women, health related issues, value of girl child, rights of women, violence against women etc. Village melas and festivals, which bring people together, should be used to popularize these messages. The media budget of the entire social sector Ministries/departments should be pooled together for this campaign.

Network of IGNOU and other agencies should also be utilized for developing suitable packages and courses on health and nutrition education.

THE CYCLE OF MALNUTRITION

The vicious cycle of malnutrition among the women of rural India perpetuates the equally vicious cycle of persistent hunger and poverty for all rural Indians.

India has the second worst rate of child malnutrition in the world, just behind Bangladesh. Low birth weight and child malnutrition are the primary determinants of ill-health and diminished capacity throughout life.

When children are born malnourished and underweight, they are at severe risk in all areas of personal development, health and mental capacity. They are physically weak and lack resistance to disease. They face a lifetime of disabilities, a lowered capacity for learning and diminished productivity.

The cost to India of this deficiency, solely in economic terms, has been estimated to be as much as US$28 billion per year in reduced GDP. This is greater than India's total annual public expenditures on nutrition and health combined.

This reality is a clear and direct result of the subjugation, marginalization and disempowerment of women throughout their lives. We should not need to focus exclusively on women as mothers in order to be committed to transforming their status. Yet, in their role as mothers, they do represent the most critical link in the chain of human well-being and development.

It is widely recognised that the health and nutritional status of a pregnant woman dramatically affects the health of her baby. A more accurate scientific understanding, however, reveals that this is only part of the story. The truth is that a woman's health, from the time she is in her own mother's womb, is the single most important factor in determining the health of her child.

With this knowledge, it is clear that traditional responses to child malnutrition, such as simply providing nutritional supplements to pregnant women, are both inadequate and ultimately futile.

If India is to interrupt the cycle of persistent hunger, the lifetime health and nutritional status of women must improve dramatically.

This, in turn, means transforming the way women are treated in the family and society as a whole:

- No longer can she eat last and least, taking whatever is left over after feeding the husband and sons.
- No longer can a girl-child be kept from the breast so that her mother may become pregnant sooner-to bear a son.
- No longer can teenage girls facing the stresses of puberty also expect to face deprivation, pregnancy and abuse.

WOMEN-INDIA'S INVISIBLE PRODUCERS

"...to fetch, to carry, to cook, to wash...year after year a submissive silent slave sold to life for nothing."
— from Silver Shackles by Maitrayee Mukhopadhyay

Rural India depends on its women for survival.

Its children and families are fed, clothed and sheltered by the labour of women. Its water and firewood are gathered by the hands of women. Its family farms and rural economy are productive because of women's work. Yet, when men are asked, they say women do nothing at all. Because of women's low social status, their work goes unacknowledged, unvalued and unsupported. Women carry a triple burden. They make indispensable contributions in all areas of rural life and economic activity, particularly in household maintenance, agriculture, and income-generating activities.

Household Maintenance

Women and girls have primary responsibility for all household work, and caring and providing for their families. They are traditionally responsible for collecting water, fuel and fodder (animal feed).

- Women hold full responsibility for cooking, cleaning and washing, and caring for children, the sick and the elderly.
- Women may cook for more than three hours per day with a biomass stove-burning wood, dung and crop residues. The smoke they inhale is equivalent to 20 packs of cigarettes per day. It causes eye and respiratory problems, bronchitis and lung cancer.

Agriculture

- Women contribute between 55 per cent and 80 per cent of total farm labour. Their work includes planting, transplanting, cultivation and weeding, watering, fertilising and harvesting.
- Women provide 50 per cent of the intensive labour in rice cultivation.
- Women account for 93 per cent of total employment in dairy production.
- In most households, women are responsible for all post-harvest processing and preservation.
- Women are generally not allowed to use agricultural implements. They perform many arduous tasks, such as transplantation and weeding, with their bare hands.

Income-generating activities

- Women are critical income earners for the family. They engage in small business ventures including silk cocoon rearing, vegetable oil extraction, spice preparation and fish farming.
- Women raise animals for milk, eggs, wool, leather and meat, as well as for use as draft animals.
- Women are involved in various paid labour activities, which are often severely physically taxing. Women's work includes cutting rocks and stones, construction, digging and carrying loads on their heads.

- Women constitute 51 per cent of total employment in forest-based small-scale enterprises such as basket, broom and rope making. Women who transport firewood on their heads may make two to three trips per day to the forest, carrying as much as 20-25 kilograms (44-55 pounds) of wood per trip.

Unequal Pay for Unequal Work

Despite their hard work, women are rarely compensated for their labours.

In a 1992 study of family-based textile workers, male children who helped in a home-based hand-loom mill were given pocket money, while the adult women and girls were not.

When women do earn an income, it is significantly less than men's. In the state of Tamil Nadu, women's agricultural wages are only 57 per cent of men's.

When women control their own income, they invest in the well-being of their children and families, while men often spend earnings on alcohol and leisure.

Improve Health: In the nations with the best health care, the life expectancy of women is 10% longer than that of men. In developing countries, however, women's life expectancy is closer to or shorter than men's. This occurs because women receive less than their fair share of health care and food, often beginning in childhood. As adults, many women do not get the food and health care needed for healthy childbearing.

Encourage Education: Over the last 20 years more and more girls have been going to school, but boys still get more education than girls. An estimated two-thirds of the 300 million children without access to education are girls. Two-thirds of the 960 million nonliterate adults are women.

Ensure Job Opportunities and Fair Pay: Most women work long and hard, and they earn less for it than men do. Even in developed countries, for example, women earn 75% or less of what men earn. Much of women's work is unpaid. Women's unpaid household labor accounts for about one-third of the world's economic production. When unpaid agricultural work and housework are considered along with wage labor, women work more hours than men.

Guarantee Legal Protection: Legal codes often sanction inequality between husband and wife. They may allow marriage of very young women, marriage without the woman's consent, unequal ownership and control over family assets including land and other property, unequal inheritance rights, and unequal access to divorce and to support after divorce. In many cases the law does not recognize women as adults with the same capacities and right to make decisions as their husbands. Laws that do protect women's rights often are not enforced.

Permit access to reproductive health care. The International Planned Parenthood Federation (IPPF) has reported that 46 of 94 surveyed countries require spousal consent for contraception, abortion, or voluntary sterilization-services used primarily or exclusively by women. Worldwide, 54 countries require a woman to obtain her husband's approval before voluntary sterilization, but only 20 of these countries also require a man to have his wife's approval.

Young women and unmarried women often have little or no access to reproductive health services. Yet surveys in eight sub-Saharan countries, for example, find that 20% to 47% of adolescent women become pregnant before marriage.

Prevent violence against women. Many women live every day in fear of violence, often from their husbands. In surveys in Chile, Colombia, Kenya, India, Mexico, Pakistan, Papua New Guinea, San Salvador, South Korea, and Thailand, 40% to 99% of women reported physical abuse by their husbands. Most of these women have no choice but to live with this abuse and fear. Leaving the marriage is often not a realistic option when women, denied education, jobs, and inheritance rights, are economically dependent on their husbands.

Unwanted sexual intercourse is a major form of violence against women. In a US national sample survey, 13% of women reported that they had been raped at some time in their lives, not counting marital rape. This amounts to one woman raped every minute. Half of these women were under age 18 when raped, and 75% knew the man who raped them. Detailed data on rape are not available from developing countries.

Fear of desertion or violence prevents women from acting in their own best interests. For example, in Egypt many women do not seek care for gynecological problems such as vaginal discharge or fistula because they fear that their husbands will divorce them for spending time and money on their own health. Threats of violence prevent some women even from participating in development projects.

Increase respect for women. Since most societies value females less than males, many women grow up believing that they are inferior to males. Such perceptions are difficult to change. For example, China has promoted equal roles and rights for women for 40 years. Still, 30% of Chinese women surveyed in 1990 thought that men are born to be more important than women, and 33% agreed that women should hold back so that they are not more successful than their husbands.

Programs to Improve Women's Lives

Programs to help women often focus on their economic or legal position. Women themselves have started many of these programs. For example, women in India formed the Self-Employed Women's Association (SEWA) in 1972 and the Working Women's Forum (WWF) in 1977 to change local ordinances that interfered with their ability to work as market traders. Both groups broadened their agendas as members began to request help with health, education, and other needs.

In Tunisia in the 1970s President Habib Bourguiba led the government to legislate better legal protection of women. In Bangladesh university professor Mohammed Yunus convinced the Grameen Bank, a private bank, to give poor women small loans.

Development planners have developed two broad approaches to assessing women's needs and designing programs to address them:

- The status of women approach compares the positions of women and men in a society or cross-nationally. After identifying the areas in which women are disadvantaged, planners design programs to address the problems.
- The empowerment of women approach aims to help women gain more control of their lives. This approach often begins with women identifying and prioritizing their own needs. Program organizers then help women to design programs that meet those needs.

Both approaches have advantages. Focusing on objective measures of women's status documents the problem for top-level policy-makers and helps motivate their support for policy changes. The United Nations has based its efforts to eliminate discrimination against women on status measures such as years of education and hourly wages. The empowerment approach may bring faster results for individual women, although usually on a smaller scale. Involving women in solving their own problems builds their skills and self-confidence and finds solutions that are locally appropriate.

Using both approaches could speed improvements for women, and in practice the two approaches are not always distinct. Program organizers can use the status-of-women approach to influence policy nationally and to evaluate its impact and at the same time can use community-based empowerment programs to begin change locally. Some of the most successful community programs at first address a need that women clearly recognize, such as the need for income, and then build skills that women can use in many areas of life.

Women's advocates are asking that development plans pay more attention to the effects of planned changes on women's lives. Some development plans have required, for example, male labor migration or female volunteer labor, which place additional burdens on women. "Gender planning," as the approach is called, considers the impact of a proposed program on women, men, and their relationship. Its goals are to ensure that development programs do not inadvertently harm the lives of men or women and to see that women's situation is improved.

A BETTER LIFE OF WOMEN

"The main thing that makes the times different, I think, is the control women have over the number of children in a family. A family can be planned now; it can live a better life. Women have more facilities for everything because of this. I began to take contraceptives when the last child was eight months old. I take the pill."

> *"...we were very poor when I was a child. We were six children, and my father didn't earn much. That is why I want just two or three children. I don't want my children [two daughters] to grow up like me-without an education. I feel very ashamed and bad about not having any education. I want my children to go to school and learn many, many things.... I want them to be independent and proud of themselves." -19-year-old Mexican woman using contraception without her husband's knowledge.*

SON PREFERENCE, DAUGHTER NEGLECT

In some countries parents tend to prefer sons and to treat them better than daughters. Boys sometimes get more to eat and more medical care, while girls are slighted in education and jobs and in some cases are neglected, abused, and even killed. While the majority of studies on son preference come from countries in South Asia and North Africa, where son preference is believed to be strongest, son preference appears to exist to some degree in other regions of the world as well. The preference for sons is both a symptom and a cause of limited opportunities for women.

Extent of Son Preference

A common index of preference for sons comes from survey responses: the ratio of the number of parents who say that they prefer their next child to be male to the number who prefer their next child to be female. A ratio also can be derived from survey responses about desire for additional children among women with different numbers of living daughters and sons. Among countries surveyed, those with strong preference for sons-indices of 1.6 or above-are Bangladesh, Jordan, Nepal, Pakistan, South Korea, and Syria. Moderate preference for sons (indices of 1.2 to 1.5) has been documented in many other countries, including the Dominican Republic, Egypt, Mexico, Senegal, Sudan, Turkey, Nigeria, Tunisia, and Yemen. Some countries, such as Colombia, Ghana, and Indonesia, show no preference, and two-Jamaica and Venezuela-show a slight preference for daughters. In most countries parents desire at least one daughter as well as sons.

Reasons for Son Preference

Why do many parents favor boys? Often the reasons are both economic and cultural.

Economic Security: In many developing countries sons are their parents' only source of security in old age. Particularly where women have little economic independence or cannot inherit property, sons are insurance for a mother against the loss of her husband's support due to death or desertion.

Where women have few opportunities to earn income, investing household resources in female children, who will marry and leave the family, is likely to have little pay-off, and so poor families tend to invest what little they have in sons. In cultures with dowry systems, such as India's, daughters are more expensive to marry off than sons.

Cultural Factors: In many countries kinship systems, tradition, and religion value males over females. In parts of Bangladesh, China, Egypt, India, and Tanzania, for example, traditional patrilineal kinship systems require women to marry out of their families of origin and then not to provide financial or even emotional support to their own parents. In both Hindu and Confucian traditions, practiced throughout Asia, only sons can pray for and release the souls of dead parents, and only males can perform birth, death, and marriage rituals.

Effects of Son Preference on Female Children

Although females are thought to be genetically more resistant to respiratory and other infectious diseases than males and more likely to survive infancy, in some developing countries this advantage rapidly disappears as female babies grow up. Females are more likely than males to die in early childhood (ages 1 to 4), particularly in South Asia, the Near East, and North Africa. Poorer nutrition and health care are important reasons.

Nutrition: In some places boys get more and better food than girls. Breast-feeding and weaning practices also seem to favor boys in some countries. In the Indian state of Punjab, for example, boys from both wealthy and poor households are better nourished than girls. An analysis of DHS data from 18 countries, however, found few significant differences in the nutritional status of boys and girls.

Medical Care: Girls are sick as often as boys, but boys sometimes receive more treatment and more medicine. For example, boys were seen 66% more often than girls at a diarrhea treatment center in Bangladesh even though the center provided free ambulance transport and treatment.

Parents bought drugs and sought medical care three times more often for boys than for girls. Girls often receive less preventive health care, as well. Studies in Latin America and India show that girls often are immunized later than boys or not at all.

Female Infanticide: Some unwanted female children are killed or abandoned soon after birth. It is not clear how common or widespread the practice is, but some demographers have long suspected its existence. They base their conclusions largely on reported sex ratios at birth. Others argue that underreporting explains the discrepancy. In China, where sex ratios show that 5% of all infant girls born are unaccounted for, some observers suspect that female infanticide accounts for at least some of these missing girls, although informal adoptions, sending girls to faraway relatives, or raising the girls covertly probably explain most of the cases.

Abortion of female fetuses. Selective abortion of female fetuses reportedly is widespread in such Asian countries as China, India, and South Korea. Increasing use of prenatal ultrasound and amniocentesis procedures, which make selective abortion possible by revealing the sex of a fetus, may be contributing to a growing gap in the number of males and females born in some countries. Although governments in China, South Korea, and three Indian states have banned prenatal gender tests to prevent selective abortions, illegal tests are available, and females are more often aborted than males.

Son Preference, Fertility, and Contraceptive Use

Does a preference for sons result in higher fertility? Do more couples adopt family planning after having a son than after having a daughter? The answers may depend on current fertility levels. In general, where most couples have large families, son preference has little impact on fertility levels because most couples will have at least one son by biological chance. As contraceptive use becomes more widespread and average family size decreases, however, in some countries the desire to have at least one son begins to affect fertility decisions: Trying for a son, many couples have more children than they would otherwise.

A recent study in Matlab, Bangladesh, indicates that son preference can have a strong effect on contraceptive use and fertility. In Matlab, where intensive family planning services are available, contraceptive prevalence now tops 50%, and couples average four children, researchers calculated that eliminating preference for sons would increase contraceptive use by 10% and continuation rates by 15%. These increases would avert nearly one birth for every two couples.

What can be Done?

Attempts to improve the position of girls in society often focus on economics. Increasing economic opportunities for women and raising the value of women's labor increases the likelihood that parents will see daughters as economic assets and not as liabilities.

Also, increasing girls' education may increase their income-earning potential and, thus, their economic value to their parents. Other recommendations include better access to food and medical care so that parents will not have to choose between male and female children in allocating household resources.

Also, better access to pension plans and other forms of old-age security that do not depend on children would relieve some of the pressure to have sons. While specific measures can help, some researchers insist that only far-reaching improvements in the cultural, social, legal, and economic position of women will improve the well-being of female children.

CHANGES IN WOMEN'S LIVES

How do women's lives differ between countries where contraceptive use is common and countries where it is rare? The Demographic and Health Surveys (DHS) are one source of information. Contraceptive prevalence varies widely among surveyed countries, from over 60% in 4 of 30 countries to 5% or lower in 3 countries. The surveys reveal that in countries where contraceptive use is widespread, women:

- Are older when they have their first child,
- Complete their childbearing earlier,
- Spend fewer years pregnant, and
- Spend fewer years with young children in the household.

Age at First and Last Births

Where total contraceptive use is above 40% (the average for use of modern methods in developing countries), women ages 25 to 29 at the time of the surveys first gave birth on average about three years later than in countries where contraceptive use is below the average. Median age at first birth in the 30 countries from about 18 years in Niger and Uganda to close to 25 years in Morocco, Sri Lanka, and Tunisia. First births come soon after marriage in most countries. Still, on average women in the countries with higher contraceptive prevalence first give birth more than two years after marriage, while women in countries with lower than average prevalence give birth about a year and a half after marriage.

Last births come sooner in countries where contraceptive use is above average levels. Where contraceptive use exceeds 40%, most women had their last births in their early thirties, while in countries with lower levels of contraceptive use, women last gave birth in their late thirties. Age at last birth for women ages 40 to 49 at the time of the survey, the age group most likely to have completed childbearing. This analysis may underestimate the impact of contraceptive use on average age at last birth, because women in this age group are the least likely to have been affected by recent rises in the use of contraception in many countries.

The median age at last birth ranges from 31 years in a few Caribbean countries where contraceptive use is widespread to 38 or 39 years in several African countries where there is little use of contraception. Of course, other factors besides contraceptive use help to determine the age at last birth, including age-related sterility, divorce, widowhood, and reduced coital frequency at older ages.

The number of years that women can expect to live after the birth of their last child varies tremendously. This difference reflects both a woman's age at the birth of her last child and her life expectancy. Life expectancy tends to be longer in the more developed countries, where also age at last birth is lower. In all surveyed countries where contraceptive prevalence is above 40% except Peru, a woman still has more than half of her life ahead of her when she last gives birth. In contrast, in most countries where contraceptive prevalence is below 40%, women average fewer years of life after their last birth than before it.

NEW ROLES FOR WOMEN

"Because I have that job, our family is better off, and we are able to raise our children in a better way," says Zanati Begum. Zanati is an especially effective and articulate family planning field worker in rural Bangladesh. "And given the situation [of large families and poverty] prevalent in the society, it is our duty and responsibility as conscientious people to help solve the problem." Zanati's example is helping to change attitudes toward women's roles among men and women in her community.

The Route to a New Role

Zanati believed in the importance of family planning before she became a field worker. After the birth of their first child, a daughter, in 1984, Zanati and her husband Sarkee decided to delay the birth of their second child. Zanati took oral contraceptives for four years before the couple decided to have their second child. Both Zanati and Sarkee thought that many of their neighbors had more children than they could afford to raise. The poverty of some large families saddened the couple. When they saw a newspaper announcement in 1988 asking for family planning field workers, they agreed that Zanati should apply. "At the beginning some of my neighbors and relatives were against my work," Zanati recalls. "They felt working as a family planning worker, going house to house and talking to people about it, was degrading. They also didn't think it was right for a wife to earn for the family. A wife's taking up a job was a sign that her husband wasn't capable of supporting his family, they thought."

But now the neighbors' attitudes are changing. "Now people realize that women, too, can take up jobs and help their communities and families," Zanati says.

Sarkee has become increasingly committed to his wife's work. At first he thought only that her small income as a field worker would benefit their family. He also knew that his friendly and energetic wife would get satisfaction from working with others. But after Zanati began discussing her work with him, he became interested in the problems of her clients. Now he feels that she should be a field worker even if she were not paid. In fact, he tells her that, if a household task would keep her from her work, he will do that task for her. Her work, he says, will prevent hunger and hardship in the community.

Sarkee is not troubled that some might criticize him. "If my wife...can do good for the society, I will allow her [to work]. No matter what obstacles come, I will overcome them. And if anyone comes and asks me directly, 'Hey, how come you allowed your wife to go outside the house?'...I will explain to them why I allowed her to do that." Besides, Sarkee says, men now recognize that small families are necessary. "Even in the men's circle...everyone says the same thing, 'We have no choice but to adopt this.'"

Learning New Skills

Zanati has learned new skills from her job. She works with the Jiggasha program of the Bangladesh government and Johns Hopkins Population Communication Services. She meets with groups of women, who listen to tape recordings of songs and dramas and discuss family planning and other maternal and child health issues.

The women enjoy this rare entertainment, and they become less timid about talking about their needs and desires. Zanati also notes, "If people know that their neighbors practice [family planning], then they are more ready to adopt. That's why the Jiggasha idea works so well."

Zanati uses her new skills in other areas of her life. "...There are things which I'd never done before, for example, going house to house, holding meetings, keeping records of each day's work.... I do try to use these skills in my personal life and even to teach them to my neighbors."

As a result of her training in counseling, Zanati encourages women to talk and ask questions. "There are certain techniques we learn in counseling....

We learn that during counseling we must give the client greater opportunity to speak.... I should help a client to select a method according to her taste--according to her likes and dislikes." Zanati feels that she has done a good job when the women whom she counsels are willing to tell their friends openly that they use family planning.

Changing Attitudes Toward Women

Zanati says that her work is helping to change community attitudes toward women. "I've set an example in the community, by taking up a job in the family planning office. In the past it was hard to imagine women coming out of their homes to work. Now many of them realize that a girl's place in the family is just as important as a boy's," she says. "That's why they've begun to send their daughters to school as well."

"Society's attitudes toward women going to work have also changed. After I've taken up a job, people have begun to realize that there is nothing wrong with women going to work and that, like men, they can contribute to their societies, localities, and families...."

Many women have become interested in Zanati's work. Some have asked her advice about working. "Two of them are now teachers at the BRAC [Bangladesh Rural Advancement Committee] semi-formal education center," Zanati observes. "Women are no longer working only at home, as they have been doing for a very long time. The reason is an increasing awareness of their place in society and the family. For example, there are women in my family who say with regret, 'If we could only take up a job like you, we would have greater value in the family and society. Most of us who look after our families don't have any authority. Our opinions are never heeded.'"

Men's attitudes are changing, too. "After I began working in the field, the men have also given up their age-old ideas about women and their place in society. For example, they used to think that women should only look after the household affairs and their children, husbands, and mothers-and fathers-in-law. But now many of them realize that women should also be educated and allowed to work outside the home and that their work can bring prosperity to the family."

Zanati and Sarkee have two daughters. They do not plan to have more children. In Bangladesh most couples wish to have sons for support in old age. But Zanati and Sarkee say that, if parents can give daughters a good education, daughters can do just as much for their parents in their old age. Zanati says that her mother-in-law used to advise her to have a son, but no longer. "I explain to my mother-in-law that since my parents educated me and since I have a job, I can give my mother two saris every year if I want. I can take all the burden."

TEN PROGRAM STRATEGIES TO MEET WOMEN'S NEEDS

How can family planning programs improve their response to women's reproductive health needs? Ten possible strategies include:

1. Meeting unmet need by identifying and overcoming the institutional, cultural, and personal barriers to family planning that women face.
2. Widening the clientele to serve neglected groups such as young people, unmarried people, and men.
3. Training personnel to respect and communicate with clients, provide good technical care, and ensure informed choice.
4. Offering more services to meet a broader range of reproductive health needs.
5. Seeking women's opinions, including involving women in program planning.
6. Helping men and women to communicate, cooperate, and share responsibility by informing and educating men as well as women about men's and women's reproductive health and by providing convenient services.
7. Presenting new images in the mass media of competent women and caring men communicating and collaborating.
8. Adding criteria for evaluation of programs and personnel to assess how well clients' needs are met.
9. Promoting capable women employed in family planning programs.
10. Speaking out on behalf of women and in favor of policies that support women's rights to personal autonomy and more opportunities.

DURATION OF THE CHILDBEARING YEARS

Where the level of contraceptive use is above average, women devote less of their lives to childbearing and child-raising. Also, within countries the length of the childbearing period has decreased as contraceptive use has spread.

Differences Across Countries: The interval between average ages at first and last births among women ages 40 to 49 ranges from just 11 years in Trinidad and Tobago and in Thailand, where contraception is widely used, to nearly twice as long in Zambia and Senegal, where contraception is little used. In Trinidad and Tobago women ages 40 to 49 averaged four children.

The first child was born when the mother was 20 years old, and the last, when she was 31. In contrast, in Zambia women ages 40 to 49 had given birth to an average of seven children. The first was born when the mother was 18, and the last, when she was 38. Because contraceptive use is increasing in nearly every country, the childbearing years probably will be shorter for women who are now in their 20s or 30s.

By comparison, US women have fewer children over a shorter period of time. In the US, where about three-quarters of married women use contraception, those born between 1940 and 1949-and thus about the same age as women ages 40 to 49 in DHS surveys-married at a median age of 20.5 years. They first gave birth a little over a year after marriage and had their last child at age 30. They gave birth to an average of 2.8 children over the course of approximately eight years, and their life expectancy at the time of their last birth was 47.5 more years.

Both the number of children that women have and the spacing of their births influence the number of years that mothers spend with young children. In countries where use of contraception is widespread, women spend an average of 14 years with at least one of their children under the age of six. Where contraceptive prevalence is low, women have young children for an average of 20 years.

Changes over time. Women's childbearing patterns have changed as contraceptive prevalence has risen. In 16 countries at least two comparable surveys have been conducted since the 1970s.

Where contraceptive use has increased most, the childbearing period has decreased most. Also, in all 16 countries the time that women had a child under age six in the household decreased, but in some countries the decline was small.

The changes are most obvious in the five countries where three surveys have been taken. For example, in Morocco, where the level of contraceptive use more than doubled between 1979-80 and 1992, women's average childbearing period decreased by almost two years. The number of years spent with a child under age six fell by almost three years. In the Java-Bali region of Indonesia, contraceptive prevalence rose from 26% to 53% between 1976 and 1991. Over the same period the childbearing period decreased by 3.5 years, and the amount of time spent with at least one young child at home declined by five years. Age at last birth declined substantially in Colombia, the Dominican Republic, and Peru, and so did the length of the childbearing period.

Because the DHS are internationally comparable surveys, they offer a unique comparison of women's lives across a large number of countries with varying levels of contraceptive use. But they cannot tell the whole story. Cross-sectional surveys such as the DHS cannot explain much of how contraceptive use affects individual women. This is because surveys usually have not recorded the sequence of events such as the timing of contraceptive use, births, and employment. Also, surveys can reveal full childbearing patterns only for women whose reproductive years have ended. As noted, these women's experience is least likely to reflect recent changes in contraceptive use.

FAMILY PLANNING AND WOMEN'S LIVES

Not enough is known about the way contraceptive use affects women's lives. Researchers know that women's education, economic position, household characteristics, and social status influence use of contraception and thus fertility. In contrast, little is known about the opposite perspective-how changes in contraceptive use and thus in fertility affect other aspects of women's lives, particularly the ability to take on new roles.

The Rockefeller Foundation funded early research on the relationship between the status of women and fertility. Findings indicated that the status of women is defined differently in different cultures and that multiple factors affect both fertility and women's status. The researchers did not find any universal relationship between the status of women and fertility.

Assessing current understanding of this issue, Sawon Hong and Judith Seltzer observed, "(1) good data and rigorous analysis are scarce; (2) the relationship is complex and varies by social, cultural, and economic setting; and (3) no simple conceptual model has yet been set forth."

To improve understanding of how contraceptive use affects women's lives, the United States Agency for International Development has funded a 5-year, US$8.6 million research project, begun in late 1993 by Family Health International. Its purposes are (1) to support social and behavioral research on the immediate and long-term consequences for women of both family planning programs and contraceptive methods and (2) to help improve family planning and related reproductive health policies and programs through increased knowledge of the needs and perspectives of women. The project will support qualitative and quantitative research in six to eight countries. In-country advisory committees will help establish the research agenda. Based on its findings, the project will recommend improvements in program design and implementation from the perspective of women's interests and needs.

WHO MAKES REPRODUCTIVE DECISIONS?

Who makes reproductive decisions? How and why are these decisions made? Family planning programs can better serve their clients, both male and female, if they can answer these questions.

They also can better find ways to help women express their needs and to help men understand and respect women's concerns.

Complex Situations, Complex Decisions

The reproductive decision-making process reflects tradition, religious belief, community norms, family structure, household economics and the value of children, and access to new ideas and innovations, all expressed in peoples' attitudes and opinions. Research on the reproductive decision-making process is limited and scattered, but a study in areas of North and South India illustrates the complexity of the process. Women in southern India are valued agricultural workers, marry later than women in the North, have more contact with and support from their parents and families, and are closer emotionally to their husbands. Their daughters are less likely to die in infancy.

Women in southern India are better treated because they marry within their own extended families-groups of people who depend upon each other for continuing support. In contrast, women in northern India marry out of their extended families into families that have no on-going relationship with the women's parents and other relatives and that permit married women little contact with their own families. Meanwhile, men's families form close, mutually supportive groups.

Most men are not close to their wives. In the northern system women have little value to their own parents and are valued by their husbands' families chiefly when they produce sons. Women in the southern kinship system are better able to make reproductive choices such as using contraception because they are more valued, less isolated, and more autonomous. They also are under less pressure to produce sons.

As this example illustrates, the extended family or the community is often the ultimate decision-maker in matters of reproduction, even in countries as diverse as China, India, and Mexico. Such influence can extend even to decisions about what contraceptive method to use.

While the web of influences on decision-making is complex, people nonetheless have perceptions of who actually makes decisions in the household or who has the most say. Here and there surveys and focus-group research have asked people who makes household decisions including decisions about reproduction.

When Men Decide

Within marriage, in many cultures men typically have more say than women in the decision to use contraception and in the number of children that the couple will have. In Ghana, for example, both Demographic and Health Survey (DHS) data and focus-group research reveal that the husband is usually the effective decision-maker about fertility. Furthermore, husbands' family planning attitudes and fertility goals usually are not influenced by those of their wives. When partners disagree on whether to use family planning, the man's preference usually dominates. In South Korea researchers found that 71% of women whose husbands approved of family planning had used contraception at some time compared with 23% of women whose husbands did not approve.

When Women Decide

Within marriage some women make the decision to use family planning. In the few studies comparing various household decisions, women seem to have more say about using contraception than about most other important decisions. In Turkey, for example, 62% of the semi-urban wives surveyed made their own decisions about contraceptive use. In general, better educated women have more decision-making power within marriage, including more influence over decisions about reproduction and family planning.

Some women decide to use contraception without telling their husbands. In DHS in African countries, a small minority of women report doing so because they think that their husbands would disapprove. In rural Nigeria, as elsewhere around the world, some women secretly use contraceptives, use patent medicines as abortifacients, or make secret trips for abortions even though they risk eviction from their homes if found out.

Many unmarried women make reproductive decisions by themselves, of course. These decisions add up; in many countries women spend much of their lives outside marriage. For example, in Botswana women older than age 20 spend an average of 46% of their remaining reproductive years unmarried. In Colombia women spend an average of 40% of their entire reproductive lives unmarried.

Discussion Between Partners and Joint Decision-Making

Married couples together sometimes make household decisions of various kinds, including the decision to use contraception. Whether a couple discusses family planning can affect the decision to use contraception.

In many places such communication is the exception rather than the rule, however. In Kenya, for example, lack of communication between spouses proved to be a more common obstacle to contraceptive use than male opposition. In a study of monogamous couples in Ghana, 35% of the wives and 39% of the husbands reported discussing family planning during the previous year. Even among women who said that they had discussed family planning with their husbands, however, 39% reported their husbands' attitudes to be different from what their husbands independently told interviewers. Still, contraceptive use was higher among the couples who had discussed the subject.

Focus-group discussions in Tanzania found that different people had different reasons for not discussing contraception. Older people did not discuss using contraceptives because they believed that God determined the number of their children or because they used abstinence or herbal medicines to space pregnancies. Women did not discuss the topic because they thought that their husbands did not approve of contraception. Married men said that discussion was unnecessary because the women decided on their own the number and timing of pregnancies. Young people did not talk about contraceptives for fear of being considered promiscuous.

Program managers need to be aware of the variety of ways that individuals and couples make decisions about contraception-a variety that reflects not only the social position of women relative to men but also the different types of sexual relationships, from long-term monogamous marriages to one-time contacts between strangers. Communication campaigns and counseling are most likely to be effective when they recognize existing patterns of communication and decision-making. In some cases that means reaching out to couples. At the same time, communication needs to address men and women as individuals. In many cases communication programs may seek to influence men's and women's roles in the decision-making process as well as its outcome.

EFFORTS FOR LEGAL CHANGE

What can be done to eliminate the inequities that women face? While laws alone are seldom enough to change women's lives, legal change can be crucial. Change can start at every level, from international organizations to local women's groups.

International Leadership

The United Nations has advocated equality between men and women since its start in 1945. The UN Charter affirms the equal rights of men and women and prohibits discrimination based on sex. The United Nations considers reproductive choice a basic human right.

In 1979 the UN General Assembly adopted the Convention on the Elimination of All Forms of Discrimination Against Women. The Convention specifies steps to prevent discrimination against women in education, employment, public life, health, family planning, and other areas. It also suggests actions to change laws and attitudes. As of June 1993, 116 countries had ratified or acceded to the Convention. Many nations attached reservations to their acceptance, however. For example, Austria, Brazil, Ireland, Jordan, Libya, Malta, Thailand, Tunisia, Turkey, and the United Kingdom attached reservations to Article 15, which gives women full legal capacity. Some 52 countries have not yet signed the Convention, including India, Pakistan, South Africa, and the United States.

The UN called attention to the need to improve women's lives by declaring 1976 1985 the Decade of Women. The 1985 World Conference on Women set forth strategy to achieve equality between men and women by 2000, and the UN General Assembly endorsed the plan. This endorsement obligates all UN members to implement measures ending discrimination against women in such areas as access to education, rural development resources, legal protection, marriage, and access to health and family planning services. In 1995 the UN will convene the Fourth World Conference on Women, in Beijing.

National Initiatives

National efforts to improve the status of women are organized in various ways. Among 50 countries answering a 1989 questionnaire from the UN Commission on the Status of Women, some had set up separate bureaus or offices for women's affairs while others gave the ministry for social welfare authority over programs for women. Eleven of 14 industrialized countries and 22 of 36 developing countries reported programs to make people aware of gender inequality. All 50 countries said that they were promoting economic equality for women. In addition, developing countries sought to improve women's access to education, health services, family planning services, and child care. Most countries identified public attitudes favoring the subordination of women as the greatest problem facing their efforts.

Specific efforts vary widely. Recently, for example, Barbados gave priority to reducing violence against women; China reported programs to involve men in family planning; and Guatemala adopted a policy to incorporate women into development efforts through specific projects.

Of course, such policies make a difference only when government leaders have the political will to carry them out. Some national leaders have championed legal reforms on behalf of women. In Tunisia President Habib Bourguiba issued a new Personal Status Code in 1956 requiring that a bride consent to her marriage, abolishing polygamy, giving women the right to divorce while limiting men's ability to divorce at will, setting minimum ages for marriage, and establishing equal rights to custody of children. Bourguiba's government also provided family planning services for men and women. In Zimbabwe the courts have enforced the 1982 Legal Age of Majority Act, which asserts equality between men and women even in matters covered by customary law.

Often policy-makers' opinions are divided, however, and inaction results. In Kenya the constitution asserts equality between men and women but at the same time allows customary law to take precedence in cases of alleged discrimination. Revisions to the Marriage Act proposed in 1979 would have required a first wife's permission for her husband to take a second wife, given women a share of the couple's property at divorce, and recognized the possibility of a woman's having custody of her children after divorce.

Heated debate arose, and the bill has never passed. As a result, customary law, which grants women few rights, takes precedence in these matters. In some cases legal advances have even been reversed. Laws giving Egyptian women the right to seek divorce within a year after her husband's taking a second wife were passed in 1979 but repealed in 1985.

Women have few opportunities to change laws and policies because their political influence is limited. So is their direct participation in policy-making. In 1987 women comprised no more than 35% of members of parliament and government ministers in any country. In fact, women rarely made up even 25% of parliamentary representation.

WOMEN'S ORGANIZATIONS

Women's organizations have been powerful agents for change. They were early advocates for reproductive choice. Women's welfare organizations in Bangladesh, Egypt, and Pakistan were pioneers in supporting reproductive health services for women. In Thailand and Ecuador in the early 1970s women's medical and nursing organizations were among the first to provide family planning services.

Around the world women (sometimes joined by men who believe in equal rights) have formed groups to see that women receive fair treatment under the law. For example, in Brazil women's rights advocates began a campaign in 1985 to influence legislators writing the new constitution. They organized vigils, sent letters to newspapers, and aired television spot announcements. As a result the new constitution gives women equal rights and protection from domestic violence. Women's advocates in Brazil, Malaysia, and Zimbabwe have helped to train police to handle domestic violence and to involve police in drawing up laws to prohibit domestic violence.

WOMEN DEVELOPMENT IN INFORMATION...

Wives are lonelier now than they ever used to be. In older, gentler times, when age still had its privileges, the old folks never harbored any guilt feelings about being a drag on the young. They either moved in, reasoning that it was high time they were supported for a change, or else they lived nearby. People moved less, and families stuck closer together.

Grandma, never having become emancipated, was always around for advice and help. (Today grandma is likely to be off fund raising or taking courses at Columbia.) I know a Polish area in Chicago where everyone in the family lives within a few blocks of the others, and there are usually two generations in each house. They may have other problems, but loneliness isn't one of them.

The young college-educated mother with a medium amount of money is the one who reflects all the problems at once. In spite of her hopes for fulfillment through her children and contentment with woman's great career, she vaguely feels that she is frittering away her days and that a half-defined but important part of her ability is lying about unused; she is guilty about her feeling of futility because of her belief in the magic medicine of love.

This is the housewife's syndrome, the vicious circle, the feeling of emptiness in the gap between what she thought marriage was going to be like and what it is really like.

Let's take a look at a fairly typical young mother. She married her husband because she loved him, and she still does. She has two children and is pregnant with a third. Whether in city or country, she is more or less surrounded by gadgets which free her from drudgery. If she is lucky, she has a cleaning woman once a week. She and her husband have enough money for a fairly comfortable life, but for time alone together are dependent on baby sitters and possibly a grandma who will help out in a pinch. If the young mother is in the country, the children play in the yard, and she watches them from the window; if she is in the city, she takes them out once or twice a day, pushing a carriage and pulling a tricycle. Talking to her friends on these outings is her solution to loneliness. Her day is full of a thousand pressures, some miniature, some large. Two of the main worries are illness and money. If everyone in the family is healthy for two weeks at a stretch, she counts herself fortunate. Every cold goes the rounds of the family, and she sometimes feels that she supports the pediatrician singlehandedly.

During the healthy periods she strives to improve her home, cook a new dish, do something about her looks, give a dinner party and a children's birthday party, go to the theater with her husband, catch up on her reading, have coffee with a friend. Her life vacillates between being very organized and completely disorganized, because she has the struggle of all women: to keep the house clean and in repair without being a shrew about people's messing it up. Because children are natural makers of havoc, she constantly strives to maintain the delicate line of balance. Usually, when the first child starts school, she is drawn into community or P.T.A. work of some kind. If she is normally conscientious, she feels she should do something, but if she is normally realistic, she knows she doesn't have time. So she does it anyway. Joining things as a virtue is a hangover from college, where well-roundedness and abundant interests were considered rungs on the ladder to heaven.

The demands of her family and community cause her to feel, as one woman put it, like a pie with not enough pieces to go around. Depending on whether or not she is gregarious, she longs for time to talk to her friends or time to be alone; I should say, the busier she is, the greater her urge to be by herself, to feel unique and separate again. Great numbers of friends are a luxury she can no longer afford; old friends often diminish in importance, which she is sorry about. But there is a limit to her capacity for giving affection, and maintaining old friendships at their original intensity requires an effort she hardly has the energy for. Besides, she is often forced into unwanted and demanding friendships with the next-door neighbor, the boss's wife, or the ladies' club chairman, and she must learn to cover up her real feelings. (To her surprise, she often ends by liking these women.) Another group of demanding relationships is required with her in-laws, and if she gets along well with them, she is lucky. If her husband now lacks the mystery and fascination of the wedding night, he is now more loved and appreciated. The occasions when they have time alone together are among her precious jewels.

In spite of this full life, the old illusions of what life was supposed to hold, the restless remnants, the undefined dreams do not die as they were supposed to. Probably every educated wife has found herself staring at a mountain of dirty diapers and asking herself desperately, "Is this all there is?" And at the same time she is embarrassed by her dissatisfaction; she, of all people, with her intelligence and realistic view of life, should be able to rise above it. But the paradox is that it is she who is least able to. She lives for a better day.

Things will be easier when this baby is born, or that one toilet-trained, or the children are all in school; and she will have time to be pretty and intelligent and young again. The mistake is in thinking that everything is going to solve itself by magic. What our girl must do, as she stares at the diapers, is to accept some of the truths about marriage and motherhood that her education and society conspired to keep from her, and go on from there. And if she would appreciate what she has, she must do it now, not next year or five years from now.

The first truth is that marriage does not automatically equal security and contentment. An unmarried friend of mine told me once that she did not see how any problem in marriage could be as bad as one outside of it, because if you had your man, anything else could be easily straightened out. We had a long argument about whether the heart sank more over a sick child or a departed boy friend, and neither of us won. She is one of a good many girls who think that three dates a week, secretarial jobs, and the responsibility of keeping themselves clothed are a nerve-shattering, frantic business, and who look forward to marriage and motherhood as a long, relaxing rest cure. "Getting married and settling down" is a valid notion for men, as it has been throughout history, but not for potential mothers. The day the doctor confirms one's pregnancy is the day to start bracing oneself for the really hard work. (I cannot convince my unmarried friends of this, but, of course, that is as it should be, or many babies might never be born.)

The truth is that, with the birth of the first child, marvelous changes take place. From that moment on, mama is no longer the center of attention; the baby is. Mama and papa will give-and willingly-and the baby will take. They will assume responsibility, earn money, employ their energy, change their lives, if necessary-all for the baby. This is no light undertaking, but the business of life is starting now, and every day of mama's life proves it to be so. And here her struggle starts.

She wants to give everything to the baby; she wants equally to hold on to herself, her intelligence and uniqueness, while the baby con-stantly tries her patience, her strength, her nerves, and roots out of her the deepest emotions she has ever known in her life. This is a whole new process, and not one that provides built-in security. It is a mistake to assume that marriage is a cure-all, a miraculous bit of psychiatry that is going to banish all the old problems overnight and, like phenobarbital, put disturbingly violent instincts to sleep. The benediction of church and state is not enough to still the quality of excitement that comes from strangeness and the idealization of a still-unknown experience. These things, after all, were part and parcel of sex before marriage, and half its value. Sex in marriage makes up in intimacy what it loses in mystery, but this does not mean that mystery is no longer attractive. The most embarrassing lust for the least likely person can exist in the best-adjusted P.T.A. member in town. Whether or not anything is done about it is another story, but probably most of the time nothing is. We take marriage very seriously; our Puritan heritage is still very much with us; and we fear the wages of sin. Besides, the communities of young married couples are built for decency and togetherness, and the woman who considers taking a lover simply has no place to go.

All of the notions about peace being intrinsic in the state of marriage have to do with the happiness-togetherness cult, the great American dream, the return to the hearth. The peak of all earthly satisfaction is said to be found in the family, popping corn together in matching pajamas, not in hard work and self-denial, or even in the self-knowledge that came with the Freudian age. In our unending search for panaceas, we believe that happiness and "success"-which, loosely translated, means money-are the things to strive for. People are constantly surprised that, even though they have acquired material things, discontent still gnaws.

An Englishman said to me recently, "You Americans live on a much higher plane of expectancy than we do. You constantly work toward some impossible goal of happiness and perfection, and you unfortunately don't have our ability just to give up. Really, it's much easier to accept the fact that some things can't be solved." He is right; we never accept it, and we kill ourselves trying. The feeling of futility of the housewife is based on a history of high expectancy, a faith in external things, and an inability to see that the rewards are found within oneself. It is a paradox that the achievement of a home and family is so often regarded by women as the consummate solution for human ills, when actually the responsibilities it entails are enough to reduce some people to nervous wrecks. Marriage, entered upon maturely, is the only life for most women. But it is a way of life, not a magic bag of goodies at the end of the road.

The fact is that marriage and motherhood bring forth deeper and more staggering emotions than any experience before marriage. There is nothing soothing or secure about the feeling, familiar to all mothers, of wanting to murder one's child and really feeling capable of it, and then the next moment dissolving into the deepest love and repentance. There is nothing soothing about the insane annoyance that one can feel at some irritating habit of a loved one, or at loathing the knowledge of what he or she is going to say; one feels trapped by a total ability to see-mystery gone forever. It can be painful to find oneself isolated, in marriage, with problems that have always been shared with mother or girl friends, and to realize that there are some things that even one's husband cannot be told. This is the hard lesson of discretion. And there is nothing soothing to participants or onlookers about the spine-chilling habit of some couples who goad each other to a fever pitch of irritation, with repeated fingernail rasps on each other's well-known sensitive spots-all in the name of playful affection. It is frightening to see how close emotions are to the surface and how little it takes to make destruction.

And it is equally frightening to know suddenly how complete love is and how much one gives to it, to see how little one can really stand when someone in the family is sick, and to know how quickly one can be torn apart by nothing at all. A young mother said the other day, speaking of young mothers in general, "It always amazes me how vulnerable we are and how we, who are supposed to be so responsible, are such preys of our own feelings." In a family of love, one must become infinitely flexible to withstand the continuous jounce of emotion.

This is the muscle that develops, not superefficiency or physical strength, and it is the weariness of this muscle that causes young mothers to want to run away and hide in a solitary place where nothing can jar the heart. The second truth is that a girl does not need a college education to take care of babies and keep house. I recall a lot of talk at college among engaged girls that bringing up children is a vastly complicated business which makes full use of a mother's brains and energy, and that no man on earth has a position as responsible and delicate as that of being totally in charge of the education of minds, souls, and bodies of two or three important human beings. Well, for one thing, mother is not totally in charge, though she may like to think so. The influences of father, school, doctor, friends, neighborhood, city, or country are equally important. Besides, mother is not really in charge of herself enough to be in charge of her children. What the children learn is what mother is, not what she thinks she is. For another thing, the job is hardly complicated and delicate, at least at first. It is the simple, nerve-wracking, mindless, battering-ram process of trying to teach a savage to use a fork. It requires bloodless patience, a deadly will, enormous physical stamina, and a stable disposition, but no precision instruments. It takes strength and determination. For the fact is that motherhood makes the heaviest demands in what might be called the areas of least experience.

I would be surprised if there were a single college-educated mother who has not been struck by the total uselessness of her liberal education when it comes to housewifery. Instead of distilling pearls of knowledge from a large body of facts, she must now master a whole new set of domestic facts: how to roast a chicken, remove gum from the rug, take a child's temperature, keep the shine on the Sheraton table, iron a blouse, or even change a tire or build a bookcase. Some of these necessities are positively shocking. The care of dirty diapers and the job of keeping the oven clean call for a strong-minded unfastidiousness; even more does the whole process of having a baby, which is certainly nature at its rawest. Learning all of these things calls for a day-to-day resourcefulness and is a new and rather frightening responsibility.

Choosing a house and everything that goes into it, and a school, and a competent doctor are decisions that the young mother makes without adequate knowledge, and she can ill afford mistakes. If her husband is sympathetic, he helps her with these decisions. If not, she gropes her way along and takes the blame when that lovely color for the living-room walls turns out to be bilious salmon pink in the sunlight. And this calls for a brand-new virtue, too; the ability to adapt oneself completely, in about thirty seconds flat, to an entirely new viewpoint. Around a house, no achievement is very permanent, and the day can turn inside out before one's eyes. The salmon-pink walls must suddenly be repainted, the baby sitter suddenly fails, the clean living room is no longer clean, the elevator in the apartment building breaks down, and mother and baby carriage are trapped for the day on the seventh floor.

BACKGROUND

The National Commission on Population which was set up to review, monitor and give directions for the implementation of the National Population Policy with a view to meeting the goals set out in the Policy constituted eight Working Groups on the following subjects related to population stabilization in the country:

I. Strategies to Meet Unmet Needs;

II. Primary and Secondary Education in relation to Population and Civilization;

III. Registration of Births, Deaths and Marriages;

IV. Media for Information, Education and Communication and Motivation;

V. Role of Panchayati Raj Institutions and Self-Help Groups;

VI. Mainstreaming of Indian System of Medicine and Homeopathy into the Health System;

VII. Task Force on Monitoring;

VIII. Advisory Group on Tribal Communities.

Four Sub-Groups have been constituted under the first Working Group on Strategies to meet the following specific unmet needs:

a) Sub-Group on Strategies to Address Unmet Needs of Contraception;

b) Sub-Group on Unmet Needs on Maternal and Child Health;

c) Sub-Group on Strategies for Unmet Needs for Public Health, Drinking Water, Sanitation and Nutrition; and

d) Sub-Group on Empowerment of Women, Development of Children and issues for Adolescents.

The Sub-Group met twice under the Chairpersonship of Smt. Margaret Alva, Member of Parliament and Chairperson of

Parliamentary Standing Committee on Empowerment of Women. During the course of the deliberations of the Sub Group, two important developments took place-first, the provisional results of Census 2001 were published and National Policy for Empowerment of Women was approved by the Government. The Sub Group considered both the developments and deliberated on various issues of empowerment of women and development of children and adolescents in the context of the National population Policy.

The Sub-Group felt that the 'unmet needs' of empowerment of women and development of children and adolescents cover a whole gamut of issues which cut through the terms of references of all the Sub Groups and of the Working Groups and, therefore, there is bound to be considerable degree of overlapping in the terms of reference and deliberations of this Sub-Group. The issue of empowerment of women and development of children and adolescents is not a side or peripheral but a core issue for stabilizing the population growth of the country.

DEMOGRAPHIC TRANSITION

The demographic transition of the country in the recent years has brought the issues of women and children into the forefront of the country's development strategy. From a "high birth rate-high death rate" country of the pre Independence era, which provided fodder for the theory of Malthus, India had reached the stage of " high birth rate-low death rate" in the early fifties, which contributed to the high rate of growth of population. This continued till the beginning of the eighties, with a decadal growth rising to 21.51% in the fifties, from 13.31% in the previous decade, followed by 24.80% in the sixties and 24.66% in the seventies, despite all the national efforts made to contain this growth.

The transition to the phase of "low birth rate-low death rate" has started at a very slow pace, with population growth sliding to 23.85% in the eighties and 21.34% in the nineties. If the goal of National population Policy of bringing TFR to the replacement level has to be achieved by 2010, the growth rate of population has to be brought down to 10.7% during the current decade, which is a very tall order and can not be achieved unless the issues of women, adolescents and children are brought to the centre stage of our development planning.

The changing demographic profile of the country indicate a few important trends which will have significant bearing on the position of women and children of the country. First, although the percentage of child population below the age of 14 has declined from 37.76% in 1991 to 34.33% in 2001, the absolute numbers of children are still on the rise. The population of children in the age group of 0-6 has increased from 150.42 million in 1991 to 157.86 million in 2001. Likewise the population in the age group of 7-14 is projected to be 170.34 million today as compared to 161.94 million in 1991. Together they constitute 31.9% of the country's population-a huge 328.20 million out of 1.02 billion-the largest number of children in any country anywhere in the world. The adolescents in the age group of 15 to 19 constitute another nearly 10% of the population. Together they constitute the most important potential human resource and it is the health, nutrition, education and well being of these children and adolescents that will determine the future of the country.

The second trend in the country's demography is the declining sex ratio. The overall sex ratio has declined almost consistently over the years-from 972 females per 1000 males in 1901 to 933 in 2001-although the numbers had improved marginally by 1 point in 1951, 3 points in 1981 and 6 points in 2001, but sliding by 5 points in 1961, 9 points in 1971 and 7 points in 1991. The decline of sex ratio have been particularly striking in the age group of 0 to 6 years in recent years. Census 2001 has registered this decline by 18 points-from 927 in 1991 to 945. This decline has been registered in all the States and Union Territories except Kerala, Mizoram, Sikkim, Tripura and Lakshadeep. The decline has been very sharp in prosperous States like Punjab, Haryana, Maharastra and Gujrat. `n Punjab the gap in the sex ratio has widened to more than 200 per 1000 children. Unfortunately, the trend could not be arrested by rising female literacy during the decade. This is reflective of a deep seated prejudice against the girl child in the country. Countering this trend should be one of the priorities in the National Socio Economic Goals of the country.

While the female sex ratio among the children is declining, it is increasing among the aged, due to increased life expectancy among the females, leading to a strange gender asymmetry in the population pyramid of the country. With the gradual weakening of family based social security and absence of any strong alternate system, the care of the aged and particularly of the widows, is increasingly assuming the shape of a national problem to be reckoned with in the coming years.

The age pyramid of Indian population will swell in the centre in the years to come. At present 58% of Indians are in the age group of 15-59 years. This will increase to nearly 64% during the next ten years-from 596 million at present to 708 million by 2010, even if TFR reaches its replacement level. The implication of this transition in terms of additional needs of food, water, energy, health care, education and employment will be enormous. At the same time, the gradual increase in literacy particularly among the females on the one hand and the rise in the mean age of marriage of girls on the other, would mean that more and more girls will demand employment, particularly in the organized sector. New types of demands will be placed on the country's educational and training institutions for building capacity and skill of the workers and particularly of the female workers and of those who will be employed in the self employed and informal sectors.

The national demographic features often conceal substantial differences between States and between regions and sub regions within the same State in the achievement of basic demographic indices. These differences are conditioned by factors such as illiteracy, poverty, inadequate access to health and family welfare services etc, which often coexist and reinforce each other. At one end of the spectrum is Kerala with IMR and TFR comparable to many developed countries, but there are districts within the same State like ldukki and Malappuram where IMR and CBR are higher than the national average. At the other end are the States like Bihar and Uttar Pradesh (including newly created Uttaranchal an Jharkhand) which have the worst HDI indices in the world, but with districts like Almora and Ranchi with IMR and CBR much lower than the national level.

The co-relationship between various indices have also been conditioned by a complex web of 'other' factors which need to be studied in depth. Kerala and Tamil Nadu, for example, have achieved replacement level of fertility well before CPR of 60% was reached, whereas, in spite of a developed health infrastructure and CPR much above 60% Punjab is yet to reach that level. Inspite of low female literacy, Andhra Pradesh will be achieving replacement level of fertility much ahead of States with higher literacy rates. Maharastra, Haryana and Punjab have higher SDP than Kerala and Tamil Nadu, but are much behind the southern States in the rates of female literacy, infant mortality and fertility.

These suggest that different strategic interventions are required in different States and in different regions and sub regions within the same States for reaching the desired goals of population stabilization. The Sub Group felt that concerted attention should be paid on 5 BIMARU States (Bihar, Madhya Pradesh, Rajasthan and Uttar Pradesh) plus Orissa which account for nearly 44% of the total population of India and which are anticipated to contribute 55% of the population growth in the next decade. Here again district and sub-district specific strategies and action plan should be worked out.

CONCEPTUAL ISSUES

National Population Policy has rightly looked at the issue of population stabilization not as a technical issue that has a technical fix. Population stabilization cannot be achieved by mere physical provisioning of contraception mix or emergency obstetric care. It is critical to involve people-and enable women in particular-to have a say in decisions relating to reproduction and livelihood. This brings in the issues of reproductive rights of women and of the larger conceptual issues of gender equality and of empowerment of women within and outside the household.

The linking of the issue of reproductive health with Women Development in Information... recognizes that underlying the issue of good health and nutrition for women, we need to examine the issue of power and the nature of gender relations between men and women within the family and community. Here the following conceptual issues need to be highlighted.

Defining Women's Health and Meeting Women's Health Needs: While there have been intense debates attempting to distinguish "women's health" as a more holistic concept than "reproductive health", the issue perhaps is to clearly define what is meant, for our purposes, by women's health and to locate the discourse within a framework of rights. While decision making linked to reproduction and regulation of fertility is important, meeting health needs of women through a system that is sensitive to the differential needs of men and women and their differential access to health care also needs to be taken into account. There are some aspects regarding organizational issues of health delivery which need to be specifically addressed. The division of the health delivery system in terms of two structures-family welfare and health-is not very conducive to a holistic approach to women's health.

Enhanced Awareness and Information: Linked to Women Development in Information... is the issue of raising awareness about rights-legal literacy, rights to education and health and enhancing information sharing about basic issues. Various studies have indicated that the knowledge of women and adolescent girls about their bodies, and reproductive functions is very limited. Substantial systematic efforts need to be made for enhancing women's and adolescent girls understanding and awareness about various issues.

Linking Health and Reproductive Rights to Other Issues Related to Human Rights: It is essential to recognize the connection between women's health and food security and other economic and environmental conditions. For example, lack of access to water impacts on hygiene, heavy load bearing leads to occupational diseases, lack of nutrition impairs productivity and so on. Therefore the issue of access to safe contraception cannot be delinked from the larger issue of access to food, water, shelter and the issues of sustainable livelihood and a safe environment.

Involvement of Men and Changing Power Relations in Family and Society: In view of the fact that we are laying emphasis on reproductive rights, informed choice and autonomy, it is important that attention is given to underlying social issues which relate to decision making and lack of choices at the level of the family. This involves the social conditioning of roles and responsibilities which one learns from one's 'culture'. It also means trying to address the structural/ fundamental inequalities that exist and give rise to certain situations. For example, it is important that solution to anemia etc. is not viewed as a problem, which can be solved by distributing folic acid, but also as an issue of inadequate nutrition, which also has socio-cultural determinants.

Women's Participation: For an empowerment approach to be well integrated into health programmes it is important that women's participation is incorporated at each stage of the programme and issues regarding power structures are also dealt with. The entire conceptual shift from targeted family planning to reproductive health, which is based on informed choice, is to allow women to voice their preference and needs. However, for women to be able to speak out within the family and community social factors have to be taken into account and conditions create for an enabling environment which would allow this to happen.

STATUS OF WOMEN'S HEALTH

The experience of economic progress, political developments and social transformation of the last 50 years, indicate that although women of India have made major gains in terms of decline in maternal mortality and rise in life expectancy, increase in female literacy and employment, mobilization through self help groups and representation at the grassroots level democracy etc., large gender gaps still exist in almost every sphere of life, which do not empower women to have informed choices on their health and nutrition. India accounts for nearly 25% of the world's maternal deaths. Every year about 1,25,000 Indian women die from pregnancy-related causes many of which are preventable. Poor maternal health results in low birth weight and premature babies. More than 7% of the new born babies perish every year. Nearly 2.3% of the babies who survive the first year perish before they complete five years. The number is more in case of female babies.

The mean age of marriage at the national level is 19.5 years, but about 17.4 percent of girls are married below the age of 18 years. Corresponding rates show marked rural (20.3%) and urban (7.4%) difference. 8.3% of fertility in India is contributed by mothers below 19 years of age and this is also linked with pregnancy wastages ranging form premature death, still birth, neonatal deaths, low birth weight babies and maternal morbidity.

Micro Studies have indicated that women do not get adequate nutrition during pregnancy and lactation. The dietary intake of women in the lower economic group is deficient by 500 to 600 calories. In the above 7 years age group there are gender differences in consumption of cereals, pulses, and milk products. In the above 18 years groups, gender difference is quite prominent in the intake of energy rich food. According to an assessment of underweight and stunted growth of children (1997), in the age group of 1-5 years, almost half (49.1 %) of the girls were underweight and 20.3 per cent were severely underweight. Stunting was observed in 56 % percent of girls. The Body Mass Index (BMI) indicates that more women (36.1 %) than male (28.6%) are affected by various stages of Chronic Energy Deficiency.

Research has provided enough information on women's morbidity linked with the environment like indoor air pollution, iodine deficiency of soil/water, flurosis and arsenic related disorder, use of fossil fuels etc. The spread of Tetanus, Pneumonia, Dysentery, Typhoid, Cholera, Plague do not need any further research to prove their relationship with environment and sanitation. The brunt of all these fall disproportionately on women. Several domestic chores as also occupational work of many kinds affects the women and leads to an incurable state of health. This is true both at household level and at the work place specially in the unorganised industry sector where maximum number of women earn their livelihood.

Chronic Mental depression and neurosis in girls and adult females is quite wide spread, but the present health care delivery system and social attitude are ill equipped to tackle them especially in rural areas.

Studies have indicated that women are biologically and epidemiologically more vulnerable to AIDS. Male to female transmission of HIV is twice as efficient than female to male. Moreover, majority of Indian women being anemic, transfusion of blood during child birth is quite common making the women more susceptible to the contact. Besides social factors like lack of control over their own body, early marriage and repeated pregnancies, lack of information, poverty induced/forced prostitution, promiscuity of husbands etc. make them more vulnerable to this disease. The impact of HIV and Aids on women is also much more severe and critical. First, inter-generational transmission of the disease takes place through women. Secondly, the rejection and ostracisation of women and girls are much more than for males. Further, women and girls suffer disproportionately from the burden of the disease. The traditional gender role of women in caring for the sick make them more susceptible to the disease. Girls of AIDS affected families often have to leave the school to care for the sick.

Women are the victims of a whole plethora of violence committed against them-infanticide, torture, rape, molestation, battering, trafficking, prostitution, forced marriage, dowry death, custodial violence and so on. This is a reflection of the deep rooted 'gender ideology' of society. Often the crimes are committed by people who are close to the victims and are traditionally supposed to be their protectors. But the victims, especially the sexually abused girls and women, face the brunt of the act more than the abuser. Only a miniscule of the acts of violence committed against women are covered under legal provisions and the bulk of them go unreported. Complex and lengthy legal procedures, often involving substantial expenditure, poor rate of conviction and lack of support from relatives and community are the important reasons for under reporting of crimes against women. Even then the crimes committed against women in relation to the total crimes, has increased from 11% in 1996 to 13.5% in 1998.

Poverty in general, and extreme poverty in particular, has a significant gender dimension. Studies has been revealed that (i) the percentage of adult women exceeds the percentage of adult men below the poverty line, both in rural and urban areas; (ii) the percentage of children in the 0-4 age group in poor households exceeds that of non-poor households, and (iii) in both urban and rural areas, disadvantaged groups of women from Scheduled Castes and Tribes constitute a high proportion of the poor. Incidence of poverty is positively co-related with IMR-a poor couple perceives an additional child to be an investment, both as security against probable mortality of the surviving child and as a potential wage earner. Significant co-relation between spread of female literacy and decline of fertility has been observed throughout the country although there are regions where fertility has declined despite prevalence of illiteracy. A lot of gains have been made in the recent years in female illiteracy. For the first time the number of absolute illiterates has declined and rate of growth of female literacy has outpaced that of males. But still 45.84% of females in the age group of 6 to 50 are illiterates. The gap between male and female literacy is still as wide as 22 percentage points.

THE STATE OF INDIAN CHILDREN

India is to home the largest number of children in the world. Nearly one third of its population-328.20 million in absolute terms-is children below the age of 15 years. About 45% of its population are minors i.e, below the age of 18 years. The country had formulated a National Policy for Children in 1974 and ratified the United Nations Convention on the Rights of the Child in 1992. A National Plan of Action for Children (NPAC) was also drawn up in 1992, which had set goals for various indicators to be achieved by the year 2000. But most of these goals have remained unfulfilled, although significant improvements have taken place in all the crucial indicators like infant and child mortality rates, school enrolment ratios, drop-out rates, levels of mal-nutrition etc. Infant mortality has remained around 72 per 1000 live births with no significant improvement in the nineties unlike in the eighties. This is much below the average of 6 in developed countries, 64 in developing countries and the world average of 59. There are significant disparities across States, within the States and among castes, communities and other ethnic groups. Kerala for instance, has IMR of 13 per 1000 live births against 94 in Madhya Pradesh: The Infant mortality rate among Scheduled Castes is 24% higher than the national average. Like-wise, the rural and urban differentials also continue to be very high-46 in urban areas as compared to 78 in rural areas. The underlying reasons of high infant mortality are early marriage and childbearing, lack of birth spacing, inadequate maternal nutrition, inadequate antenatal care, and large proportion of deliveries lacking supervision by trained birth attendants.

The Child Mortality Rate (CMR) of India is also very high 25 children out of every 1000 who survive the first year die before they complete 5 years. India ranks 49 out of 189 countries in CMR i.e, if the worst is ranked 1, India is 49th. This reflects the inability of families to look after their young children. Despite efforts being made under the Integrated Child Development Services programme, malnutrition continues to remain a principal underlying cause of morbidity and mortality in under-5 children. This is because intrauterine growth retardation caused by inadequate nutrition during pregnancy cannot be corrected later on. It is an alarming fact that one out of three children are born in India with low birth weight (<2500 g). Coupled with unsupervised delivery and delayed complementary feeding, unhygienic sanitary practices and lack of access to safe drinking water, the average child succumbs to acute respiratory infections and diarrhea.

Malnutrition constitutes a major threat to the development potential of young children. Although surveys conducted by the National Nutrition Monitoring Bureau, Hyderabad have confirmed that there has been a declining trend in severe and moderate degrees of malnutrition amongst children, the micro-nutrient deficiencies, viz. Vitamin A, iron and iodine have been affecting children in various degrees. The national data indicates that although the proportion of nutritional blindness has reduced drastically, yet the sub-clinical deficiency of vitamin A still continues. Other health concerns of the children are vaccine preventable diseases, birth asphyxia, injury and disability, Mother to Child Transmission (MTCT) of HIV and iodine deficiency disorders. While India has achieved great success with the Pulse Polio Campaign, reports indicate that this has affected routine immunization under the Universal Immunization Programme where the coverage has slipped in recent times. Birth asphyxia is linked to lack of resuscitation facilities during delivery. Many cases of congenital birth defects and mental retardation are caused due to neglect at the time of birth, which are preventable.

A growing incidence of HIV positive mothers in the general population suggests that problem of HIV infected children may soon emerge as a serious problem to be reckoned with. The rate of transmission from a HIV positive mother to her child varies between 15 to 40% with increased risk if the child is breastfed. A child infected at birth, unlike in the case of adults with HIV has a short window period of 3-5 years before the infection overwhelms the developing immune system of the child.

Education is a right of every child. The Directive Principles of State Policy enshrined in the Constitution of India require the State to provide free and compulsory elementary education to all children up to the age of 14 years. Although there has been a substantial increase in the enrolment of children at all levels of schooling, yet 100 million children are estimated to be out of school. Most of these children are vulnerable to neglect. The NSS survey of 1977 has indicated that child labour in the country has increased to 17 million as compared to 13.6 million in 1981 and 11.3 million in 1991. As many as 4.15 lakh children live on the streets in the mega cities of Bangalore, Mumbai, Calcutta, Delhi, Hyderabad and Chennai and are exposed to all types of exploitation.

3

Development of Contraception use Helps Women Plan

INTRODUCTION

Women who can decide if and when they will become pregnant are better able to plan other aspects of their lives. In the short term women who use contraception effectively may have more choice about the use of their time because they have fewer children. Women may be better able to make plans to take new educational, economic, and other opportunities. Also, in the long term society in general and women themselves may change their expectations of how women lead their lives. Young women probably benefit most from being able to control their own fertility.

The Changing Needs of Young Women

Young women's lives are changing. Almost everywhere in the developing world, more women are delaying marriage. In 29 of 36 countries that have conducted Demographic and Health Surveys, the percentage of women who had married by age 20 was at least 10% lower among women ages 20 to 24 than among the oldest women interviewed, usually those ages 45 to 49. As women delay marriage, they have more opportunity to complete their education, to develop remunerable skills, and to choose their husbands or to choose not to marry at all.

Avoiding unintended pregnancies is critically important to allow women to make these choices, especially in cultures where unplanned pregnancy precipitates marriage or where premarital births have particularly disastrous social or economic consequences. In Latin America and the Caribbean, the Young Adult Reproductive Health Surveys (YARHS) document that many women are sexually active before marriage but are not consistently using contraception. For example, in a 1985 survey in Mexico City, 13% of women age 15 to 19 and 44% of men reported premarital intercourse. Only 22% of the women and 31% of the men used contraception at their first sexual experience, however. Among unmarried women ages 15 to 24, half of all first pregnancies were unintended. Among married women in this same age group, 11% of first births were conceived before marriage.

Nevertheless, offering contraceptives to unmarried adolescents and young adults remains controversial. Some parents and policy-makers assume that the availability of contraception will lead adolescents to have sexual relations before marriage. This assumption is one reason that, formally or informally, many family planning programs refuse to serve unmarried young people.

In fact, data do not suggest that the availability of contraceptives encourages early sex. Most research on the subject comes from the US and other developed countries. For example, an international comparison found that sex education and contraceptive services were more available in Europe than in the US. Sexual activity among adolescents, however, was about as prevalent in the UK, France, and the Netherlands as in the US, while the US teenage pregnancy rate was much higher. Another US study found that teens who had a sexual education program in their school delayed intercourse and were less likely to become pregnant. Still other studies have found no link between the presence of contraceptive clinics in the schools and levels of sexual activity among students.

Contraception and Education

For many young women the most important fork in life's path is the divide between education and early pregnancy. It is true that many barriers stand between young women and an education. Some parents think that it is wiser to educate sons because there are more and better-paying jobs for men than for women. Also, some girls are taken out of school to work at home. Some families are not willing to educate girls if the school is distant or the teachers are male.

Still, once girls reach puberty, the greatest threat to their staying in school may be pregnancy. Students who become pregnant often drop out of school, or they are expelled by school authorities-a fate that does not befall male students who father children. In many African countries pregnancy is the most common reason that girls leave school and the main reason that the school-leaving rate is higher for girls than for boys.

To ensure that girls are not forced to leave school due to unwanted pregnancy, girls need to be able to refuse unwanted sexual intercourse and to have access to contraceptives, information, and counseling if they choose to be sexually active. Also, schools should help young women continue in school, not expel them, even if they are pregnant or have a child.

Policies that help young women avoid pregnancy and stay in school could help change attitudes in the long run. Parents and communities might be more willing to invest in girls' education if they had more confidence that their daughters would not become pregnant and leave school. Also, as more women complete an education, and as more women hold paying jobs, the perception of women's potential is likely to change, helping to break the vicious cycle that holds women back.

Some young women recognize that avoiding pregnancy protects their futures. For example, in a Kenyan study female students of high socioeconomic status viewed contraception favorably. Those who ranked in the top quarter of their class were nearly four times more likely than other female students to have used contraception at their most recent act of intercourse. These young women could afford contraceptives and recognized that an early pregnancy would endanger their chances for academic success and economic security.

Children benefit in various ways from their parents' use of contraception. Education appears to be one area in which women pass on the benefit to their daughters: Both sons and daughters from small families have better educational opportunities than children from large families. In a Thai community, in families with three or fewer children, 44% of the children went to lower secondary school, and 31% went to upper secondary school. By comparison, in families with four or more children, 24% went to lower secondary school, and 14% went to upper secondary school. In this study couples with small and large families were matched for wealth, religion, residence, parents' educational attainment, and parents' ambitions for their children's education. All couples had had access to modern contraceptive methods throughout their reproductive years. Similarly, in Matlab, Bangladesh, children in small families stayed in school longer because they did not need to care for younger siblings at home. Still, in both Thailand and Bangladesh parents provided more education for their sons than for their daughters.

Contraception and Employment

The relationships among women's status, employment, and childbearing are complex. Some statistical studies find lower fertility associated with more female participation in the labor force, while others find the opposite. Such inconsistency is not surprising, given the variety of jobs and occupations, demographic and household characteristics, cultural forces, and socioeconomic circumstances around the world.

While statistical research into women's labor-force participation and women's use of contraception has not produced clear findings, the conceptual links are clear. With effective contraception, women are better able to work when they need to without the interruption of unplanned childbearing. Women also may find the burden of household work somewhat lightened. In addition to caring for children, women nurse the sick. Women in developing countries raise 50% to 90% of their families' food. In most rural areas women spend long hours carrying water, gathering fuel, and preparing and cooking food. How spacing and limiting births influence the daily lives of women working in the home also deserves research.

Wherever unplanned pregnancy would limit the types of work available to women, effective contraceptive use may help provide women with broader opportunities to obtain the economic security of a job. When a woman cannot be sure of avoiding pregnancy, her occupational choices often are limited. She may have to find employment that can be combined with childcare, that permits flexible hours, and that is easy to enter and leave frequently. Such jobs typically earn low, static wages. Most such jobs are in the informal sector of developing economies--for example, agriculture and petty trade. Even in the formal sector of developed countries, such jobs as nursing and teaching have been held mostly by women since employers did not care if pregnancy forced teachers or nurses to leave after a few years on the job. Seen as jobs that young women held until they had a family, these professions have commonly been paid less and offered less opportunity for advancement and less status.

More detailed studies, rather than large-scale statistical analyses of fertility levels and labor force participation, may offer a clearer view of how contraceptive use and employment are linked. For example, in Nigeria researchers found that young unmarried women out of school were using contraception in order to work longer before marriage. In one area studied, 75% of single women ages 18 to 25 were using contraception, more than five times the contraceptive prevalence of married women in the same age group.

Of course, many factors other than contraception affect women's employment. Women's autonomy within the family is one such factor. In some countries cultural norms call for women to remain at home no matter what their own preferences are. Also, some employers discriminate against women, partly because employers assume that women's commitment to their jobs is weaker than men's. Nevertheless, in modernizing economies women are an increasingly important part of the labor force. Where contraception is widely available and its use is accepted, employers can be more confident that female workers will not be forced to leave because of unplanned pregnancies. At the same time, however, the possibility that a woman may become pregnant is not legitimate grounds for denying her a job.

When women have access to contraception and new economic opportunities, many take advantage of both. In Bangladesh the Grameen Bank offers poor women small loans for income-generating projects. The women attend regular meetings at which they receive advice on their projects. They also learn the "Sixteen Decisions"-resolutions to make changes in their lives including planting vegetables, educating their children, and having small families. Women who have taken advantage of this new economic opportunity are more likely to be using contraception than women who are not receiving loans.

HOW CAN FAMILY PLANNING PROGRAMS BENEFIT WOMEN?

Contraceptive use protects women from the health risks of unwanted pregnancy and gives women more control over their own lives. Family planning programs help women primarily by providing contraceptive methods. What more can family planning programs do to meet women's needs? Women interact with family planning programs only briefly and infrequently. Still, in addition to providing contraception, those brief contacts can be designed to strengthen women's abilities to fulfill current roles and take on new ones. Program managers can seek to:

- Encourage respect for women,
- Provide a range of reproductive health care, and
- Design program activities to strengthen the skills that enable women to take new opportunities.

Encouraging Respect for All Women

By showing respect for women, family planning programs help women build self-confidence and self-esteem and thus strengthen their ability to make their own decisions and to act in their own interests. Also, showing respect for women as clients sets a good example for the community.

Family planning programs have an excellent opportunity to promote respect for women. Unfortunately, some programs have missed that opportunity-perhaps because program personnel share widespread social attitudes that denigrate women, because a program focuses on enrolling more clients rather than meeting clients' needs, because personnel are simply not aware that courtesy is important, or because service providers have too little time for each client. Program managers can encourage respect for clients in several ways:

- Ensure informed choice. Programs that help women make their own informed choices about their fertility show respect for their clients' right and ability to make decisions. To ensure informed choice, managers can see that clients are (1) offered a choice of methods, (2) given the information they want about each method, and (3) allowed to choose the method that they want, provided there is no medical reason to withhold it.

- Communicate respectfully. All personnel, no matter what their function, can act politely and in a respectful, friendly manner with all clients at all times. Program personnel demonstrate their respect for clients by paying attention to what clients say, answering their questions fully, never belittling their concerns and questions, and understanding and honoring their clients wishes. Also, programs must be sensitive to clients' modesty and preserve client-provider confidentiality.

- Train staff. Program managers can train staff to think of clients' needs and to communicate with clients. Staff also can learn how to communicate respect.

- Reward respect. Managers can reward personnel who treat female clients respectfully. They can measure the success of programs and providers by client satisfaction rather than just by numbers of clients. To measure client satisfaction, managers can survey clients about the care that they received. Whether clients return for further services when needed also indicates whether they are satisfied.

- Improve staff morale. Family planning personnel may treat clients poorly if personnel themselves have to work with insufficient time, supplies, space, or pay. If so, managers can acknowledge the problems, remedy them if possible, and at the same time make clear that the staff's frustrations are not an excuse for treating clients disrespectfully. Also, public promotion that enhances the image of providers, along with training, improves morale and inspires staff to live up to their new image.
- Set an example. Managers are role-models for other program personnel. If they do not treat clients and staff with respect, they cannot expect their staff to do so.

Clients know when they are treated with respect. Among Chilean women interviewed at a family planning clinic run by the Instituto Chileno de Medicina Reproductiva (ICMER), "being treated like a human being" was the most frequently identified element in high-quality care.

In a clinic run by the Bangladesh Women's Health Coalition, a woman commented on the care that she had received: "I'd heard about family planning before, but not this way. This is the only clinic where I was asked to sit down and where I was treated as an equal. If I knew about it in this way, do you think I'd have six children?" People who are treated with respect develop self-respect. Brief contacts with a family planning program are not likely to revolutionize women's lives. Still, for some women, contact with high-quality family planning services can be a start; for others, a step forward; and perhaps for a few, a big step.

A young mother in Chile credited a family planning service with improving her self-esteem: "I am valuing myself more. I am realizing that I am really worth something. I am a person, and I should take care of myself..."

OFFERING OTHER REPRODUCTIVE HEALTH CARE

A reproductive health approach to family planning services can improve women's health and therefore women's choices. Judith

Bruce and Anrudh Jain define a reproductive health care approach as one that helps clients reach their fertility goals in a healthful manner. This approach focuses first on ensuring that clients receive high-quality family planning services and then on offering additional services to help women meet multiple health needs at the same time and place.

To attain high quality, family planning services require two components: respectful, helpful interaction between provider and client and technically skilled personnel. To assure high quality, family planning programs can (1) determine the services that they can offer, (2) develop locally defined standards of care, and (3) establish quality-monitoring procedures. For example, those who counsel clients about contraceptive use must be trained to explain whichever methods are offered, to understand clients' needs, and to help them consider their options. Those who perform medical procedures need technical training. All training should raise providers' skills to a demonstrated standard of competence. Monitoring and supervision reinforce quality standards to assure that programs offer an informed choice of methods, hygienic care, and safe medical procedures. AVSC International has developed the COPE technique and the Population Council has developed the Situational Analysis approach to evaluate the quality of both client-provider interaction and providers' technical skills.

Many medical professionals favor a reproductive health approach because they see a visit to a family planning clinic as a rare opportunity to inform, screen, and treat women for a variety of reproductive health conditions, such as certain common sexually transmitted diseases (STDs) and conditions of pregnancy. Also, girls and adolescent women can be counseled about nutrition, anemia, and general health to help prevent later pregnancy-related morbidity and mortality. Some programs, too, may want the convenience of dealing with multiple health needs on one clinic visit.

Women often see little distinction among family planning, other reproductive health needs, and still other health needs, including their children's. When family planning personnel cannot help, some women feel that program personnel are not really interested in their health. In the ICMER clinic in Peru, women wanted a clinic visit to be an opportunity to learn more about their reproductive health and how to protect it. They preferred to discuss all their health problems with one provider.

Meeting a variety of needs encourages women to use services. For example, in Tunisia a family planning program recognized that new mothers have multiple concerns-about their new infants' health, their own health, and their ability to breast-feed. Therefore a clinic in Sfax began to offer neonatal, postpartum, and family planning services on one visit. Women are encouraged to come to the clinic on the fortieth day after giving birth, the traditional day on which a new mother first leaves the house. In 1987, 83% of postpartum women came for this visit, and 56% of these women adopted a family planning method. The approach is now being applied nationwide.

Not all women want all services, however. For example, some women may want a contraceptive method but not a pelvic exam or Papanicolaou smear. Requiring clients to accept services that they do not want could discourage them from getting any services at all.

In counseling women, programs also might broaden their focus beyond preventing pregnancy and disease. For example, women have a right to refuse unwanted sexual intercourse but often cannot do so. Helping women with such matters requires learning more about their private lives.

Ruth Dixon-Mueller argues that providers cannot truly meet women's needs for contraception, disease prevention, or safety from violence without knowing something about how each client is sexually active. Providers may need to find out, for example, if a client has multiple sexual partners or is forced into unwanted sexual acts. Few family planning providers are prepared to elicit such information, which must be discussed in a sympathetic and reassuring manner. Training and a new way of thinking about the providers' role will be required. Of course, clients should not be required to disclose intimate information if they choose not to.

Weighing program options. Each program must determine its own ability to offer new services. Some programs may be strained to capacity, already serving as many clients as possible. For such programs, the scarcity of resources limits how much more they can offer. Other programs may want to attract more clients. For these programs, broadening services-and improving quality-may help. In choosing which services to add, each program has to assess clients' needs as well as program resources.

Still, some general principles apply to making these decisions. Elizabeth Maguire, Acting Director of the Office of Population, United States Agency for International Development, urges that family planning programs consider adding other reproductive health services "that will benefit the most women at an affordable cost and have the highest public health impact". Under these criteria a common, serious condition that is easily treated or prevented would have highest priority. Providers and other public health experts should involve clients in deciding which conditions are deemed serious, but without abandoning their professional judgement.

Many family planning managers are considering whether to offer services for sexually transmitted diseases. Adding STD services to family planning services can be appropriate because (1) many people need care, (2) combined services would be convenient for clients, (3) most STDs can be treated, (4) counseling could help women avoid STDs, and (5) most family planning programs offer condoms in any case.

Also, STDs are spreading and have serious health consequences. It is now known that infection with the AIDS-causing human immunodeficiency virus (HIV) is more likely in those with other STDs. Some family planning programs may find it difficult, however, to add STD services.

Of course, family planning program managers can choose among several different levels of STD services: (1) prevention-information, counseling, and providing condoms and spermicides; or (2) in addition, initial screening and referral of suspected STD cases for diagnosis and treatment elsewhere; or (3) diagnosis and treatment as well as prevention and initial screening. The potential for impact and costs differs at each level.

Treatment after a septic abortion is also a serious need because so many women die from unsafe procedures. At the 1984 International Conference on Population in Mexico City, delegates urged governments to help women avoid abortion and to treat them humanely if they have had an abortion. Policy-makers can reduce the number of abortion deaths by improving treatment for septic abortion and by linking post-abortion care with contraceptive counseling and services. While offering contraception to all who want it, family planning programs can reduce abortion by reaching out especially to women at high risk of unwanted pregnancy, including adolescents, and by providing post-abortion counseling and family planning services in hospitals where women receive post-abortion treatment.

Around the world a variety of reproductive health programs are developing. For example, some affiliates of the International Planned Parenthood Federation (IPPF) in Africa and Latin America provide counseling and referrals for clients with STD symptoms. In Colombia the Asociación Pro-Bienestar de la Familia (Profamilia) offers contraceptive methods, screening for sexually transmitted diseases, sex counseling, clinics for men, AIDS prevention, and even legal services to low-income men and women.

In Bolivia a coalition of 18 public and private health institutions recently launched a national campaign to promote reproductive health services. The Bolivian National Reproductive Health Program encourages couples to use services that will improve family health including reducing the high maternal mortality rate.

These services include family planning, prenatal care, safe delivery and post-delivery care, breastfeeding promotion, and abortion prevention. To inform people about these services, the organizations, with technical assistance from Johns Hopkins Population Communication Services (JHU/PCS), have developed a campaign logo, clinic signs, posters, radio and television spots, in-clinic videos, client-provider materials, and audio cassettes for play on buses. The campaign tells couples that they have the right and responsibility to protect the health of women and children.

Strengthening Women's Skills

Women often need to build skills and self-confidence before they can take on new opportunities. Family planning program activities that strengthen women's assertiveness, communication, and decision-making skills can help prepare women to obtain fair treatment and to take new opportunities. In the process of delivering health services, high-quality family planning programs can help to build such skills by:

- Helping women learn to make informed choices in new areas of their lives,
- Supporting women's choices,
- Encouraging women to recognize their strengths and to build on them,
- Improving women's skills at communicating with their husbands and with people outside their families, and
- Creating new images and models of competent women and caring men.

These skill-building efforts do not necessarily require major new training, large new expenditures, or more staff. Much can be done in the everyday process of serving clients. A change of attitude and a change of emphasis can make a lot of difference.

Self-awareness can be the first step. Whether services meet women's needs can depend on providers' most basic assumptions about women and men. For example, if providers assume that women are solely responsible for contraceptive use, they may design services that make it difficult for men to obtain information and services. If, instead, providers assume that both men and women need services, they are more likely to design services that both men and women can use easily. Making informed choices.m Women make many decisions throughout their lives, but they may need to gain confidence in making new kinds of decisions, such as decisions to control their fertility or to seek new social roles. In a Mexican study young women with unplanned pregnancies seemed to be women with little awareness that they could make decisions for themselves. They were less likely than nonpregnant young women to know about contraceptives, to have discussed sex with their girlfriends, and to have aspirations and plans for the future. Women surveyed in parts of such countries as Bangladesh, Ghana, Jordan, Mali, Nigeria, Pakistan, and Tanzania say that they do not participate in decisions about having children. Many say that they obey their husbands' wishes or the will of God.

Reproductive health programs can help women make wider choices. By discussing reproductive needs and goals with clients, providers can give women practice in assessing a situation and making thoughtful decisions. Since making fertility decisions may be unfamiliar to some clients, the process requires skill and patience on the part of the provider. Ideally, the provider imparts information, listens attentively, encourages discussion, helps clients recognize their own needs, and answers clients' questions. The clients themselves make the decisions about whether and when to have children and how to carry out their plans.

Supporting women's choices. Respecting clients' wishes builds women's confidence in their own decision-making and their right to make decisions. For example, many women already know what contraceptive methods they want before they come to a family planning provider. Honoring a woman's preference is important to her satisfaction with family planning. In Indonesia, for example, 91% of women who were given the method that they chose were still using that contraceptive method after one year compared with only 28% of women who were given a method that was not their first choice. A 6-country IPPF study also found that women were more likely to continue contraceptive use when they received the method that they wanted.

Women's choices reflect their own needs. Providers cannot assume what women need or want. For example, in Peru some women in focus groups said that they preferred the rhythm method because it gave them the right to make choices about when to have sex. Also, its use implied the intelligence to take charge of one's life. Women chose this method because it requires cooperation between sexual partners, and that cooperation enhanced the relationship.

Therefore, to create the best services, managers can ask clients what they want and design programs and train staff accordingly. Even better, they can directly involve female clients and community members and groups in planning and monitoring services. Such a client-oriented approach is rare. Indeed, providers' biases often block access to contraception and to a choice of methods. Often because of misinformation about methods, providers may favor one method over all others or shun certain methods. Because of negative assumptions about clients, particularly about women, providers may deny clients a choice of methods or discourage use of methods that require clients to act-for example, using barrier methods at each act of coitus or taking an oral contraceptive tablet daily.

Recognizing women's strengths. Successful counseling helps women identify their strengths and build upon them in planning their lives. In India group leaders from the Institute of Health Management ask groups of women who is the most important person in their homes. At first, the women never mention themselves. Then the group leaders recite a list of household chores and ask the women who does each chore in their homes. The women repeatedly answer that they do the chores. When the leaders ask again who is the most important person in their house, the women laughingly answer that they are most important. Good counseling can help women recognize that they already plan their time, save money or grain, and care for their families and homes. Building on these skills, women may learn to plan other aspects of their lives, including their reproductive lives, in which they may have depended previously on others. Recognizing their own managerial role in the home, women can have more confidence applying these skills elsewhere. A manual prepared by the United Nations Educational, Scientific, and Cultural Organization (UNESCO) suggests an exercise to help women build their self-esteem: Women list their skills, such as planning their time and organizing their families. Then they say how those skills would help them in a business situation.

Improving communication skills. Family planning programs can help women speak up on matters that concern them. In particular, programs can encourage and enable women, and men, to talk about contraceptive use and reproductive health. Women's discussion groups have been the approach most widely used to help women bring up and discuss these issues.

To help women learn to talk about family planning, a program in rural Bangladesh designed with assistance from JHU/PCS organizes volunteer discussion groups. The program was set up to reach more people than family planning field workers could reach in home visits and because women were isolated and unaccustomed to discussing family planning with each other or with their husbands. The discussion groups, called Jiggasha ("to enquire" in Bangla), are formed for men and women separately. Leaders and meeting places are chosen to take advantage of the existing networks of communication in the community.

The Jiggasha meetings have encouraged women to discuss and use family planning. About 65% of participants report that, after attending several meetings, they have discussed family planning with their husbands or with other women in the group, and about 50% report talking to people outside the group or to a family planning field worker. Some 30% of the women began to use a modern contraceptive method, and 20% visited a health clinic.

In Bolivia in the early 1990s client-provider materials produced to improve the quality of reproductive health services and counseling contributed to communication between spouses. Before-and-after surveys found that significantly more clients had talked with their spouses about family planning after seeing and receiving the materials--95% compared with 84% before they had seen the materials in clinics. By comparison, the increase among those who had not seen the materials-from 83% to 88%-was not statistically significant. Later a video drama entitled Hablemos en Pareja (Let's Talk Together) was produced and shown in clinic waiting areas to help clients overcome barriers to communication between spouses.

Couples may find talking about family planning and reproductive health easier if they have discussed the subject first with someone of their own sex. Programs such as Jiggasha can help. For example, women in a rural area of northern India could not talk to their husbands about sexually transmitted diseases, even though they feared that their husbands might infect them. Health advisors organized the women into groups that discussed the problem and decided how to approach their husbands. After practicing the conversation in groups, the women were better able to talk with their husbands.

Family planning providers can help couples communicate better if they are aware of social conventions. For example, in Mexico a survey revealed that couples thought it immodest for the wife to start a discussion of family planning. These couples said that husbands should start such discussions and decide whether the couple uses a family planning method. In response, family planning providers designed counseling services for men and women advocating that women start discussion and that the couple make a decision together.

Strengthening communication skills is important to women and men who want their partners' support and cooperation in planning their families and protecting their reproductive health. For some, discussion may be a necessary step to taking an action they desire. For example, according to DHS data from six African countries, women who approved of family planning were more likely to use a modern contraceptive method if they had discussed family planning with their husbands in the year before the interview than were women who approved of family planning but had not discussed it. Studies in Java and South Korea have found that the more often couples discuss family planning, the more likely they are to use a contraceptive method. Discussion between partners may make continued contraceptive use easier, too. In the IPPF 6-country study, women who thought that their partners agreed with their use of a family planning method were significantly more likely to continue using that method than women who did not know that their partners approved. Although studies link spousal communication with contraceptive use, the nature of the link is not obvious. It is not always clear whether more communication leads to more contraceptive use or, instead, couples talk more about contraception because they already use or plan to use a method. Also, some couples may not have an immediate reason to discuss family planning-for example, the woman is pregnant, the couple wants a child, or they have no access to contraceptives. New images of women and men. It will be easier for women to take new opportunities when society respects them as strong and competent. Men will find it easier to help women when they see positive images of men who support those qualities in women. Family planning communication can provide these images by portraying competent women and caring men in radio drama, videos, films, advertisements, and users' testimonials.

ENCOURAGING MEN'S COOPERATION

Women's situation will improve faster if men help. Protecting reproductive health particularly requires commitment from both men and women. While a woman can control her fertility without a man's cooperation-and many do-men's understanding and help make contraception and family planning easier and widen the choice of methods that a couple can use. Also, to prevent sexually transmitted disease, a woman must have the cooperation of her male sexual partner, who must remain faithful to her or use condoms. What can family planning and reproductive health programs do to encourage men's cooperation?

Changing Times and Changing Attitudes

Encouraging men's cooperation can start with understanding men's points of view. Many men approve of family planning and contraception. Even where few people use contraceptives, such as Burundi, Ghana, Kenya, Mali, and Pakistan, at least half of men surveyed approved of contraception. Still, many men have negative attitudes about women choosing and using contraception. Some men fear that contraceptive use will make their wives independent of their control. They fear that their wives will have sex with other men if they no longer risk pregnancy. Some men may be unwilling to have their wives adopt family planning because they themselves know little about it. Some do not want their wives talking with strangers about sex and reproduction. Some worry that contraceptive use will harm their wives' health or their own (3). Some oppose contraceptive use for religious reasons. Some men think that large families reflect their masculinity or their wives' faithfulness in serving them.

These male attitudes about contraceptive use are part of some men's broader fears. Traditional social norms often have required men to maintain the honor and position of their extended family, village, religious group, or other social organization. Therefore men feel responsible for the behavior of their wives and children and think that women have no right to make decisions for themselves.

Men are not alone in imposing limits on women. Many mothers, even wealthier, better educated women, prefer sons and take better care of them (1, 374). In some places women dominate their sons' wives, pressure them to have many children, and even physically abuse them.

Paternalistic traditional norms are no excuse for the mistreatment of women, however. Violence against women, including violence from their husbands and other family members, can be condemned by religious and political leaders and prohibited by law, and the law, enforced. Also, legal changes in a variety of areas affecting women's well-being can be the catalyst to changing community norms.

Economic and social changes, too, are requiring couples to be more flexible about gender roles. More and more, both partners must produce income to support the family. As a result, men are finding that a wife with many skills can help support the family. In 1990 women made up 42% of the paid labor force in the developed world and 33% in the developing world. The need for women to earn income has changed gender roles. In the US some husbands and wives are arranging to work different hours, and more men are caring for the children. In 1991, 20% of children under age five were cared for by their fathers at home while their mothers went to work.

Some men find that they have gained through improvements in their wives' status. For example, in Colombia the Instituto Colombiano Agropecurio provides poor women with small loans and on-going help with planning and decision-making. The women and their husbands have worked together to make their enterprises succeed and to take care of their homes. Both husbands and wives said that they benefited from the project. The women became more self-confident and knowledgeable about dealing with local institutions such as schools and markets. Their new confidence made them better advocates for the family. In Zimbabwe and other areas of Africa, husbands report that their wives' employment as family planning field workers enhanced the prestige of their family. These men support their wives in their new positions even if the women do not bring in additional income.

ENCOURAGING MALE RESPONSIBILITY

Reproductive health programs can help men cooperate with their sexual partners to avoid unwanted pregnancies and to prevent sexually transmitted diseases. Specifically, programs can:

- Inform men about family planning, reproductive health, and contraceptive methods,
- Encourage and improve communication between spouses,
- Design convenient services for men,
- Provide contraceptive choices for men, and
- Promote images of male role-models who cooperate with women both in the family and in the community and who share the burden of ensuring reproductive health.

Informing Men: Many men want to know more about contraception and family planning and to be more involved. For example, in Malaysia, Nigeria, and Turkey, most men surveyed wanted to learn more about family planning. In Peru men in focus groups complained that false stereotypes of dominating men (machismo) limited their opportunities to obtain information about sexuality and family planning. In Tunisia men often accompanied their wives to the family planning clinic but then waited outside, talking among themselves. When asked, some said that they would like to be more involved. Men commented, "We are made to feel like strangers." "We are pushed aside...," and "From the way we are treated, one would think that this doesn't concern us."

Women, too, want men to have information. In Chile women asked that men be allowed to come to the classes at the clinic. One woman said that her husband did not always believe her and that she would "love to have him come to some of the talks."

Men need information about contraceptive methods for women as well as about those for men. Well-informed men can use a method themselves or support their partners in using a method. Well-informed men also can talk with their wives and cooperate in assessing their needs and choosing a family planning method.

Men especially need information about sexually transmitted diseases since men play a big role in the spread of sexually transmitted diseases including AIDS. Although there is much variation among cultures, except for female prostitutes men are likely to have more sexual partners than women. Men have more control over condom use. Men are more likely to control the frequency of sexual relations and the possibility of abstinence within a relationship. To reduce risk, men can: (1) reduce the number of sexual partners, (2) use condoms, and/or (3) practice sexual fidelity or abstinence.

Encouraging Communication between Spouses: Men can support women's choices better when couples can talk about reproductive health and family planning. But surveys show that even men who approve of family planning do not always discuss it with their wives. For example, in Burundi 94% of surveyed men approved of contraceptive use, but only 48% had discussed it with their wives in the preceding year. Family planning communication campaigns can change men's role in contraceptive decision-making. The Zimbabwe Male Motivation Project in 1988 and 1989 sought to inform men, promote more favorable attitudes, increase contraceptive use, and promote male involvement and joint decision-making. The project appeared to increase condom use particularly. Its impact on men's attitudes about decision-making was ambiguous, however. Men who heard the campaign radio soap opera, attended a lecture, or saw a pamphlet were more likely to say that the man alone should make the decision to practice family planning. At the same time, these men also were more likely to say that the couple should decide jointly how many children to have. Researchers concluded that future campaigns should put more emphasis on joint decision-making and discussion between spouses.

Some family planning programs welcome husbands and wives who seek family planning counseling and services together. While counseling a couple, a provider can encourage the woman to ask her own questions and express her own opinions. The provider also can encourage the man to understand and respect the woman's opinions and choices. Program managers seeking to improve women's situation need to make clear, however, that the program also welcomes women and men who come alone, does not require a husband's permission before serving a woman, and keeps the names of clients and all information about clients confidential, even from spouses.

Designing Convenient, Appealing Services: Men cannot share responsibility for reproductive health and family planning if services and information do not reach them. Few men go to facilities that offer services primarily for women. Men must be reached in other ways. There are five main approaches:

- *Separate Clinics*: Male-only clinics can inform men about all family planning methods and provide condoms and vasectomy. Separate male clinics have been successful in Asia and particularly in Latin America, including Brazil, Colombia, Guatemala, Honduras, Mexico, and Peru. Some offer a range of reproductive health services including care for sexually transmitted diseases and infertility.
- *Better Service for Men at Existing Clinics*: Some conventional family planning clinics have hired male staff, offered hours

convenient for men, and offered additional reproductive health services for men. In Colombia Profamilia serves men at its women-oriented family planning clinics as well as in clinics for men only.

- *Workplace Services*: In India, Kenya, the Philippines, Turkey, and elsewhere, employers or trade unions provide family planning services to workers, often as part of broader health services. Other possibilities include working with male-oriented educational or fraternal organizations, cooperatives, or the military.
- *Community-based Services*: Male community-based distributors can provide men with condoms and information about family planning. For example, in 1987 the Katibougou Family Health Project in Mali recruited men from the community who distributed condoms from stocks kept in their homes, just as female community health workers distributed supplies to women.
- *Commercial and Social Marketing*: Commercial sales have long been men's chief source of condoms. To make supplies more affordable and to increase promotion, social marketing programs, which sell contraceptives at subsidized prices through established commercial outlets, operate in more than 20 countries. Men can buy social-marketing condoms along with other goods. In many Muslim countries particularly, men do the household shopping.

Providing Contraceptive Choices: Currently, there are only two contraceptive methods for men-vasectomy and condoms-and there are two methods in which male cooperation is crucial-periodic abstinence and withdrawal. Research on new methods for men is underway, but it is unlikely that a radically new male method will be available for at least 10 years. In the meantime, family planning programs and the private practitioner should make sure that current methods are readily available. In most developing countries neither condoms nor vasectomies are widely used. Just under 5% of married couples in developing countries use each of these methods. Condoms probably are more widely used outside marriage than in marriage, however, and use may be growing because of concern about AIDS. Neglect by policy-makers and providers may help explain the low prevalence of vasectomy. Where the procedure is accessible and promoted, men use it. For example, in Colombia the annual number of vasectomies performed by Profamilia rose by 77%, to more than 1,000, after the organization opened its first two men-only clinics in 1985. In 1991 Profamilia's eight men-only clinics performed about 5,000 vasectomies.

Promoting Male Methods and Men's Services: Promoting men's family planning methods and services boosts their use. For example, in Turkey a social marketing campaign to promote condoms involved a television comedy, video tapes, sponsorship of a soccer team and tournament, billboards, and gift packs to medical schools. The program sold 4.5 million condoms in 1991, its first year of sales. Men's response suggests that some men are willing to take responsibility for contraception if programs make the effort to reach out to them.

Social marketing programs have been directed more to men than to women. They have emphasized the economic value of small families. They also depict men as the protectors of their families. While most promotion has touted condoms, some social marketing programs now address advertisements for oral contraceptives to men as members of the "contraceptive decision-making team."

In Morocco radio and print advertising, display boxes, and posters depict condoms as offering men the opportunity to share responsibility for reproductive decision-making.

Promotion also has Brought Men to Clinics: In Colombia Profamilia has promoted its men's services in the mass media and through field workers. In Brazil Pro-Pater increased the number of vasectomies performed monthly in 1989 at its Sao Paulo clinic by nearly 80% with television spots, billboards proclaiming that "vasectomy is an act of love," and resulting press coverage.

Promoting Positive Images: Family planning communication can depict new images of men as well as of women. Also mass-media depictions of couples discussing family planning and making joint decisions suggest to the public that such discussions are appropriate. They also suggest to both men and women how to discuss family planning and sex and can even provide an occasion to start discussion.

Men's Organizations are Involved, Too: In Jamaica, Fathers Incorporated assists men who want to help children. The group points out that in the past men have been seen solely as providers of goods for their children. To change that image, group members are holding workshops to promote men as care-givers as well.

DEBATE OVER POLICY

Many people involved in family planning policy and programs seek to balance a variety of concerns. Most agree that couples and individuals should be able to plan the number of their children and the timing of their births.

They do not always agree, however, on how to prioritize the goals of family planning programs. Some focus primarily on reducing the rate of population growth; others, on the reproductive health needs of couples and individuals; and still others, on adhering to ethical or religious beliefs. In preparation for the International Conference on Population and Development (ICPD) in Cairo, September 1994, many voices have spoken up, advocating differing, but not always mutually exclusive, priorities.

Population Growth: Those concerned about rapid population growth emphasize that:

- Rapid population growth threatens the progress of all other efforts to improve the standard of living.
- Environmental resources are threatened by increasingly large populations.
- Family planning programs should provide services to as many people as possible as soon as possible.

- Family planning programs should focus first and foremost on providing contraceptive supplies and services.

Needs of couples and individuals. Those concerned about the needs of couples and individuals emphasize that:

- The preferences, satisfaction, and safety of current family planning clients should receive higher priority than increasing the number of contraceptive users.
- Family planning services should be part of programs that help women and men not only with avoiding pregnancy but also with a range of other reproductive health needs.
- Reproductive health care programs should devote more attention to improving the quality of care that they offer.
- Family planning programs should help women to achieve equity in society as well as to meet their reproductive goals and health needs.
- Environmental degradation and resource conservation should not be addressed primarily by emphasizing limitation of childbearing in developing countries.

Strongly felt ethical and religious beliefs underlie many people's differing positions on population and family planning issues, including the positions of people concerned about population growth or about the needs of couples and individuals. Some advocates, however, particularly identify themselves as speaking from an ethical or religious point of view.

Ethical Considerations: Those concerned primarily about ethical considerations emphasize that:

- All individuals and couples should have the right to make their own decisions about their fertility, free of coercion or pressure.
- Family planning programs should not set targets for numbers of new contraceptive users, incentives for contraceptive use, or field workers' quotas that might result in pressure on people to use contraceptive methods.

- Clients should be given an informed choice of contraceptive methods.

Religious beliefs. Some, but not all, who express a religious viewpoint emphasize their contentions that:

- Abortion is not acceptable.
- Only married couples should have access to contraceptive methods because sexual activity outside marriage is immoral.

Alone among major religions, the leadership of the Catholic Church objects to all contraceptive methods other than periodic abstinence. This position seems to have had more impact on policy-makers and the availability of services in some countries than on the attitudes of individual Catholics.

Labels Polarize Positions

Most policy-makers and advocates recognize that many of these viewpoints are legitimate and yet prioritizing program goals is necessary. In the public debate, however, labels are often used-sometimes unfairly and inaccurately-to imply that individuals and groups advocate extreme positions, ignore other points of view, or have malicious intentions. For example, those who focus on rapid population growth are sometimes labeled "population controllers" who disregard women, and those concerned with reproductive rights are sometimes portrayed as "radical feminists" who ignore the consequences of rapid population growth. As a result, positions have sometimes become polarized, focusing on disagreement rather than on the broader areas of accord.

Seeking Common Ground

In reality the serious debate concerns allocating scarce resources to achieve the multiple goals of meeting clients' needs, slowing population growth, and protecting the environment in ways that respect individuals' religious, ethical, and cultural beliefs.

Can population policies both satisfy demographic goals and advance individual rights? A growing number of experts and policy-makers argue that conflicts, although they cannot be completely resolved, need not be as great as they sometimes appear. Suggested approaches include:

- Base national population policy on human rights as well as economic concerns. Policy often focuses on the economic benefit to all citizens of slower population growth. Policy-makers can emphasize more strongly, at the same time, that control over one's own fertility is a human right and that providing services that satisfy clients is as important a program goal as reducing total fertility rates.
- Focus on unmet need. Millions of women do not want more children, want to delay their first or next pregnancy, or need better reproductive health services. High-quality services that meet these people's existing needs would increase use of contraception, lengthen continuation, and in the process often reach demographic goals.
- Support public policies that indirectly reduce population growth. If policies support roles for women other than childrearing and make these roles socially acceptable and economically independent, some women may choose to have fewer children. Also, women who can provide for themselves and their children can better protect themselves from coerced sex and unwanted pregnancy. Changes that support more options for women include ending policies that encourage parents to favor sons over daughters, eliminating arranged marriages of young girls, enacting and enforcing minimum marriage ages, eliminating policies or tax provisions that favor large families, and assuring equitable male financial responsibility for women and children during marriage and after divorce.

FAMILY PLANNING-AN ASSET FOR WOMEN

Women want better lives for themselves, their children, their families, and their communities. They want to do their best in their current roles as mothers, wives, workers, and community members.

Many women also want new opportunities in life-chances to learn, to make their own decisions, to have more say in the course of their own lives. Women want to have choices. Family planning is one important way that women can take control of their own lives and make more choices possible. Choices are essential to human dignity. Without choices and without opportunities, a person cannot hope for a better future. Without choices, a person can have little self-respect. A person imprisoned is punished by being denied choices; a person denied choices is punished even without being imprisoned.

Although poverty and lack of education often limit choices and opportunities for both men and women in the developing world, in general women's choices are especially limited. Social norms, often embodied in a husband, parent, or mother-in-law, prevent many women from having much say in their own lives or much autonomy to choose their own paths.

Even if women were allowed to make choices, social and economic options and opportunities are often beyond women's reach. As a result, compared with men, women have less health care, less education, fewer choices of jobs, poorer pay, and less legal protection.

Family Planning Can Help

Family planning can help women meet their needs-both their practical need to perform conventional roles more effectively and their strategic need to find new roles and opportunities. By enabling a woman to control her own fertility, contraceptive use can help meet a woman's practical needs in several ways. Safe contraception contributes to good health: when women avoid unwanted pregnancy, they avoid the risks of childbearing or abortion. In the developing countries one woman in every 50 or so dies from causes related to childbearing. Also, birth spacing helps her children survive. In addition, contraceptive use may give a woman more choice in the use of her time by helping her avoid unwanted pregnancy, childbearing, and childcare. With better health and more control over her time, a woman may be able to do more in her customary roles for herself, for the children she chooses to have, and for her community.

Beyond meeting these practical needs, contraceptive use can help to meet women's strategic needs. Women who are healthier and have more control over their time are in a better position to take advantage of education, employment, or other opportunities if they are available. Also, by planning their pregnancies, women may find that they can plan more of other aspects of their lives.

Contraceptive use is often necessary but seldom sufficient to change a woman's situation in life. When a woman controls her own fertility, she may have more choice about the course of her life. Whether she can make changes in her life, however, depends on her personal circumstances, social norms, economic development, and law, among other factors. Changes in many households and throughout society will be needed before women can realize their full potential.

Family planning programs also can help meet women's needs, both practical and strategic. Of course, they do so chiefly because they provide contraceptive methods. In addition, programs can design high-quality services so that to some degree they may help women meet strategic needs. For example:

- Family planning programs can demonstrate to the community that women have a right to be informed and to have their decisions respected.
- Programs can help women recognize the value of their own opinions by seeking and heeding women's views and advice.
- Programs can help women practice making decisions in new areas and learn interpersonal skills needed to pursue their own interests.
- Programs can expand services to meet a broader range of women's reproductive health needs.
- Programs can help men both to play their part in contraception and to understand and appreciate women's new roles.

- Programs can provide women with income and skills by hiring, training, and promoting women and by offering them opportunities for leadership.

In these ways family planning programs help prepare women to make decisions and choices that formerly were not available to them. Of course, family planning programs cannot singlehandedly solve all the problems confronting women, but they can seek ways to help.

FAMILY PLANNING SAVES LIVES

Each year an estimated 500,000 women die of complications due to pregnancy, childbearing, or unsafe abortion. All but about 6,000 of these deaths occur in developing countries. Where poor health, frequent childbearing, and little access to good medical care are a way of life, an early death is too often a woman's fate. Contraceptive use can help protect women's lives and health by avoiding pregnancies. It is one of three crucial measures to improve maternal health: (1) reducing the number of pregnancies, (2) reducing the likelihood of complications during pregnancy, and (3) improving outcomes for pregnant women with complications. Reducing complications and improving outcomes require access to better obstetric care, more health care for poor and rural women, and improvements in women's living standards. Currently, emergency care often is unavailable.

Women who do not want to become pregnant can reduce their exposure to the risks of pregnancy and childbirth by using effective contraception. In this sense, using contraception is a strategy that women themselves can adopt to protect their health. Family planning and concern about maternal health have long been linked. The hope to relieve women's suffering and save lives inspired early advocates of contraception in both developed and developing countries. Now, worldwide, policy-makers recognize the importance of contraceptive use to women's health. The Draft Program of Action of the International Conference on Population and Development asserts that countries "should seek...reductions in maternal mortality through measures to reduce high-risk births, including births to adolescents, eliminate all unwanted births and all unsafe abortion, [and] expand cost-effective obstetrical and gynaecological care...". Answering a 1989 UN questionnaire, 62 of 67 countries wishing to modify fertility levels cited improving family well-being as a rationale.

Causes of Maternal Deaths

Pregnancy is the main reason that women of reproductive age die at higher rates than men. In Matlab, Bangladesh, the mortality rate for women ages 15 to 44 was 26% greater than for men in this age range. Some 30% of all women's deaths between ages 15 and 44 were related to childbearing. This study, conducted between 1976 and 1985, is one of the few long-term, detailed examinations of maternal mortality rates and causes.

The World Health Organization (WHO) defines a maternal death as "the death of a woman while pregnant or within 42 days of termination of pregnancy, irrespective of the duration and the site of the pregnancy, from any cause related to or aggravated by the pregnancy or its management but not from accidental or incidental causes." Behind the direct causes of maternal mortality-obstetric complications and unsafe abortions-lie the conditions of women's lives: inadequate care during delivery, chronic disease and malnutrition, poverty, isolation, and unwanted pregnancies.

Better care at childbirth and more access to that care would substantially reduce maternal mortality rates. Most maternal deaths occur among poor women who live in remote areas. Studies in Cuba, Egypt, Indonesia, Jamaica, Tanzania, and Turkey have demonstrated that maternal mortality is higher where access to a hospital is more difficult. When access improves, death rates drop. For example, in Oran, Algeria, the maternal mortality ratio fell 42% between 1971-75 and 1976-80 after fees for public hospital services were waived, a policy that greatly reduced the number of home deliveries.

Yet many women give birth without any trained help. For example, in 12 of 26 countries surveyed by the Demographic and Health Surveys (DHS) between 1986 and 1989, women had received no trained assistance in half or more of all births in the five years before the survey.

Chronic diseases and malnutrition leave many women unable to meet the physical demands of pregnancy. For example, anemia, often a result of poor nutrition, affects about 40% to 60% of pregnant women in developing countries excluding China-more than twice the percentage in developed countries. (By comparison, about 20% of men have anemia.) Malaria, sexually transmitted diseases, and infectious hepatitis also cause serious problems for many pregnant women and, unless treated, may kill them or their infants.

A woman's age and parity affect her chances of dying in childbirth. Health risks related to age and parity have been summarized as "the four too's"-too young, too old, too many, too close together. First births and births after the fourth are more dangerous than the second through fourth births. Women under age 18 and, more dramatically, those over age 35 face greater risk than women between these ages. Of course, age and parity are not risks in themselves; they stand in for the higher likelihood of specific risks associated with age and parity. For example, pregnancy can be dangerous to very young women because their pelvises are not yet large enough to accommodate birth. Many of these specific conditions can be managed if high-quality delivery care is available.

Some family planning programs have emphasized serving women in these high-risk age and parity categories, particularly older, high-parity women. The Mexican social security system found that this emphasis interested more doctors in family planning and thus helped expand contraceptive services. Still, the "four too's" do not justify overriding women's own informed decisions about whether and when to have children or to pressure them to use a contraceptive method that is not their preference.

Deaths from unsafe abortion. Many women resort to abortion to prevent unintended births. Because abortions are illegal in most developing countries, many women seek them clandestinely and undergo unsafe procedures. Even in some places where abortion is legal, poor-quality services put women at risk.

An estimated 10 to 20 million illegal abortions are performed worldwide annually, and an estimated 100,000 to 200,000 women die as a result-about one in every 100. These deaths account for 20% to 40% of all maternal deaths. In some Latin American cities abortions account for over half of maternal deaths. In Romania unsafe, illegal abortions were responsible for 86% of maternal deaths. After the procedure was legalized in 1992, the overall maternal mortality ratio fell in the first year to 40% of the 1989 level. Women who survive an unsafe abortion may suffer chronic pelvic pain, chronic pelvic inflammatory disease, and/or infertility. They face a greater risk of ectopic pregnancy, premature delivery, and other adverse health consequences in the future. The majority of deaths due to abortion can be prevented. Access to effective contraceptive methods reduces unwanted pregnancies. The procedure itself is safe if the practitioner uses safe techniques.

While contraceptive use can greatly reduce unwanted pregnancies, it cannot eliminate them. An estimated 25 million women become pregnant each year due to failure of their contraceptive method. Many women, especially young women, become pregnant as the result of forced sexual intercourse. A smaller number of women develop health conditions that make continued pregnancy unsafe. Many of these women will choose an unsafe abortion if they do not have access to a safe procedure.

Incidence of Maternal Deaths and Illnesses

While the number of maternal deaths is often estimated at 500,000 per year, the true number may be even larger. In many developing countries official statistics underreport maternal deaths, perhaps by one-fourth to one-half. Many maternal deaths go unreported. Others are attributed to other causes. Often deaths are reported but causes are not.

Even less is known about the extent of maternal illnesses in developing countries. A frequently cited estimate is 16 illnesses for each maternal death-a figure based on a 1980 study of one village in India. Applying this ratio to the entire developing world yields an estimate of eight million cases of nonfatal maternal complications every year. Such complications are often chronic and debilitating.

Maternal mortality is usually expressed as the maternal mortality ratio-the number of maternal deaths per 100,000 live births. The maternal mortality ratio measures the risk of dying that a woman faces each time that she becomes pregnant. This ratio is often mistakenly called the maternal mortality rate. (A ratio compares the numbers of two differing events; a rate compares a part to the whole.)

Maternal mortality ratios range widely, from an estimated 12 maternal deaths per 100,000 live births in North America to more than 700 per 100,000 in some parts of sub-Saharan Africa. For the developing world as a whole, maternal mortality is estimated at more than 400 deaths per 100,000 live births, while the ratio is below 30 per 100,000 in the developed world.

Due to poor health and poor health care, many women in developing countries face much greater risk in each pregnancy than most women in developed countries. They also face this risk more often because, on the average, they have more pregnancies. Thus the lifetime risk of maternal death-a statistic that reflects both the risk per pregnancy and the number of pregnancies-is far greater in most developing countries than in developed countries. Between one-fourth and one-third of all deaths among women in their reproductive years in developing countries are related to maternity compared with only one-half of 1% in the US. In the developing world as a whole, any one pregnancy is, on average, about 16 times more likely to kill than in the developed world. And the higher fertility levels in developing countries double that relative risk over a woman's lifetime. Thus the average woman in developing countries is about 30 times more likely to die from pregnancy-related causes than the average woman in a developed country.

Contraception can Safeguard Women's Health

While family planning programs should not be treated as a substitute for urgently needed improvements in delivery care, reducing the number of pregnancies that women have in their lifetimes also substantially reduces the risk of maternal mortality and morbidity, particularly where fertility rates are high and health facilities are poor or unavailable. The study in Matlab, Bangladesh, illustrates how fewer pregnancies results in fewer maternal deaths. In 1977 more intensive family planning services, including home visits by trained female family planning workers, were introduced in selected Matlab villages. In these test villages the percentage of married women using contraception rose from 8% in 1976 to almost 40% by the end of the study in 1985.

In comparison areas, where services were not expanded, the rate rose much less, from 5% to 17%. By the end of the study, maternal mortality in the test villages had fallen to less than half of that in the comparison villages-even though there was no change in the risk of dying from any one pregnancy. Contraception and psychosocial stress. Lack of control over one's own life is a major cause of stress. Thus the use of contraception can improve women's emotional health by providing more reproductive control and greater choice about childbearing. Also, because using contraception, like other preventive health practices, reflects an orientation to the future, it can be an important step toward overcoming fatalism and lack of self-worth.

In some circumstances, however, obtaining and using contraception can itself be stressful, especially where modern contraceptives are not yet widely accepted. A woman may worry about visiting a family planning clinic and undergoing questioning or a physical examination. She may fear disrespectful treatment or negligent care. She may also fear that visiting a clinic or using contraception will provoke her husband's anger or will bring criticism from her family, her in-laws, or others. She may experience painful or worrying side effects from using a contraceptive method. She may hear frightening false rumors about the dangers of contraceptive methods. Family planning managers must recognize these possible stresses and develop strategies to relieve them. As contraceptive use becomes the community norm and as services improve, using contraception may become less stressful.

Spacing Pregnancies Improves Children's Health

A child's serious illness or death is a common event in many places and a cause of great stress and grief. Couples can reduce their children's health risks by spacing births. Children who are born within 17 months after the preceding birth are about twice as likely to die before age 5 as those born 24 to 47 months after the preceding child. Even children born after an interval of 18 to 23 months are about one-third more likely to die than children born 24 to 47 months after the preceding child. In Brazil and Egypt the child mortality rate could be cut by up to one-third if all births were spaced more than two years apart.

Many women are having their children closer together than they wish. The World Fertility Survey (WFS) and Demographic and Health Surveys (DHS) indicate that 90% of women who plan to become pregnant would like to space their children at intervals longer than 24 months. More than one-third, however, have a second birth within 24 months.

Research also shows that children are more likely to die if their mothers are younger than age 18. According to the WFS and DHS, delaying the first birth until the mother is at least 18 years old reduces the risk of the first child's death by an average of 20%. In the Dominican Republic, Egypt, Mexico, and Peru, delaying childbearing at least until the age of 18 would reduce the risk of the first child's death by 30%.

4

Changing Attitudes to Women's Political Participation

INTRODUCTION

Considerable attitudinal changes towards women's traditional exclusion from political participation at both the community and higher levels are evident among the settled tribes. Three major processes have contributed to such change. Perhaps the most significant ones have been the political struggles of the tribals themselves. During the most dynamic phase of the Jharkhand Mukti Morcha's movement in the mid-1970s in the Chotanagpur plateau, women were encouraged to form women's associations in every village to fight against the `internal' enemies of polygamy and rampant alcoholism among men to revitalize tribal society. Large numbers of women were active participants in this struggle.

Secondly, under the ambit of different government programmes, mahila mandals (women's associations) have been formed in many villages as forums for reaching development inputs to women. Women's associations were also formed during the total literacy campaign for increasing literacy among women. Under the Bihar Education Programme, which is now being extended to all districts of the state, trained women animators organize women's associations for literacy and dealing with their other problems. Under the Government of India's DWCRA (Development of Women and Children in Rural Areas) scheme, women's groups are being organized in many villages for income generation activities. The reservation of one third seats for women in PRIs has had a visible impact in MP. Due to no panchayat elections having been held in Bihar for 19 years, such impact is less evident in Bihar. Other government programmes, such as JFM and Watershed Development, under which new village institutions are being promoted, are also encouraging women's participation in community affairs.

Lastly, there have been many NGO initiatives to organize and mobilize women. These include women's savings and credit groups, and advocacy groups for women's rights and against domestic violence.

Although uneven, the cumulative impact of all these interventions has increased acceptance of women's participation in government or NGO promoted groups and community institutions. The traditional male-only village assembly has either learnt to co-exist with such new institutions or has started to transform by accepting women in its ambit. Women still do not attend the traditional male gatherings unless specifically invited. When invited by the male leaders, they often turn up in large numbers. In the context of the continuing high levels of illiteracy among tribals, educated tribal women enjoy special respect in their communities and are gaining acceptance in leadership roles.

TRENDS OF CHANGE IN WOMEN'S RIGHTS

Despite women not having inheritance rights to land under customary law among most settled tribes, various social arrangements have existed to ensure adequate care of women in situations of widowhood, breakdown of marriage, single women and for families having only daughters.

Thus, widowed women acquired use rights to their husband's property for maintenance for life. On their death, the property passed into the hands of the husband's nearest male relatives. Both unmarried daughters and daughters who returned to their paternal homes due to breakdown of marriage, similarly acquired use rights in their paternal property for life maintenance. In the case of families having only daughters, sons-in-law could inherit their parental property if they agreed to settle in their wife's paternal village. Severe social sanctions for violation of these norms reduced the vulnerability of women in such situations.

The weakening of traditional institutions has reduced such traditional social protection enjoyed by tribal women. The rising value and scarcity of land are leading to a breakdown in women's maintenance rights. Several incidents of women inheriting land being labelled witches and being hounded out (occasionally even killed) by male relatives to grab the land, have been reported from the Jharkhand area. The worst sufferers in this category are widowed women in the age group of 55 and above.

During the field visits, it was found that unmarried daughters of Ho families are now allocated only one acre of their paternal land for life maintenance, while the rest is divided equally among the brothers, irrespective of the total size. Given the taboos against women ploughing, sowing and building roofs, such women remain dependent on their male relatives both for cultivating the land and for shelter. With many such women continuing to live with one of the brothers after the parents' death, their status and condition within such households needs to be understood better.

There were also indications that the number of daughters remaining unmarried may be increasing for a variety of reasons.

WOMEN HEADED AND WOMEN SUPPORTED HOUSEHOLDS

In most of the villages visited, an effort was made to identify the number of women headed and women supported households to understand their status and food security situation. In the limited time available it was difficult to communicate the concept of women supported households (with the man either away, sick or prone to excessive drinking), due to which the villagers only estimated the widows in their villages. Between 7 to 10% of the households appeared to be headed by widowed women. The percentage of women supported households must be considerably higher in villages with rampant alcoholism and male migration. While in the case of some widows, land ownership had been transferred to their names, in others it had been transferred to their sons. Among the Gond Manjhi tribe in Pathalgaon, the widows now receive only 50% of their husband's land, the other half going to the woman's younger brother-in-law. In a mixed Oraon-Dehadi Korwa village, the tradition had changed to no land being transferred to the widow's name with all of it being given to the sons. In most cases, daughters inherited land only when there were no sons.

CONTROL OVER INCOME AND AGRICULTURAL PRODUCE

Traditionally, ownership and control over income earned through one's labour from non-private property strictly belonged to the person who expended the labour. Thus income from collection and processing/sale of NTFPs from forest lands belonged to the man, woman or child who had invested the labour in the activity.

In the case of produce or income from private land owned by the men, by and large the ownership rested with the land owner. This is most strictly observed among the Munda. Among the other tribes, although the ownership generally rests with the male `head' of the household, its management and control were shared by husband and wife. Due to tribal women's major role in trade and marketing, and having primary responsibility for household provisioning, they have also been the effective `managers' of household income and agricultural produce.

THREATS TO WOMEN'S INCOME AND STATUS

Women in all the villages visited, categorically stated that they kept and controlled their own income (usually from wages, NTFPs and petty processing/ trading). As far as the husband's income was concerned, while some said that even the husbands handed over their incomes to their wives for household maintenance, in other cases, it either depended on individual husbands or the men kept their income in their own hands (see Table below).

Women's ability to retain control over their incomes and their traditional status are being increasingly threatened by some of the following factors:

* *Alcoholism:* With increasing marginalization and alienation, excessive alcohol consumption has become widespread among tribal men. Not only do the men's incomes decline but they start snatching even the women's earnings. Resistance invites domestic violence and abuse. Household food security becomes a major casualty.
* *Migration and Bigamy:* In areas with high male migration, the men tend to bring other women back with them, throwing out their wives. With traditional institutions for regulating such behaviour at the weakest in such areas, the issue of women's land and inheritance rights is acquiring a new dimension. Tribal women's land rights are also becoming an important issue with a minority of educated women gaining geographical and social mobility. A number of NGOs are working on the issue.
* Stereotype assumptions governing development interventions. As the majority of government programmes continue to target only men as the presumed `heads' of households, traditional gender relations, characterized by greater balance and complementarity, are being affected.

STATE GOVERNMENT POLICIES FOR WOMEN

MP is one of the few Indian states which has framed a state policy for women. Among other things, the policy advocates Women Development in Information... through increasing their access, ownership and control over productive assets, skills and resources and increasing their presence and participation in institutions at managerial and decision-making levels. Due to the important role of forests in local livelihood systems, the policy has a specific section on women and forests. This advocates ensuring that payment for NTFPs such as tendu leaf18 must be made directly to the women collectors, and that their membership of primary Tendu Leaf Cooperative Societies and representation in their managing committees should be increased and the proportion of women phad munshis19 increased to 50% by the turn of the century. New 'community' institutions also promoted by government have had some beneficial impact on creating space for women's participation in community affairs.

HOUSEHOLD TYPOLOGY, PERCEPTIONS AND PRIORITIES

Typology of Households

For this study, households were subdivided into four socio-economic strata:

* the poorest of the poor: nearly all the Primitive Tribal Groups, the landless households and the female headed/ supported households with young children;
* the very poor: nearly all the remote forest dependent villages practicing upland farming systems, all the other female headed households, all the marginal farmers independently of the production system, and some of the small farmers not having access to any lowland;
* the poor: most villages practicing mixed production systems and small farmer households having some fields in lowlands;
* the less poor: small farmer households and other farmers, especially those having access to lowland with an assured source of irrigation.

PERCEPTION OF POVERTY AND WELL BEING

During the PRA exercise, an attempt was made to understand, from the perspectives of tribal women and men, the dimensions of poverty and well being. Independently of the tribe, caste or gender, landlessness (or very small holdings), followed by dependency on wage labour emerged as the main indicators of poverty. Subsidiary ones, in descending order, were lack of (or few) livestock, not enough food from the farm, no access to drinking water and low levels of literacy.

Indicators of well being for men from settled tribes were: (i) assured source of water though construction of tanks, water management, and/or lift irrigation (ii) access to good supply of improved seeds, (iii) regular monthly income and (iv) having a school in the village. Settled women's perception of well being were: (i) food self-sufficiency, (ii) access to health and education, and (iii) having a large number of livestock.

Indicators of well being of men from PTG's were: (i) permanent rights to land, (ii) protection of crops from wild animals and (iii) easy access to NTFPs. For PTG women (i) having access to food throughout the year, (ii) good housing conditions and (iii) no consumption of alcohol by men emerged as indicators of well being.

PRIORITIES AT VILLAGE AND HOUSEHOLD LEVEL

According to the PRA exercise, water management (construction/ rehabilitation of tanks and construction of check dams and other forms of community irrigation), emerged as the overwhelming priority of all sample villages. Land development support for the uplands and better roads were the other priority for males of settled tribes.

Priorities for women were: (i) availability and proximity of fuelwood and water, (ii) availability of good quality seeds, (iii) education and (iv) proximity of a public distribution shop.

Priorities for men from PTGs were: (i) permanent title to land; (ii) license to collect NTFP, (iii) availability of good quality seeds and (iv) bullocks for ploughing. For women from PTG tribes, priorities were: (i) local employment opportunities; (ii) education for children; (iii) access to a public distribution shop; (iv) availability of seeds, and

(v) construction of a causeway on the stream to allow passage of people during the rainy season.

1. In a Birhor village in Angara block for example, the majority of households were found dependent on seasonal migration for several months each year.
2. The relatively higher literacy rates among the ST population in Raigarh/Jaspur districts compared to those in Surguja district are attributed to the work of Christian missionary organizations.
3. All information on health and nutrition is based on the 1992-93 NFHS (National Family Health Survey).
4. Underweight prevalence among pre-school children in Kerala is 28.5 % compared to 62.6 % in Bihar.
5. Poor nutrition, excessive alcohol consumption and the lack of safe drinking water and health facilities in their settlements due to their small, scattered and remote nature, makes the situation grave for the PTGs if they become afflicted by an infectious disease.
6. By tradition, the Pahari Korwas also abandon the house in which a death has taken place.
7. In the interior Mutu village in Manora block, the tradition of both the women and the men getting together to discuss village affairs was found to be intact. In addition, groups of neighbours were continuing to work collectively on each others' private lands for agricultural operations.
8. In a Ho village in Tonto block, a number of younger men, not related to the traditional leadership, had heard about the movement for tribal self rule (TSR) and had taken the initiative to form a village association to organize the villagers. 2 of the 9 members of the managing committee they had formed were women.

9. In a mixed tribal and caste village in Bagicha block, although the community spirit was still alive, considerable socio-economic stratification had developed within the village. Ghasi Scheduled Caste members of the community were landless and the poorest while four Muslim traders were engaged in money lending and an Oraon teacher had accumulated 50 acres of land.

10. In Dharamjaigarh block of Raigarh district, a `Samaj Panchayat' of 23 villages of the Rathia Kanwar community was being held. The woman chairperson of a village forest committee (VFC) had gone there to raise the issue of her daughter, married into another village, being made to do what she considered an unreasonably high amount of work by her in-laws.

11. The decision about the Lo Bir Sendra (annual hunt) among the Santhals, about transplanting and wage rates among the Hos and seasonal management of cattle grazing among most communities, continue to be taken in Gram Sabha meetings.

12. One NGO working in the study area in Bihar, has been facilitating the development of such village women's associations which take up cases related to women's land rights, promote collective action against alcoholism and domestic violence, support income generation through NTFP processing and increase awareness among women about the legislation related to tribal self rule. Interestingly, initially they encountered strong resistance from traditional male leaders to women's active participation in the Gram Sabhas on grounds of its being against tribal `cultural traditions'.

13. Ragi (finger millet), Marua (Eleusine), Gundli (Panicum milare), pearl millet, other minor millets.

14. In the four villages within or near forests where PRAs were done in Bihar, as many as 91% of the total households were

found dependent on collection and sale of firewood from the forests, an activity primarily done by women.

15. The mission came across only a couple of cases where the local wage rate for women and men was the same.

16. In Raigarh district, the only women beneficiaries were the minuscule minority of female landowners. The participation of women even in village-based training programmes was 1-5%. Only 3.5% of the beneficiaries of tank leases for fisheries in Raigarh district were women.

17. In the case of maize, however, the woman sows the seed walking behind the man on the plough. Women can also sow vegetables possibly due to vegetable cultivation being a recent introduction to the local cropping pattern.

18. Leaves of the Tendu tree, primarily collected by women and used for rolling cheap Indian cigarettes called Bidis are one of the economically most important NTFP in the study area. The annual turnover of the trade runs into many Rupees.

19. Local agents appointed for collecting tendu leaves on a commission basis.

When women are educated, they are far less likely to fall victim to violence, poverty, or the scourge of AIDS. Women who have control over their economic assets are better able to avoid risky sexual and abusive relationships.

One key element in U.S. efforts to reduce women's vulnerability is promoting property and inheritance rights for women, which we do on the ground in many countries and in U.N. deliberations.

In many ways we support entrepreneurship and women's integration into the mainstream of economic life. One of our greatest commitments is to micro-finance programs. Over the last few years our investment in these small loan and technical assistance programs--about three-quarters of which go to women--has topped $130 million. This simple tool--which may be a $100 loan to stock a stall in a market or acquire a sewing machine--gives millions of women the means to better their own lives, the lives of their families, and the economy of their countries. Huge gains for women can come from tiny investments.

To have an impact on the legal and social structures of any country, women must be a part of the political process. My own greatest accomplishment has been developing and leading negotiations at the U.N. General Assembly for a U.S. resolution urging countries to expand opportunities for women to participate in the political process. The resolution, passed by consensus with 110 co-sponsors, offers concrete steps countries and civil society can take to help reach this goal. Now I am helping to implement it in many countries.

President Bush has said, "respect for women is both a non-negotiable demand of human dignity and a foreign policy imperative of the United States."

In my work, I have seen things that have shocked and saddened me. I have met women who have energized and inspired me. And I am very proud of the work that the United States is doing to increase hope, human rights, and fundamental freedoms for women and their families.

WOMEN INTO THE SEX TRADE

A short play staged by a Filipino theatre group has become a popular feature on the international conference circuit, given the powerful message it conveys-women are abused when they are lured into the international sex trade by criminal gangs.

Written by Maria Paulin-Ballesteros, the play draws a parallel between women subjected to sexual exploitation and a chicken dish that is a favourite in the Philippines, 'lechon manok'. And Paulin-Ballesteros describes her work, titled We're Syndicated, Ma'am, as a 'fowl play'.

This Filipino human rights activist was inspired to write the play after attending an international forum, where three Filipino women narrated their plight after being forced into the sex trade in Nigeria.

And the response the play has received-through its live performance or a videotaped account, in Asia, Europe and North America-has satisfied Paulin-Ballesteros.

'While Filipino consumers crave the lechon manok, male customers around the world are going crazy over their young women,' she told a Filipino newspaper in an interview. Paulin-Ballesteros' concern has been echoed by other human rights activists, who are equally worried about the rapid rise of women being transported around the world for the sex industry. Currently, according to available reports, close to two million women have been forced into 'sex slavery'.

In February, Regan Ralph, the executive director of the women's rights division of the United States-based Human Rights Watch (HRW), underscored the urgency for an international response to such abuse during his testimony before the US Senate's committee on foreign relations. HRW has been involved in documenting and monitoring this 'serious human rights violation' for many years, Ralph revealed. 'We have reported on the trafficking of women and girls from Bangladesh to Pakistan, from Burma to Thailand and from Nepal to India.'

In his view, the current trafficking in women is 'a slavery-like practice that must be eliminated', since it involves the 'illegal and highly profitable transport and sale of human beings for the purpose of exploiting their labour'.

He even exposed its prevalence in the United States. In August 1999, for instance, a trafficking ring was broken up in the southern state of Georgia that transported up to 1,000 women from several Asian countries into the United States and '(forced) them to work in brothels across the country'. Similar evidence was presented in late February at a public hearing before the European Parliament. Close to 500,000 women are smuggled into Western Europe every year, experts said. According to researchers, nearly 60% of the women forced into the sex industry in some Western European countries are controlled by Russian and Albanian criminal networks.

No Control

The situation in Britain illustrates this scenario. According to research conducted by the University of North London's Child and Women Abuse Studies Unit, six out of 10 women in London's brothels have been 'trafficked' from countries such as the Ukraine. The study added that the 'criminal gangs trafficking prostitutes are not confining their activities to major cities'.

And once the women arrive in Britain, they are informed by the gangs responsible for their journey that they owe the gangs 'thousands of pounds for accommodation, fees to the brothel and advertising'.

In most cases, the manner in which women have been trapped into the sex industry hardly differs, say rights activists. The woman is approached with the promise of a good job in another country, 'and lacking better options at home, she agrees to migrate'.

Once overseas, however, she is delivered to her employer. In these new surroundings, the woman has 'no control over the nature or place of work, or the terms or conditions of her employment'.

What is more, when the woman learns she has 'been deceived about the nature of the work', she finds escape 'both difficult and dangerous', given the coercive and abusive situations in the brothels.

Kevin Bales, a lecturer in sociology at the University of Surrey, in Britain, sees this explosion of 'modern slavery' as a result of many factors, among which are 'corruption' in governments and the 'silence' that has encouraged it.

In his book, Disposable People: New Slavery in the Global Economy, Bales argues that the international community needs to perceive the difference between modern slavery and slavery as it was known before the Atlantic slave trade of 200 years ago.

'If you insist on defining slavery as 'the legal ownership of one person by another' then slavery has pretty much disappeared. But the key to slavery is not ownership, but control through violence...(or its threat). Couple that with economic exploitation in which someone is paid nothing and you have a good working definition of the new slavery that encompasses about 27 million people around the world,' he says. Human rights groups, too, have brought to light that aspect of the sex industry. The United Nations Office of the High Commissioner for Human Rights (UNHCR), for instance, defines trafficking as a situation where someone is persuaded, tricked or forced into leaving their country for the promise of a 'better life', only to end up in forced or slavery-like conditions.

But to guarantee the rights of these women, most rights groups feel that new international standards are required, including a broadening of the definition of 'trafficking', harsher punishment for those involved in the international trafficking of women, and guaranteeing that the victims have an opportunity to seek 'remedies and redress for the human rights violations they have suffered'.

And rights activists have stepped up their efforts to achieve such guarantees from the international community, given a projected UN convention that is due to be taken up this year-the UN Convention on Transnational Organised Crime. To end this cycle of human trafficking, they add, the language of this convention should not be watered down. For that would be 'extremely detrimental to women'.

Marwaan Macan-Markar is a correspondent for the Inter Press Service, with whose permission the above article is reprinted.

OLDER WOMEN'S HEALTH: FACING THE CHALLENGES

The health concerns of older women require special attention, especially in a changing social milieu in which there are fewer people around to care for them.

In a region where women continue to be valued less than men, older women's health reflects their life-long experience of discrimination, deprivation and neglect. The older women of Asia-Pacific today faced similar situations of poverty, malnutrition, poor health care, physical overwork and unhealthy work environments in their younger years. Along with high infant mortality rates, they faced high maternal mortality, maternal morbidity and reproductive tract infections. To add to all these, few of them received immunisation as children or benefited from the public health interventions that have developed since. Consequently, the diseases of the older years such as maturity onset diabetes, Alzheimer's disease, osteoporosis, stroke, heart disease, arthritis and cancer are superimposed on an already compromised state of health. These are acute issues facing the societies of the Asia-Pacific region. As life expectancy increases and fertility rates continue to decline, the region would see in the coming years more older persons, particularly older women, needing care and fewer people available to care for them.

Recognising this growing trend, the 1995 Beijing Platform for Action emphasised that older women's '...health concerns require particular attention. The long-term health prospects of women are influenced by changes at menopause, which, in combination with life-long conditions and other factors, such as poor nutrition and lack of physical activity, may increase the risk of cardiovascular disease and osteoporosis. Other diseases of ageing and the interrelationships of ageing and disability among women also need particular attention.' In an effort to call for the non-marginalisation of older people, which includes older women, the United Nations declared 1999 as the International Year of Older Persons, with the theme, 'Towards a Society for All Ages'.

Diverse Realities, Common Problems

Traditionally, women gained value, status and authority within their family and community as they became older, for their wisdom and nurturing role as grandmothers. With modernisation and urbanisation, traditional families are giving way to nuclear families- a single set of parents, their children and a grandparent or two. In this setting and with the growing need for families to have multiple incomes to survive, grandparents, especially grandmothers, have become convenient babysitters whose medical needs are addressed within the economic constraints of the family. Such a responsibility comes at a time when these women expect to have the freedom to focus on their own needs and begin to experience a range of health issues related to ageing. Caring for young children is a demanding task that can isolate women, particularly women who lack financial and social resources to create a support network to maintain their physical and emotional well-being. These burdens would be particularly felt by older migrant women who do not speak the local language of the host country (e.g. older women sponsored by their children to enter and stay in a foreign country).

Longer lives coupled with the tradition of marrying older men means that more women will face the loneliness and vulnerability of widowhood. With a spouse's death, older women face a significant loss of economic security. Discriminatory inheritance laws regarding parental and spousal property greatly contribute to their vulnerable economic situation. Thus, widows bcome financially dependent on their children, while single older women may have no one to turn to but the state. In several South-East Asian countries, older women who came as migrants from other parts of Asia worked in the informal sector to support their families back home. Few of them had access to state pension schemes. Today, they have practically no savings and are financially helpless.

Older women are vulnerable to violence from both their families and society. The risk increases with their loss of independence. The violence is physical and emotional. Glorification of youth in the modern culture has created negative stereotypes of the elderly, particularly older women, and they are subjected to much abuse as a result of ageism. Widows may suffer from violence by their own children or by relatives. For married older women, they may have suffered a history of violence since their younger years.

Addressing the Health Needs of Older Women

Clearly, the lack of health policies, programmes and services that address women's health needs from a life-cycle and holistic approach greatly affects their lives as they age. Special attention should be given to adequately meeting the specific physical, emotional and mental health needs of women aged 50 to 60, 70 to 80 and over 80. The views of older women are therefore important for any health policy and service development to be effective in addressing older women's realities. Mechanisms need to be put in place which would allow these women to be actively involved in the planning, design and implementation of health policies and programmes which concern their own health and that of their community. Care for older women must consider their pre-existing state of health and address their overall health-care needs instead of merely treating the immediate medical problem.

Due to their increased vulnerability in their later years, the issues of cost, quality and mobility or location of healthcare services would have to be considered carefully. Policies which promote parental care and support by the children need to be supplemented by appropriate support mechanisms (such as state-supported income security schemes), and high-quality affordable health and residential care for those older women who are unable to rely on family support. It is also imperative that boys and men are socialised into caring and nurturing roles so that the burden of caring for elders does not fall on women alone. Governments need to be committed to their social responsibility in the area of health and be ready to support effective community-based initiatives in meeting older women's health needs.

It is important to recognise that the ageing process, for some women, may be about declining health, frailty, emotional vulnerability and even senility. For other women, the ageing process may be a very positive experience. Nevertheless, decision-makers who plan policies and programmes for older women must recognise that active ageing will not circumvent the need for adequate care-giving, which can sometimes be intensive in nature. While it is true that older women have many contributions to make, their right to finally take a break from commitments and responsibilities in their old age should not be overlooked. Older women are not only survivors-they have made their contributions to society. In return, society should give them space to seek self-fulfillment.

MAKING THE HARM VISIBLE

At the end of the twentieth century, local and international forces have merged to escalate the sexual exploitation of women and girls. Policies, practices and crises are combining to increase both the supply of women and girls vulnerable to exploitation and the demand by men for women and girls to be used for their profit and sexual gratification. Sexual exploitation takes many forms, such as sexual harassment, incest, rape, child marriages, temporary marriages, female genital mutilation, pornography, bride trafficking, battering, sexual torture and prostitution. All of these practices violate women's dignity and autonomy.

Globally, one form of sexual exploitation, prostitution, is becoming more normalized and industrialized, with some powerful agents and institutions advocating for its widespread legitimization and legalization. As prostitution has increased, the demand for women and girls has resulted in widespread recruitment and trafficking to fill the brothels, bars and street corners.

In July 1997, a group of survivors, activists and service providers came together from Asia, Africa, Europe, South America, the Caribbean, North America and the Middle East to report on the situation for women and girls in their region and discuss efforts to combat sexual exploitation and provide services to victims. Participants in "Working With Women and Girls in Prostitution: Programs and Policies" focused on how sexual exploitation affects the physical health and mental well being of women and girls, and what obstacles prevent women and girls from escaping prostitution. Making the Harm Visible has its roots in that international meeting in New York City organized by the Coalition Against Trafficking in Women.

Making the Harm Visible is a collection of writings from women who are working to make the harm of sexual violence and exploitation visible. They speak out about their experiences, provide services to survivors, and create policies that force governments and communities to protect the rights of girls and women, not profit from their exploitation.

Women from every world region report that the sexual exploitation of women and girls is increasing. All over the world, brothels and prostitution rings exist underground on a small scale, and on an increasingly larger scale, entire sections of cities are informally zoned into brothels, bars and clubs that house, and often enslave, women for the purposes of prostitution. The magnitude and violence of these practices of sexual exploitation constitutes an international human rights crisis of contemporary slavery. In "Prostitution: A Form of Modern Slavery," Dorchen Leidholdt, the Co-executive Director of the Coalition Against Trafficking in Women, examines the definitions of slavery and shows how prostitution, and related forms of sexual exploitation, fit into defined forms of slavery.

In some parts of the world, such as the Philippines, prostitution is illegal, but well entrenched from providing "recreational services" to military personnel. In "Blazing Trails, Confronting Challenges: The Sexual Exploitation of Women and Girls in the Philippines," Aida F. Santos describes the harmful conditions for women and girls in prostitution in the Philippines, with problems related to health, violence, the legal system, and services. In other regions, such as northern Norway, organized prostitution is a more recent problem, stemming from the economic crisis in Russia. In "Russian Women in Norway," Asta Beate Håland describes how an entire community is being transformed by the trafficking of women for prostitution from Russia to campgrounds and villages across the border in Norway.

Political changes combined with economic crises have devastated entire world regions, increasing the supply of vulnerable women willing to risk their lives to earn money for themselves and their families. Aurora Javate de Dios, President of the Coalition Against Trafficking in Women, discusses the impact of the Southeast Asian economic crisis on women's lives in "Confronting Trafficking, Prostitution and Sexual Exploitation: The Struggle for Survival and Dignity." Economic globalization controlled by a handful of multi-national corporations located in a few industrialized countries continues to shift wealth from poorer to richer countries. In her paper "Globalization, Human Rights and Sexual Exploitation," Aida F. Santos shows us the connection between global economics and the commodification and sexual exploitation of women and girls, especially in the Philippines. Structural adjustment programs implemented by international financial institutions impose loan repayment plans on poor countries, which sacrifice social and educational programs in order to service their debt to rich nations and banks. Fatoumata Sire Diakite points to structural adjustment programs as one of the factors contributing to poverty and sexual exploitation in her paper "Prostitution in Mali." Zoraida Ramirez Rodriguez writes in "Report on Latin America" that the foreign debt and policies of the International Monetary Fund (IMF) are primary factors in creating poverty for women and children. These forces leave women with few options, increasing the supply of women vulnerable to recruitment into bride trafficking and the prostitution industry.

Social problems such as sexual and physical abuse within families force girls and women to leave in search of safety and a better life, but often they find more exploitation and violence. Physical and sexual abuse of girls and women in their families and by intimate partners destroys girls' and women's sense of self and resiliency, making them easy targets for pimps and traffickers who prey on those who have few options left to them. These factors are evident in many of the papers from all world regions in this volume, such as Jill Leighton and Katherine DePasquale's, "A Commitment to Living" and Martha Daguno's, "Support Groups for Survivors of the Prostitution Industry in Manila."

Government policies and practices also fuel the demand for prostitution, as they legalize prostitution or refuse to enforce laws against pimps, traffickers and male buyers. In Making the Harm Visible, we see how countries with governmental structures and ideological foundations as different as the Netherlands and Iran, both promote and legalize sexual violence and exploitation of girls and women. In "Legalizing Pimping, Dutch Style," Marie-Victoire Louis exposes the liberal laws and policies that legalize prostitution and tolerate brothels in the Netherlands. On the other extreme, religious fundamentalists in Iran have legalized the sexual exploitation of girls and women in child and temporary marriages and the sexual torture of women in prison. Sarvnaz Chitsaz and Soona Samsami document this harm and violation of human rights in "Iranian Women and Girls: Victims of Exploitation and Violence."

Global media and communication tools, such as the Internet, make access to pornography, catalogs of mail order brides, advertisements for prostitution tours, and information on where and how to buy women and girls in prostitution widely available. This open advertisement normalizes and increases the demand by men for women and girls to use in these different forms of exploitation. Donna M. Hughes describes her findings on how the Internet is being used to promote the sexual exploitation of women and children in "The Internet and the Global Prostitution Industry." In this milieu, women and girls become commodities-bought and sold locally and trafficked from one part of the world to another.

How do we make the harm of sexual exploitation visible? In a world where sexual exploitation is increasingly normalized and industrialized what is needed to make people see the harm and act to stop it? The women in Making the Harm Visible recommend four ways to make the harm of sexual exploitation visible: listen to the experiences of survivors, expose the ideological constructions that hide the harm, expose the agents that profit from the sexual exploitation of women and children, and document harm and conduct research that reveals the harm and offers findings that can be used for policy initiatives.

First, listen to the experiences of survivors. The contributors to this volume speak eloquently, passionately and urgently for the voices of survivors to be heard and used as the basis for a global movement against sexual exploitation. The power of survivors' testimony and their visible participation in political struggle is emphasized. The survivor testimonies of Jill Leighton, Alexia, Christine Grussendorf and Jenny speak clearly about the violence perpetrated against women and children in prostitution. In her poem, "They Are Showing Your Face," Victoria Marinelli shows us the harm of media sensationalization, which further exploits the victims of sexual abuse and exploitation. The sexual abuse, exploitation and torture of women political prisoners is recounted by Ladan Pardeshenas in "Women's Activism for Freedom in Iran" and by Aida F. Santos in the Philippines in "Memories." Malka Marcovich, in "The Violence of Silence: Survivor Testimony in Political Struggle," calls upon her experience in interviewing the survivors of Nazi Germany's "final solution" to argue the importance of survivor testimony in a movement against violence. Angel Cassidy strongly and succinctly states the need to speak out about the violence and exploitation in "Never Be Quiet." And in "Not Sex Work," Victoria Marinelli gives us her manifesto against redefining sexual exploitation as "sex work."

Second, expose the ideological constructions that hide and excuse the violence, exploitation and harm. We are bombarded with misinformation and ideological constructions of prostitution and other forms of sexual exploitation that make the harm invisible, benefit the sex industry and provide cover for the men who buy and exploit women and girls. We need to expose the explicit and implicit rationales used to justify the sexual exploitation of women and girls. Contributors to Making the Harm Visible challenge the excuses men use for exploiting women and children, and call for everyone to do the same. The oldest excuse is the biological determinist one that men have to have sex. If they don't have a wife or available partner, then buying a woman or using a child is the only alternative. Men often escape accountability for the harm they inflict by this simple, but false, assumption. The same underlying thinking applies to men in the military, who supposedly need to buy women as part of "rest and relaxation." In the papers from the Philippines and Cambodia, the presence of military personnel is sited as resulting in increased sexual exploitation of indigenous women. In "Corregidor Tales," Aida F. Santos describes the underground remnants of cells where "comfort women" were kept in sexual slavery for Japanese military personnel during World War II.

Historically, patriarchal religious ideologies have justified the sexual abuse and exploitation of women and girls in many forms, including child marriages, temporary marriages, and women's lack of sexual autonomy. In the paper on Iran, several forms of sexual exploitation of women and girls have been legally instated under fundamentalist rule. In "Trafficking and Prostitution in Bangladesh: Contradictions in Law and Practice," Sigma Huda describes the no-win situation that girls and women face after being trafficked or prostituted. In countries to which Bangladeshi girls are trafficked, such as Pakistan, the victims face long prison sentences for illegal entry into the country, or under harsh Islamic law, can be stoned to death for fornication.

Liberal ideologies about sexuality also overlook the harm of exploitation by uncritically viewing all sexual activity, including prostitution, as forms of sexual expression that should be permitted and protected as individual choices and rights. This sexual liberal philosophy merges with the neoliberal economic policies and practices to rename prostitution as "sex work." This reconfiguration of sexual exploitation is condemned by numerous contributors to Making the Harm Visible.

The contributors to this volume also ask us to critically examine explanations of prostitution that search for the cause of "self-destructive behaviors" in girls or women's personal deficits and defects. Although women in prostitution often suffer from drug and alcohol addiction, several of the authors urge us to see this as a symptom of the harm of prostitution, not as the root cause. Although, several authors discuss poverty and economic crisis as factors in compelling women and girls into prostitution, they remind us that this is what is fueling the supply, but equally important is men's demand for women and girls they can buy.

Third, expose the agents that advocate for and profit from the normalization and legalization of sexual exploitation, whether they be individual men who buy women in prostitution, or governments and United Nations bodies that advocate for legalization of prostitution or the recognition of the prostitution industry as a legitimate economic sector. The Dutch government has legalized prostitution, legalized brothels and is putting into place a system of taxation to profit from the prostitution industry. The Netherlands is the leading advocate for the legalization of prostitution and redefinition of trafficking of women to include only those women who can prove they were coerced or deceived into prostitution. In "Human Rights: A European Challenge?" Malka Marcovich describes efforts to set new standards that will deprive women of their human rights in Europe as the European Union is being constructed. Mary Sullivan, in "Marketing Women in Australia" describes how Australia is incorporating legalized prostitution into its economic and tourism plan. In "Legalizing Prostitution: Legitimating Abuse," Donna M. Hughes argues against the legalization of prostitution in Eastern and Central Europe as a way to combat the trafficking of women from that region.

Fourth, document the harm and conduct research on sexual exploitation. The harm of sexual exploitation often remains invisible until someone focuses their attention on it and documents their findings. Often issues need to be theoretically reframed and different questions posed. Several women, Jill Leighton, Jenny, and Norma Hotaling, point out that even when there are visible signs of trauma in women's and girls' lives, no one asks the simple question: "What has happened to you in your life?" The contributors use their findings to describe and analyze the forces that compel women and girls into conditions of exploitation and, often, slavery. In "Strip Clubs According to Strippers," Kelly Holsopple systematically asks women about the verbal, physical and sexual violence that they were subjected to while working as strippers. Norma Hotaling reports on research she and others have done on violence against women in prostitution in "Women in Prostitution in the United States."

In "The Health Effects of Prostitution," Janice G. Raymond surveys previous research and reports on the multiple physical and mental health problems suffered by women in prostitution, many of which lead to shortened lives or death. The contributors to Making the Harm Visible urge us to ask different research questions about the demand from men to sexually exploit women and girls and the rationales that are used to justify this violence. The Research Project on Men and Prostitution in Japan provides us with a strong quantitative base and framework on which to examine men's use of women in prostitution. In "Why Men Buy Women in Prostitution," the findings from a survey of 2000 men on their use and attitudes towards prostitution are reported.

One of the most glaring problems in combating sexual exploitation is the lack of assistance for its victims. The need for services is poignantly evident in Minerva Kalenandi's testimony, "You Need Some Place to Escape To," in which she describes being turned away from a domestic violence shelter even though she had sustained serious injuries from a pimp. Compared to services for other victims of violence, there a few services for prostituted women, resulting in women receiving little or inappropriate treatment. Since prostituted women are viewed with prejudice, they are often treated disrespectfully in treatment programs. Also, since few mainstream service providers recognize the harm in prostitution, the trauma the women have suffered is not addressed.

Innovative programs for women escaping sexual exploitation that address the harm caused to victims, though few in number, have been created in many world regions. Numerous contributors to this volume report on the services they are providing to victims of sexual exploitation. They describe innovative work and share ideas on programs and projects to assist women and girls. The founders of these programs bring a feminist analysis to the multiple problems faced by women and girls in situations of sexual exploitation. The women and girls are treated with respect and care to restore their dignity.

In "She Let Me Talk and She Listened," Jill Leighton describes how the simple act of listening can save a life. The workers and volunteers in these agencies reach out to women and girls on the street and in jails. In "Phoenix Rising," Kathleen Mitchell relates how the plan for Dignity House was conceived while she herself was in jail after being arrested for prostitution. Many of the service providers in this volume were themselves prostituted women who know first hand the lack of services for women trying to escape prostitution. In Phnom Phen, Cambodia, girls who have escaped brutality and slavery in brothels can find services at the Cambodian Women's Crisis Center. A representative from this newly found center writes about "The Sale of Women and Girls to Brothels in Cambodia."

The contributors describe model programs that provide services to women and girl victims of sexual exploitation and create a space for survivors to come to together to heal and find their voices to speak out and organize. In "Support Group for Survivors of the Prostitution Industry in Manila," Martha Daguno describes the first survivor's group to be set-up in the Philippines. Other agencies and organizations, such as BUKAL (meaning spring), and Women's Education, Development, Productivity and Research Organization (WEDPRO) are pioneers in developing services for sexually exploited women in the Philippines. Their efforts are chronicled by Aida F. Santos in "Blazing Trails, Confronting Challenges."

The involvement and leadership by survivors is emphasized in many programs. Working on an empowerment model these organizations work through peer educators. In "Casa de Passagem in Brazil," Ana Vasconcelos describes the empowerment and peer education model she uses with homeless street girls in Brazil. Norma Hotaling, in "First Offender Prostitution Program in San Francisco," describes their survivor run peer support program.

Women and girls trying to escape prostitution face fearsome odds. In "Breaking Free," Vednita Carter describes many of the obstacles the women face and their Afrocentric approach to providing services in Minnesota, USA. Pimps and perpetrators prey on the most vulnerable women and girls. Girls with disabilities are often targeted for exploitation because of their vulnerability. Claudia Vigil describes the work of the Homahi Foundation and its programs for mothers with special needs in "Prostitution and Mothers with Special Needs in Argentina." Services for victims of sexual exploitation receive little attention or support in most communities. Marlene Sandoval started the Psycho-Social Rehabilitation Center in Chile in one room in a house with no running water. She reports on the work of the center in this volume.

Some services to women escaping prostitution are combined with community education and programs that confront men's harm to women. SAGE (Standing Against Global Exploitation) in San Francisco is the 1998 winner of the Harvard University Kennedy School of Government's Award for Innovations in Government for their cooperative work with the District Attorney's office to create a program commonly referred to as "the John's School." Norma Hotaling describes their original and successful work to reeducate men about the harm they cause in "The First Offender Prostitution Program in San Francisco."

Another important aspect to ending the sexual exploitation of women and girls is prevention. Zoraida Ramirez Rodriguez describes her education and prevention programs for schools and community organizations in "Preventative Action Against Prostitution in Venezuela."

Although the women in this volume come from all regions of the world, they share common goals and attitudes. They are survivors and visionaries who are not afraid to confront overwhelming problems and remain steadfast in their work. Most of them know that their goal of ending the sexual exploitation of women and girls is nothing less than revolutionary. In "Surviving Sexual Slavery: Women in Search of Freedom," Chris Grussendorf writes graphically, with a searing analysis, about what is done to women in situations of torturous sexual abuse and exploitation in prostitution rings. She also forcefully proclaims the sustenance and aspiration of the women in resistance to sexual exploitation, "We stay alive because we are women in search of our lives; we are women in search of freedom. I stayed alive because my belief in something better than what they offered was greater than their hatred and destruction. I stayed alive because I wanted to be free, more than anything, I wanted to be free. I wanted to live in a world of respect."

Organization and activism by women is essential to create change and end violence against women and sexual exploitation. In "Women United Can Make a Difference: The Situation in Spain and the European Union," Asuncion Miura describes how women working together changed public attitudes about violence against women and created services to assist victims of battering.

Sarvnaz Chitsaz and Soona Samsami relate the importance of women's leadership in political and social activism to end of women's oppression and usher in true equality for women and girls in the world. Women must undertake the work of organization and advocacy for women because it is not in the interests of men to do this work, although there are a few men willing to stand against the oppression of women. These writers understand that when the deepest forms of exploitation, violence and oppression are named, challenged and ended and all the victims healed, there will be a true social, economic and political revolution for women.

WOMAN'S CONSCIOUSNESS, MAN'S WORLD

The capitalist mode of production has penetrated farther and deeper than any other form of production. Geographically it has extended its technology in search of markets; politically it has devised the most ingenious methods of control in its own interests; economically it has created means of production, which are wonderful in their productive capacity and terrifying in their devastation. Its industry has devoured human labor power and human intelligence. In its search for raw materials it has laid waste the land and is beginning to exhaust even the sea. Worse, its version of itself has entered the souls and spirits of millions of men and women, so we no longer know what is our own and what is alienated to capital.

The antagonisms it generates produce the shifts and fissures that make the growth of new movements possible. In quiet times the hope of liberation grows lichenlike on inhospitable rock. In times of upheaval new growths can take root. In order to change capitalism we have to understand how it is made, how it moves, and how it came into being. We have to see how it is different from, or related to, other forms of production, how it is hinged together. It is a foxy old thing, wily at dealing with the opposition it brings into being, whether its opponent is the working class or movements for black or women's liberation.

The predicament of being born a woman in capitalism is specific. The social situation of women and the way in which we learn to be feminine is peculiar to us. Men do not share it, consequently we cannot be simply included under the general heading of "mankind." The only claim that this word has to be general comes from the dominance of men in society. As the rulers they presume to define others by their own criteria.

Women are not the same as other oppressed groups. Unlike the working class which has no need for the capitalist under socialism, the liberation of women does not mean that men will be eliminated. Sex and class are not the same. Similarly people from oppressed races have a memory of a cultural alternative somewhere in the past. Women have only myths made by men. We have to recognize our biological distinctness but this does not mean that we should become involved in an illusory hunt for our lost "nature."

The oppression of women differs too from class and race because it has not come out of capitalism and imperialism. The sexual division of labor and the possession of women by men predates capitalism. Patriarchal authority is based on male control over the woman's productive capacity, and over her person. This control existed before the development of capitalist commodity production. It belonged to a society in which the persons of human beings were owned by others. Patriarchy, however, is contradicted by the dominant mode of production in capitalism because in capitalism the owner of capital owns and controls the labor power but not the persons of his laborers.

In order to act effectively we have to try to work out the precise relationship between the patriarchal dominance of men over women, and the property relations which come from this, to class exploitation and racism. In order to understand the traces of patriarchy which have persisted into the present, it is essential to see what part patriarchy played in pre-capitalist society. The dominance of men over women in the past was more clearly a property relation than it is now. When a man married in a society in which production was only marginally beyond subsistence, he married a "yoke-fellow" whose labor was crucial if he were to prosper. Her procreative capacity was important not only because of the high infant mortality rate but also because children meant more hands to labor.

The family was a collective working group. The father was its head, but for survival the labor of wife and children was necessary. The introduction of individual wages and the end of the ownership of people in serfdom did not dissolve the economic and social control of men over women. The man remained the head of the family unit of production and he retained control over the ownership of property through primogeniture. Both his wife's capacity to labor and her capacity to bear his children were still part of his stock in the world. Moreover, the notion that this was part of the order of things was firmly embedded in all political, religious, and educational institutions.

Although capitalism temporarily strengthened the control over women by middleand upper-class men in the nineteenth century by removing them from production, it has tended to whittle away at the economic and ideological basis of patriarchy. As wage labor became general and the idea spread in society that it was unjust to own other people, although the exploitation of their labor power was considered perfectly fair, the position of the daughter and the wife appeared increasingly anomalous. Ironically, middle-class women came to the conviction that their dependence on men and the protection of patriarchal authority were intolerable precisely at a time when the separation of work from home was shattering the economic basis of patriarchy among the working class.

The factories meant that the economic hold of men over women in the working-class family was weakened. Machinery meant that tasks formerly done by men could be done by women. The woman's wage packet gave her some independence. Ideologically, however, men's hold persisted among workers and was nurtured by the male ruling class.

Subsequently by continually reducing the scope of production, by developing the separation between home and work, and by reducing the time spent in procreation, a great army of women workers has been "freed" for exploitation in the commodity system. This integration of married women into the labor market has been especially noticeable in the advanced capitalist countries since the Second World War.... The result in terms of women's consciousness at work is only now beginning to be felt. While the dissolution of the extended kinship networks has produced in the nuclear family a streamlined unit suitable for modern capitalism, it has forced an examination of the relationships of man to woman and parent to child.

The struggle of the early feminist movement for legal and political equality and the assumptions it has bequeathed to women now, despite the degeneration of its radical impulse, have strained the hold of patriarchy in the capitalist state, though without dislodging it. The power of the working class within capitalism and the growth of new kinds of political movements recently, particularly for black liberation, have touched the consciousness of women and brought many of us to question the domination of men over women. This has taken a political shape, in the new feminism of women's liberation.

The development of contraceptive technology in capitalism means that ideas of sexual liberation can begin to be realized. The fact that sexual pleasure now need not necessarily result in procreation means a new dimension of liberation in the relation of men and women is possible. It also removes some of patriarchy's most important sanctions against rebellion. The right to determine our own sexuality, to control when or if we want to give birth, and to choose who and how we want to love are central in both women's liberation and in gay liberation. All these are most subversive to patriarchy.

However, although capitalism has itself eroded patriarchy and has brought into being movements and ideas which are both anti-capitalist and anti-patriarchal, it still maintains the subordination of women as a group. Patriarchy has continued in capitalism as an ever present prop in time of need. Although women are not literally the property of men, the continuation of female production in the family means that women have not yet even won the right to be exploited equally. The wage system in capitalism has continued to be structured according to the assumption that women's labor is worth half that of men on the market. Behind this is the idea that women are somehow owned by men who should support them. Women are thus seen as economic attachments to men, not quite as free laborers. Their wage is still seen as supplementary. If a woman has no man she is seen as a sexual failure and the inference is often that she is a slut as well. She also has to struggle to bring up a family alone, on half a man's income. This very simple economic fact about the position of women in capitalism acts as a bribe to keep women with men: it has no regard for feeling or suffering and makes a mockery of any notion of choice or control over how we live. It also means that women make up a convenient reserve army which will work at half pay and can be reabsorbed back into the family if there is unemployment.

Equal pay is obviously only the beginning of an answer to this. The inequality of women at work is built into the structure of capitalist production and the division of labor in industry and in the family. The equality of women to men, even the equal exploitation of women in capitalism, would require such fundamental changes in work and at home that it is very hard to imagine how they could be effected while capitalism survives. Our labor in the family goes unrecognized except as an excuse to keep us out of the better jobs in industry and accuse us of absenteeism and unreliability. This separation between home and work, together with the responsibility of women for housework and child care, serves to perpetuate inequality. Women, as a group in the labor force, are badly paid and underprivileged. This is not only economically profitable to capitalism, it has proved a useful political safety valve. It is quite handy for capitalism if wives can be persuaded to oppose their husbands on strike or if men console themselves for their lack of control at work with the right to be master in their own home.

Because production in the family differs from commodity production we learn to feel that it is not quite work. This undermines our resentment and makes it harder to stress that it should be eliminated as much as possible not only by technology, but by new styles of living, new buildings, and new forms of social care for the young, the sick, and the old.

In capitalism housework and child care are lumped together. In fact they are completely different. Housework is drudgery, which is best reduced by mechanizing and socializing it, except for cooking, which can be shared. Caring for small children is important and absorbing work, which does not mean that one person should have to do it all the time. But we are taught to think there is something wrong with us if we seek any alternative. The lack of facilities for children and the rigid structuring of work and the division of labor between the sexes again makes choice impossible.

Propaganda about our feminine role helps to make us accept this state of affairs. Values linger on after the social structures which conceived them. Our ideas of what is "feminine" are a strange bundle of assumptions, some of which belong to the Victorian middle class and others which simply rationalize the form patriarchy assumes in capitalism. Either way the notion of "femininity" is a convenient means of making us believe submission is somehow natural. When we get angry we are called hysterical.

Thus, although capitalism has eroded the forms of production and property ownership which were the basis of patriarchy, it has still retained the domination of men over women in society. This domination continues to pervade economic, legal, social, and sexual life.

It is not enough to struggle for particular reforms, important as these are. Unless we understand the relationship of the various elements within the structure of male-dominated capitalism, we will find the improvements we achieve are twisted against us or serve one group at the expense of the rest. For example, the wider dissemination of contraceptive information and the weakening of guilt about our sexuality have meant a major improvement in the lives of many women. However, the removal of fear alone is not enough because relations between the sexes are based on the ownership of property—property consisting not only of the woman's labor in procreation, but also of her body. Therefore, while class, race, and sex domination remain a constituent element of relations between men and women, women and women, and men and men, these relations will continue to be distorted. Sexual liberation in capitalism can thus continue to be defined by men and also continue to be competitive. The only difference between this and the old set-up is that when patriarchy was secure, men measured their virility by the number of children they produced. Now they can apply more "suitable" means of assessing masculinity in a use-and-throw-away society and simply notch up sexual conquests.

There are other examples of feminist reforms being distorted by the structure of capitalist society. We are far from the situation of baby farms and state-controlled breeding, but these are the lines along which pure capitalism, shorn of the remnants of earlier forms of production, would develop. Similarly, one group of women can be bought off at the expense of another, young women against old, middle class against working class. If we are ready to settle for a slightly bigger bite of the existing cake for a privileged section, we will merely create gradations among the underprivileged. We will not change the context in which women are inferior. For instance, in Britain there has been some discussion about giving women better jobs in management and promoting secretaries because they will work harder for less pay. Capitalism is not based on the organization of production for people, but simply on the need to secure maximum profit. It is naive to expect that it will make exceptions of women.

It is impossible now to predict whether capitalism could accommodate itself to the complete elimination of all earlier forms of property and production and specifically to the abolition of patriarchy. But it is certain that the kind of accommodation it could make would provide no real solution for women when we are unable to labor in commodity production because we are pregnant: socially helpless people protected in capitalism are not only treated as parasites who are expected to show gratitude, but are under the direct power of the state. Also class and race cut across sexual oppression. A feminist movement that is confined to the specific oppression of women cannot, in isolation, end exploitation and imperialism.

We have to keep struggling to go beyond our own situation. This means recognizing that the emphases that have come out of women's liberation are important not only to ourselves. The capacity to bring into conscious combination the unorganizable, those who distrust one another, who have been taught to despise themselves, and the connection that comes out of our practice between work and home, personal and political, are of vital significance to other movements in advanced capitalism. Similarly, the comprehension in women's liberation of the delicate mechanism of communication between the structures of capitalist society and the most hidden part of our secret selves is too important not to become part of the general theory and practice of the Left. Women's liberation has mounted an attack on precisely those areas where socialists have been slow to resist capitalism: authoritarian social relationships, sexuality and the family. We have to struggle for control not merely over the means of production but over the conditions of reproduction.

The problem about how a revolutionary theory can come out of a day-to-day practice defined by the existence of capitalism has long bedeviled revolutionary socialism. The concept of the Leninist party as the conscious embodiment of an alternative has become dubious because the party in reality will still express the viewpoint of sections which are the stronger within capitalism, most obviously men, for example. Moreover, the party itself can become absorbed in the immediate problem of surviving within capitalism rather than in the task of exposing contradictions and seeking revolutionary transformation. The mobilization of new groups within capitalism against a specific form of oppression is thus very important, but more important still is the means of translating the experience of one group to another without merely annexing the weaker to the stronger.

Thus it is not just groups that have a position of power at the point of production in the advanced sectors of the capitalist economy, but the organization of groups whose consciousness spans several dimensions of oppression that becomes crucial in a revolutionary movement. This is not an idealization of weakness. Women as a group are extremely vulnerable within capitalism, but because of our social situation we are forced to find the means of going beyond our own specific oppression. The blocks against us are very real; male domination permeates every organization within capitalism including trade unions and revolutionary groups, and the problem of how to safeguard our autonomy while making a strategy of organizing with men is a persistent dilemma in the women's movement.

Nor is this an evasion of the urgent problem of making an offensive organization which is capable of overcoming the tremendous resources of the advanced capitalist state. The substitution of the women's movement for such an organization would be most evidently absurd. Although we have the capacity to go beyond our own predicament, and although alternatives must be continually drawn out of our day-to-day struggle to defend women against capitalism, neither our structure, nor our politics, are the same as those of a revolutionary organization. We come into women's liberation out of our specific predicament as women, not as people who necessarily are committed to the creation of socialism. We are, moreover, essentially a partial orgar ization representing a specific group.

There are no short-cuts. The making of a revolutionary socialist organization that is capable of taking the offensive without being either absorbed or smashed, which can at once safeguard the interests of the groups within it and not simply reproduce the structures of authority and domination that belong to capitalism, is a gigantic task. Autonomy and cohesive organization in the face of repression go uncomfortably together. The models of the past can help us, but do not fit the special problems of the modern capitalist state. However, the political process of making an effective movement for the liberation of women-which means a movement in which workingclass women are in the majority-is an essential part of this task.

5

Media Commercialisation and the Women's Market

INTRODUCTION

India is not only a country of diversities in the economic and social spheres, but also in gender inequality and inequity, leading to poor status and social injustice. Status can be ascertained from the extent of control that she has over her own life derived from access to knowledge, economic resources and the degree of autonomy enjoyed in the process of decision-making and choice at crucial points in her life cycle. Socioeconomic suppression of women affects not only the woman but also the country as a whole. Women's status and autonomy are important aspects of empowerment. Sustainable social development can improve the status of younger generation but empowerment needs more than that. This paper aims to identify some of the factors, which can help to measure empowerment of women in the midst of social development.

An Analysis of Indian States of each of DPT and polio vaccines), crude birth rate, total fertility rate and crude death rate. Women Development in Information... indicators Variables exclusively related to women were considered for the construction of the composite index. The following 14 such indicators were included - % female literates (age 6+), median age at first marriage, women regularly exposed to any media, women in the workforce in the past 12 months of the survey, women involved in decision-making about own health care, women with access to money, median birth interval between the most recent birth and the previous birth, median age at first and last birth, women currently using modern contraception, women not anaemic, women who received all recommended antenatal care (three or more antenatal checkups -with the first checkup within the first trimester of pregnancy, two or more tetanus toxoid injections and iron and folic acid tablets or syrup for three or more months), delivery attended-by a health professional and women without any reproductive health problems.

Indicators selected were not in uniform units of measurement. Individual analysis of independent variables would not provide an integrated dimension. To obtain a single composite index using such variables, there is a need for standardization of the indicators. The statistical techniques presented by Narain et al were applied for standardization and construction of the composite indices for each state.

METHODOLOGY

This study relates to the four southern states of India. The required data relating to the selected variables were taken from the published reports of NFHS-II 1998-99, India.

Among the four southern states, Andhra Pradesh, Karnataka and Tamil Nadu are mega states with a population of over 50 million consisting of over five per cent of India's total population. Kerala is a big state with more than 10 million population or one per cent of India's population.

Social development indicators The following 11 indicators representing social well-being of the people were included for each state. General literacy rate, % of urban population, under five mortality rate, % of households with drinking water (piped or hand pumped), % of households with toilet/latrine facilities, % households with electricity, % households living in pucca houses, % children aged 12 to 23 months who have received all vaccinations

The value of composite index is non- negative and it lies between 0 and 1. The value of index closer to 0 indicates the higher level while the value of index closer to 1 indicates the lower level.

RESULTS AND DISCUSSION

State-wise distribution of the indicators of social development and Women Development in Information... for social development the health and fetility indicators in general is better in Kerala than in the other three states, while Karnataka's infrastructure facilities are better as compared to the other states in the south.

However, women in Kerala were found to be the least in the workforce. Contraceptive use and age at first and last birth showed no significant difference between the states.

The composite index values vary from 0 3472 in Kerala to 0 5464 m Andhra Pradesh This means Kerala has the highest level of social development followed by Karnataka (0 4704), Tamil Nadu (0 4944) and Andhra Pradesh the least with 0 5464 The indices constructed by using the indicators relating to Women Development in Information... have also shown lower values for Kerala (0 2999) and higher for Andhra Pradesh (0 6872) Tamil Nadu got the second position with a value of 0 4484

SOCIAL WOMEN'S DEVELOPMENT EMPOWERMENT

Comparing the indices for each state the data shows that Kerala has better social development as well as higher women's status In Karnataka, although there is social development, women's status does not show remarkable achievement On the other hand, in Tamil Nadu women seem to have better status compared to social development index In Andhra Pradesh both are at a poor level

It can be concluded that in Karnataka and Andhra Pradesh there is a need to improve the condition of women as also other developmental indicators, while m Tamil Nadu there is a need for greater attention to be given for other development, Karnataka calls for more specific programmes to improve the status of women

The overall results indicate that mere social or economic development will not improve the status or autonomy of women Special measures have to be taken to make them equal partners to progress and development.

WOMAN'S FUTURE POSITION IN INDIA

To be strictly logical one should not treat of woman apart from the rest of the human race, for this is in a manner to admit that women are a distinct class, not affected by conditions, environment, etc., as men are. But we find a "woman question" actually existing. A great deal of discussion has been going on as to what is proper for woman, what her real nature is, and how many of the duties and privileges of man she should be admitted to. Women do not occupy the same position, socially, politically, economically, or intellectually that men do, and her powers are not equal to her brother's. She is daily reproached for trying to be other than she is, and reminded that her very nature forbids her presuming to climb out of the subserviency and inferiority which are now undeniably her portion. Thus a "woman question" is forced upon us whether we will or not. It is to discover, if possible, whether she may ever become equal to and like man without perverting her inherent nature, that this inquiry is made.

It is impossible to ascertain whether there ever was a time when woman stood an equally strong intellectual and physical being, on an equal footing with man, or not. If it ever existed, its memory is now very hazy. Yet there are writers who refer to it as a fact. August Bébel, in "Woman: Past, Present, and Future," refers to it thus: "We have no grounds for assuming that in this primitive state men were physically or mentally superior to women.... Certain savage tribes were governed by women instead of men owing to the superior strength of the former.... Primeval woman, although the equal of man in bodily and mental power, nevertheless became his inferior when periods of pregnancy, birth, and lactation forced her to look to him for assistance, support, and protection."

And in a more mystical sense Olive Schreiner refers to the time: "And he answered: 'Listen and I will tell you. Ages and ages long she has lain here, and the wind has blown over her. The oldest, oldest man living has never seen her move; the oldest book records that she lay here then as she lays here now. But listen! Older than the oldest book, older than the oldest recorded memory of man, on the rocks of language, on the hard baked clay of ancient custom, are found the marks of her footsteps. Side by side with him who stands beside her, you may trace them, and you may know that she who now lies here once wandered free over the rocks with him.'"

Matilda Joslyn Gage, in her "Woman, Church, and State," lays great emphasis upon the days of matriarchy, when women, as mothers of the race, ruled the people. But we have no evidence that any such period ever existed. Letourneau shows that cases have been where inheritances descended and relationships were determined through the women of the tribe. Accompanying this usage, a certain importance adhered to the mothers of the tribe. It is true, women attained powerful and prominent positions in the old civilizations that have come and gone. The mythical lost Atlantis was peopled with great women of divine aspect. There were queens in the days of Solomon; and the Helens, Cleopatras, and Hypatias of history dot the dark pages with glints of a glory to come. A matriarchy never existed; cases of matriarchy have been known. Woman never stood beside man his equal in all things; women have ruled in isolated instances.

Be that as it may, woman's subordination came to be complete. She was first knocked down, dragged away senseless, and made a slave. She was bought and sold, or traded; she became a thing, a piece of property, a bond slave. Her degraded position among men became a custom, then an institution, then a tradition. There were centuries of "dark ages for her, into whose gloom no ray of light ever pierced, and from whose depths little has come down to us to tell the sombre story."

Slowly, very slowly man developed in intellect and acquired a rude knowledge of art. The woman in his tents could not remain very far behind him, and in time arose to some degree of companionship. That he treated her with a little kindness, and even appealed to her in times of weariness or perplexity for sympathy or counsel, was due, not to his traditions and creeds conceived in another grade of civilization, but to changed conditions and his own developed nature. There might even have arisen a "woman's rights question" in those old Mosaic days, had not the priests, who feared any loosening of their control over the people, issued a "Thus saith the Lord," and so riveted her chains for another three thousand years. "Thy desire shall be unto thy husband, and he shall rule over thee," settled the problem for the time.

"Economic dependence is the basis of all slavery," Bébel says; and he is right. All forms of slavery had their inception in some kind of economic dependence, but the slavery often exists long after the dependent condition has passed away. A thing, once established, once made an institution, is very apt to outlast the economic phase which determined its existence, and become a very troublesome matter. Institutions are crystallized ideas; they stand still: people grow--grow beyond and outside of them. Yet there they remain, unwieldy, mischief-breeding; to get rid of them at all is to tear them out by the roots at great cost of life and suffering. The bonds made ages ago, by economic conditions prevailing at the time, have become sacred; they bear another strength than that which they possessed when first formed. Though no longer with any economical basis for existing, they are even more effective in power than when first established.

Individually men are not to blame for the inferior position of women. They accepted a condition, a chain of customs, as they found them. Though long past the time when constant danger from without rendered it necessary that his whole family give him implicit obedience, the habit of expecting filial deference is fixed. Though the days of absolute property in wives have gone by, the sense of proprietorship in and responsibility for wives still prevails. That sentiment which played upon the superstitious fears of woman, setting a sort of mental watchdog to guard the master's property in his absence as well as when present, still exists in a modified form in the demand for perfect chastity in woman not expected man. The old feeling of ownership, which led men to seclude their women, has softened into that modern sentiment which would keep women guarded from the public gaze in every respect. The stern commands of old are toned down into "what is expected of womanly women," but that expectation is as binding as any chain or title deed to person could be.

Thus, through ages of subserviency, of which there were many grades, women have come to be what they are: emotional, since any prominent display of other faculties has been unnecessary in that "sphere to which it has pleased God to call her;" deceitful, since deceit has been her only weapon; illogical, since the encouragement of her reasoning powers would have often placed her in direct opposition to her master; vain, since her personal charms were long the only qualities for which she was considered; weak-minded, since strong brains were not desirable in that function to which man wished to limit her. So from long persisting conditions woman has come to be the creature she is.

But the change in woman's position and in the manner in which woman is considered during the last fifty years has been a remarkable one. We scarcely realize its greatness until we begin to compare the prominent women of today with women of the last century. It is perhaps correct to say that Mary Wollstonecraft began the modern woman's-rights movement. Her work, "The Rights of Women," written toward the close of the last century, is read more widely now than at the time of publication. It was many years before an organized effort was made to secure political equality for women. The movement, which has lasted through the lifetime of some of America's noblest women, though a little too narrow for modern sociological students, has been a great element in the remarkable change. Unconsciously it has builded better than it knew, and helped to widen the field and elevate the aspirations of women far more than the originators ever intended.

The introduction of machinery has been the most potent factor in the transition. When the work of the world was done in the home, when the spinning-wheel, the loom, the soap vat, the "pig-killing," the bake oven, and the slender needle were institutions in every household, naturally "woman's place" was at home. But spinning-wheel and loom turned into great cotton and woollen mills; the pork-barrel became the vast packing-houses of our large cities; the needle was reserved for mending, and great clothing establishments took its place; the old lye barrel gave way to immense soap factories; and family ovens were relegated to the past, for the bakeries that now supply the staff of life.

It was no longer profitable to make these things in the seclusion of the home; and women followed the machines and went in great crowds to the factories. The demand for women's work came at a time when a new restlessness was pervading the inner sanctum of the home. Secluded and protected, kindly treated though they might happen to be, women began to feel that they were not living full, true lives. They felt that all their faculties were not being developed, that all their powers for giving and receiving happiness were not being called out. Though the duties of motherhood might for the time being occupy all their time and energies, it was also true that not all women were mothers of children, nor were the mothers always mothers of young children. A woman's life stretches over many periods, as does man's. In a lifetime she is capable of being much more than a mother, as man is expected to be much more than a father.

The restlessness was natural. Women came out into the world and became acquainted with each other and with their working brothers; they took a broader view of life; and something of that feeling of fraternity to which men had attained in their clubs, lodges, and unions, began to take lodgment in their breasts. For the "old" woman had no conception of the brotherhood of the human race. She loved her own passionately, and she loved her immediate friends; she loved her church and believed in a vague way that she "loved all men," as a good Christian should. But of the real solidarity of the human race, of the truth that "an injury to one is the concern of all," she had no conception. The "new woman" has a very fair realizing sense of this great social truth today. And therefore, though she may be more of a slave in the factory than she was in the narrow confines of home, she has come up higher. She has reached greater opportunities for full, well-developed existence; and though she makes some mistakes, she is far advanced in her evolutionary progress.

But as yet she is no happier, and men are not pleased. They think she has taken their places in the workshop, in the office, and at the business desk; they fear to lose the sweet, clinging, fragile, wheedling little creature they imagine they love; and they have not reached a conception of what the free, self-poised, capable, womanly woman of the future will be. They are not very well satisfied with the crude sample of the "new woman;" and they are in a manner drawing away from her in the consciousness of a lofty superiority which never needs a transitional stage.

Women themselves are not happy, because they are not yet accustomed to the new order--an order that is as yet chaotic and undefined. Just out from the unwholesome hothouse air of their old seclusion, the atmosphere of comparative freedom and independence strikes too harshly upon them, and they shiver. They cannot go back, and they cannot yet breathe easily. They can do wonders in adaptation, but they cannot find their equilibrium in half a generation of partial freedom. The adjusting process hurts; it always does.

What is it that woman wants? What is it she hopes to attain? What is it she lacks that men are not willing to give? It is no wonderful thing; nothing preposterous or presumptuous. She simply wants to be a human being, not a slave, not a toy, not a queen. She wants the equal personal liberty that every man demands in order to become a fully developed, well-balanced, happy, and useful being. Only this and nothing more.

With this emancipation--this "liberty to do whatsoever one wills so long as one [does not infringe] on the equal right of others to do as they will"--she needs not even the chivalry of old. Kindness, sympathy, love from equals she needs in common with man. She needs not that spirit of worship which some men who think they are "advanced" seem willing to pour out upon her; she needs not that undue devotion on account of her motherhood which many good people believe is right and just; she needs not that right which Robert Ingersoll declared she must possess when he said: "Women should have all the rights that men possess and one more--the right to be protected." The right to be a human being includes that right when necessary. If every individual in the world possesses an equal right to life, liberty, and the pursuit of happiness, the right of opportunity at nature's table, the right to develop to the highest she is capable of becoming, the rights of motherhood and womanhood are conceded. No better protection is needed than that which any enlightened human being will naturally give to another if circumstances make it imperative. A free woman will not choose to be "protected" in the old sense. Protection has ever been an implication of weakness and a willingness to occupy a subordinate position. Nations which call upon other nations for protection must needs give up for that protection some portion of their independence; and industries that can flourish only under "protection" create slaves in their turn.

A great fear seems to exist that if women were perfectly free to become whatever they see fit many dire calamities would happen. Woman would become "mannish;" she would lose her delicate sense of morality; and she might slight that one great duty to which she has been almost wholly consigned for so many ages. But why do we hesitate to trust woman free, when she has fulfilled so many precious trusts in bondage? I have no fear that motherhood and love is a great part of the sweetness of life, and free women are not likely to yield up any part of their happiness.

This one great fear seems to lie at the bottom of every objection to the full freedom and equality of woman--the fear that she will refuse to do her duty by the human race. It is the last prejudice, the last of the old traditions, that man is willing to let go. He will go so far as to admit the right of suffrage, to accept equal property rights, to grant equal opportunities in all the fields of human activity, but he cannot rid himself of that sacred old tenet: that a woman cannot be a good wife and mother if she have any other interest in life besides her home and children. Even very radical thinkers still at times declare that "woman's crowning glory is motherhood;" and only insist on equal opportunities and unequal consideration that she may be more fully and perfectly the mother. I am aware that I am proving myself a startling heretic to generally accepted ideas, but I most emphatically dissent.

I am aware that throughout the realm of nature the one blind impulse of every living thing is to reproduce itself. Everything else seems to be sacrificed to this one object. In the lowest living organisms individual identity is completely lost in the separation which creates two where one existed before. A little higher up in the scale extinction follows reproduction; and for many degrees in the ascending gamut the sole purpose of existence seems to be simply reproduction. But as the higher forms of life evolve, in both the animal and the vegetable kingdoms, more and more of life is utilized in other ways. Trees live to give shelter and shade, and they minister to our sense of beauty through many years; the higher animals have many uses, and many years of animal enjoyment, aside from the function of reproduction.

In the lower grades of human life the power of reproduction seems the most important part of existence. But as the race advances, develops, acquires knowledge, the existence of its members becomes rich and full with the wealth of life itself. The individual becomes an emphasized, distinct identity. It is something to the world that a bright, sound individual lives, acts, and thinks, even though it is never reproduced. The male portion of the race already feel as though fatherhood were a mere incident in their lives, and would be insulted were you to intimate that fatherhood should be the crowning glory of their lives. They know that they possess powers and capabilities that the world needs and appreciates, and that fatherhood, blessed though it be, is not the fullest and best manifestation of their existence. The idea is in every way as applicable to woman as to man. Why should all the faculties and energies of woman be turned to the fulfilment of this one function of her being?

It is flattering to man to think that it takes all of a woman's whole life to carry out her duty to him and his children. But if he only knew it, the entire devotion of her powers to this one purpose is the poorest preparation for wifehood and motherhood that can be made. Even the man himself feels a sort of undefined contempt for the woman who is nothing but wife and mother. A woman becomes morbid who simply retires within herself to brood over her fitness or unfitness for her "crowning glory." It is distorting, dwarfish, narrowing. Her child is unfavorably affected by this intensity of thought centred upon its embryonic existence. It is like that unwholesome "self-analysis" which has ever made up so great a part of the old religious creeds, and which still crops up in modified forms in the "new philosophies."

Let the woman live for herself, not for unborn children. Let her fill her life to the brim with happiness, knowledge, mental and physical activity; let lofty emotions and vigorous thoughts fill her being; let her whole existence expand to its fullest extent; let her forget her motherhood; she will be the better mother for first being a perfect woman. And to be this she must first be free. It will not do to ask what she will do with her freedom, to criticise, to judge; one must only wait. "The cure for the evils of liberty is more liberty."

Do not fear for the result. The trend of human evolution is upward and onward. The plant allowed to grow freely, in the sunlight, with warm rich soil and pure fresh air, will develop to its very highest possibilities. Cramp it, interfere with it, abstract either light or warmth, and it becomes a stunted, pale, sickly growth. Looking upon it, no one could tell what it might have become under proper conditions.

Do not fear that woman thus freed would become a poor mimicry of a poor sample of a man. To become "mannish" is in the eyes of conventional society worse than to commit a crime. But what do we mean by this term? If it is anything reprehensible, believe me, it is as bad in man as in woman. Does it apply to the manners, morals, or the intellect? It is very vague at best. For those qualities which we call "good" are as beautiful in man as in woman. We love bravery, self-poise, strength, honor, truthfulness in one as well as in the other. We love gentleness, kindness, sympathy, tact in both sexes. We see today timid men and brave women; weak-minded men and strong-minded women; deceitful men and truthful women; vain men and self-forgetful women. Under equal and similar conditions the virtues and vices would be diffused much more equally. For I hold another heresy: that there is no sex in intellect, sentiment, or morals. The same environment, the same treatment, the same teachings would result in a similarity of characteristics. There will never cease to be variety, but we should not find a greater tendency toward any particular group of faculties in one sex over the other.

True, some scientific scholars declare that it is a physical impossibility for woman under any condition to become man's equal in physical and mental strength, or to become free from her emotional disturbances and sensitiveness of nerves. The shape, size, and quality of the brain, they say, preclude this; her peculiar functions, the time and energy necessary to the bearing of children and the nourishing of them, prevent a change from her present nature. Nevertheless this is not a demonstrated truth; no one knows by actual experiment whether it is true or not. The fact that all human creatures are the subject of environment and of hereditary conditions signifies that woman is no exception. There is every reason to suppose that under like conditions with men, women would develop in a manner as men do. Woman's peculiar functions should not create the sharp distinctions now seen. Weakness, dependence, emotionalism, vanity, deceitfulness have been cultivated in woman; these traits have been considered her greatest attractions; tradition, custom, public opinion have fixed them upon her, and it will take long to eliminate them.

There is no reason why woman should devote more of her time and energies to motherhood than man does to fatherhood. Work, activity, interest in other things, both while carrying and nourishing children, are better than idleness. No special training, no particular occupation or exercise of one's faculties, or the cessation of activities, are necessary as a preparation for motherhood. The life which makes a woman all she is capable of being as a human being is the only one essential to the rearing of good children. So little is required of a mother that need interfere with ordinary duties and occupations, that it is difficult to see how motherhood should have, in itself, such a wonderful differentiating effect.

Woman has been considered too much as woman, and not enough as a human being. The constant reference to her sex has been neither ennobling, complimentary, nor agreeable. Either as slave, toy, pet, or queen, this ceaseless thinking of her sex instead of herself has been degrading. To finally arrive at her best she simply needs consideration as a fellow member of society.

Do not fear liberty. Just now the results of the beginnings of freedom do not seem very satisfactory. Woman seems to be an intruder; she cannot overcome at once the prejudices that had their inception in the time of her complete economic dependence. She herself is dissatisfied. She is not as lovable perhaps. She has lost some of the charm of clinging womanhood which at best man only heeded in his leisure moments, and has not yet gained the poise and individuality that will draw him to her as a companion. She is dissatisfied with the old gallantry, and has not yet attained the spontaneous recognition and respectful love she longs for. But this will come. There will be a time when men and women, equal human beings, clasping hands and looking each other in the eyes on a level--not leaning on each other, but upright--will feel a true fellowship; and mutual admiration and respect will exist between them. Then will love be sweeter, purer, more beautiful than the world has ever known.

THE UNIVERSAL MISSION OF WOMAN

Woman's essential mission in the world is to be for mankind a living example of the spirit of total dedication to God. To love God with her whole heart, her whole mind, her whole strength, and to radiate that love to the world--this is the universal task of woman. It is true that every human being is made for the love of God and is meant to be totally consecrated to His praise. In what sense, then, can we say that it is the particular mission of woman to be both an example and guide of man along the way of dedication?

There are two poles, two principles in human nature. Father Gerald Vann, O. P., in his recent book, "The Heart of Man," distinguishes these two basic tendencies as "man the maker" and "man the lover." Both principles are present to some extent in every human being, but man the maker is realized most perfectly in man; man the lover in woman. It is the maker who asserts, who imposes his idea and his will on the surroundings. The race takes its forward motion along the way of organization and invention from him. It is man the lover who gives, who yields his own will and gladly surrenders not only his will but his very self to the beloved.

Mankind has always recognized that love plays a far greater role in woman's life than in man's. Every woman when she looks into her own heart finds there the deep desire to surrender herself completely in love. Woman is by nature total in her giving; love absorbs her whole being. Byron was expressing the common experience of mankind when he wrote:

"Man's love is of man's life a thing apart

'Tis Woman's whole existence."

In relation to God, we must all fulfill the role of the lover, awaiting the divine initiative, surrendering completely to the divine will. As C. S. Lewis writes so beautifully, "Our role must be always that of patient to agent, female to male, mirror to light, echo to voice. Our highest activity must be response, not initiative. To experience the love of God in a true and not an illusory form is therefore to experience it as our surrender to His demand, our conformity to His desire." Christian tradition has often expressed man's relation to God in the beautiful phrase: the soul is the bride of Christ. But woman's nature has the greater innate affinity for the bridal role, for the act of loving surrender. That is why woman has been throughout Christian history a symbol and example of the spirit of complete consecration to God. Woman's natural capacity for wholehearted giving of herself in love is the basis for her glorious supernatural vocation. It is her function to help to lead mankind to God by becoming herself a radiant example of total dedication to His will.

The lover's surrender opens the way for the action of God's grace in the world. "The world can be moved by the strength of man, but it can be blessed in the real sense of the word only in the sign of woman," writes Gertrude von Le Fort. It is first of all to Our Lady that these words apply. In her, the universal mission of woman, the lover, was fulfilled most completely. Her "fiat" is the perfect expression of the creature's wholesouled surrender to the creator, and through her surrender the fullness of blessing entered into the world. These words may be applied, too, to the universal task of womankind, for it is the function of every woman to re-echo the "fiat" of Mary and thus to become a source of blessing to humanity.

Woman as Mother of Mankind

Woman helps to lead society Godward by her direct service of mankind as well as by her example. Total dedication to God implies wholehearted service of man. A loving care for one's neighbor is but the necessary practical expression of a genuine love of God. In woman, the care for one's neighbor has the character of maternal love, with its warm personal devotion and generous sacrifice of self. Spiritually as well as physically, woman is the mother of mankind, the fountain and nurturer of life.

Through her relation to "man the maker" woman exercises a strong spiritual influence on the whole of a culture. Man leaves the imprint of his personality in the creations of his mind--works of science and art, monumental buildings and commercial empires. But woman's masterpiece is life itself. She is not interested in abstract or technical achievements but in persons, and in bringing persons to God. She stays in the background, the great inspirer, whose warm sympathy and encouragement spur man on.

Intuitively she perceives what is best and noblest in his proposals and helps to develop it. With her deep awareness of the sacramentality of life, she helps man to see matter as the image of spirit, inspiring him with her vision of the divine poetry of creation and the symbolism of human action.

In the life of every great man one finds this vital influence of a noble woman-Monica and Augustine, Paula and Jerome, Scholastica and Benedict, Clare and Francis, Blanche of Castile and King Louis, Clothilde and Clovis, Beatrice and Dante. Woman's influence is subtle and hard to define but nonetheless real. When she no longer fulfills her role as spiritual mother, culture becomes gross, materialistic, brutal, and loses grace and beauty.

The Three Spheres of Woman's Dedication

Woman must needs fulfill her universal mission of dedication to God and loving service of mankind in some concrete set of circumstances. There are three spheres in which she can carry out her primary task: religious life, marriage, and single life in the world. In the designs of God's

Providence, some women in every generation, the "first fruits," are meant to consecrate themselves to God in religion; most women are called to dedicate themselves to Him in marriage; and very few are intended for the life of the unmarried woman in the world. But whether she becomes a nun, a mother of a family, or a single woman in the world, her essential function remains the same: to be a living example of the spirit of surrender and love, the spiritual mother of mankind.

The virgin consecrated to God by her vow of chastity has always been regarded with highest honor in Christian civilization. Consecrated virginity diffuses a fragrant atmosphere of purity and spiritual integrity throughout society, which contributes to preserve the sanctity of marriage and the dignity of womanhood. The greater the respect and esteem shown to virginity in a society, the higher the position of all women will be. It is significant that the Protestant revolt which has had so many unfortunate consequences for the position of woman began with Luther's attacks on virginity and his liquidation of convents and monasteries.

The topic of woman's contribution to society through the religious life, however, demands a separate article for adequate treatment. The present discussion will be confined to the role of woman in marriage and in the single life in the world.

Woman in Marriage

Woman's nature is admirably adapted to her functions as wife and mother. The responsibilities of the family develop her powers and mature her spiritually, mentally. and physically.

Spiritually, a woman becomes mature through surrender, through finding the particular role in which she can accomplish her total dedication to God. The young woman who has found her vocation in life in marriage and is wholly given to her task of bringing her family to God is a mature person whatever her age. She will have that air of serenity and peace which are the sign of the basic fulfillment of her being.

The woman who has never surrendered wholeheartedly to any purpose outside herself remains immature all her life, like a bud which never unfolds itself. In marriage, woman can develop a spirit of selflessness which makes her dedication deeper and richer with the years. Her service to her family both expresses her love of God and increases her power of loving. The woman who has no outlet for her love, no one for whom she can spend herself, is apt to become hard, bitter, selfish, because she has no one but herself to consider. The woman who is constantly concerned with the needs of her family can unfold the qualities of love, tenderness, and unselfish devotion which make her truly great and truly happy.

Mentally, a woman's mind matures under the stimulus of the varied practical activities she performs for those she loves. In the concrete, living experience of the family, she can develop sound judgment and a keen insight into human nature. Lombroso's observation can readily be verified.

"The mother of a large family who has had no time to study, having been occupied with her children and her household, has more life, more breadth of ideas, than the old maid of the same age who has done nothing else than to potter about at universities and libraries." The responsibilities of her family life exercise all woman's mental powers. Her intuition and powers of observation are called into play constantly to discover the unexpressed desires of her family, particularly the needs of the helpless child. She has need of her intuition, too, as well as her tact, to help her solve the hundred problems of human relations and practical affairs that arise in the course of her day. Providing for the family helps to develop woman's natural ingenuity and inventiveness.

It is to the ingenuity of women intent on meeting the needs of their families that we owe the discovery of many of the most important arts: horticulture, for example; the creative arts of weaving, pottery, basketry; the domestic arts of food preparation and preservation; the uses of medicinal herbs in healing.

Physically, too, marriage and child bearing represent a development and completion for the normal woman, giving her new beauty and vitality. The mother of a large family experiences a physical fulfillment with the birth of each child which gives her fresh vigor and health.

Dr. Alexis Carrell observes that women attain their full development as a rule only after the birth of several children. He writes in "Man The Unknown": "Women who have no children are not so well balanced and become more nervous than the others. The importance to woman of the generative function has not been sufficiently recognized. Such function is indispensable to her optimum development. It is therefore absurd to turn women against maternity.

The Gigantic Task

In a well balanced society, where the family performs all its proper functions, the home is a society in microcosm, presenting all the problems of human relations, all the variety of human activities. The home is at once an economic and industrial center, preparing goods for family use; a school in which the young are introduced to the universe; a sanctuary for rest and relaxation; a temple dedicated to the praise of God. It is woman's function to organize and direct this complex undertaking, a role which demands intelligence talents and spiritual qualities of a high order. Chesterton describes the vastness of woman's task in the family in the following passage from "What's Wrong With the World":

"To be Queen Elizabeth within a definite area, deciding sales, banquets, labors, and holidays; to be Whiteley within a certain area, providing toys, boots, sheets, cakes and books; to be Aristotle within a certain area, teaching morals, manners, theology and hygiene: I can understand how this might exhaust the mind, but I cannot imagine how it could narrow it. How can it be a large career to tell other people's children about the Rule of Three and a small career to tell one's own children about the universe? How can it be broad to be the same thing to everyone, and narrow to be everything to someone? No; a woman's function is laborious but because it is gigantic, not because it is minute."

One of the greatest of woman's responsibilities is her task as educator, transmitting the fundamental heritage of civilization, the traditions of culture and religion, to the new generation. The child receives his first introduction to civilization from his mother. The first formation of his mind and character belong almost entirely to her. She gives the child his first concepts of reality, his basic acquaintance with his mother tongue.

The child's ideas of God, of right and wrong, of repentance for faults, his first meeting with God in prayer--all come through the mother's teaching. She socializes the young human being, training him to honesty, courage, generosity, developing self-control, responsibility, and all those other virtues without which society cannot exist. She molds the men and women of the future. No other influence is as strong as the mother's in forming and preparing human beings for life.

Woman not only transmits the foundation of culture to the child; she is the great keeper of tradition in society, the custodian of manners and morals, conserving the gracious customs and fundamental standards of the race. She inspires and enforces the code of social behavior as, for example, the great chatelaines of the middle ages upheld the noble code of chivalry, and the hostesses of the seventeenth century salons cultivated the refinement of taste and manner. She keeps alive those religious customs and traditions in the home and community which link the daily life of man to God by so many intimate bonds. She is the guardian of the moral standard, especially in all that concerns the family. In this respect, as in so many others, the modern woman has abrogated her traditional role with tragic consequences for society.

It is impossible to exaggerate the importance for society of woman's achievement in the family. The family is the foundation of all the larger social structures, the basic cell on which all other agencies depend for the very existence and first formation of their members. A nation can flourish only to the extent that it is composed of healthy, flourishing families. But the family can endure only if the woman spends herself wholeheartedly to create a real home. If the woman looks down upon her function and neglects her task in the family, nothing can take her place; the family will disintegrate and with it the whole society. This should be abundantly clear to us when we see how powerless the most elaborate schools and the most advanced methods of social work are in the face of the rising tide of juvenile delinquents from neglected and broken homes.

It is superficial to think as women that we must be in the forefront of public affairs, politics, or business to influence the course of the world. "Not in the branches of a tree but in its roots do force and power reside," writes Gertrude von Le Fort. Woman is at the very roots of social life. If she keeps the sources of life pure and healthy, the entire social order will be renewed and reinvigorated by her effort.

Woman in Single Life

The other sphere through which woman can carry out her mission is the state of single life in the world. In normal times, only a few women are called to this vocation. But in our time, due to the war and to other abnormal social conditions, many women will remain unmarried. We should realize that this circumstance falls within God's Providence, and that He has destined the single woman to fulfill an important role in the modern world.

The task of the unmarried woman is, by her whole hearted surrender to God, to make virginity spiritually fruitful in the world.

In embracing virginity, she should radiate purity and nobility of soul. Her very existence, like that of the virgin consecrated in religion, should be a strong positive influence upholding the dignity of womanhood and the sanctity of marriage.

By developing her capacity for spiritual motherhood, she should become a source of strength and comfort and inspiration to mankind. Never has the world been so full of misery, so desperately in need of the healing influence of woman's love. The mission of the unmarried woman in this time is to give the full riches of her maternal love and devotion to alleviate the sufferings and renew the hope of mankind.

In order to accomplish her vocation, the single woman must find an appropriate sphere in which she can carry out her dedication to God through loving service of human beings. She must strike out on new paths, searching for types of work in which she can use her womanly talents and develop her woman's nature. In the education and formation of the young; in agriculture, tending growing plants and animals; in the care of the sick, the weak, the poor, the helpless, woman finds fields of activity appropriate to her capacities as nurturer of life.

Unfortunately, work as it is carried on in these fields today often affords small opportunity for the use of woman's characteristic talents. In medicine, in education, in social work, we suffer from depersonalization, from too much large scale organization and mechanical routine, from too much concern with the physical aspects of the process. We need women to pioneer in these fields again, bringing with them their gift for warmly personal service and creating truly womanly occupations. We need women who will help to restore the emphasis on the spiritual, and who will make the work of healing, of teaching, of relieving the distressed a full expression of living charity between human persons.

How did We Lose the Concept of True Womanhood?

As we look over the modern world we may be tempted to echo King Solomon's cry: Who shall find a valiant woman? On every hand we see modern women turning away from this type of the greathearted woman. How does it happen that we have lost the concept of the woman of love and sacrifice and have accepted the ideal of the professional woman in its place?

Three major factors have contributed to the destruction of the womanly ideal: the Reformation, and the consequent secularization of western culture; the Industrial Revolution; the Feminist Movement. The Reformation was an ultra-masculine movement with small regard for woman's qualities and woman's functions. As society lost its Catholic sense, it lost also the concept of total dedication, the understanding of the sacramentality of life, the regard for the sanctity of marriage--all principles intimately connected with woman's mission and dignity. At the same time, "the masculine desire to dominate the woman found expression in the law." Public opinion looked down upon woman's sphere. "Kirche, kuche, and kinderstube" ("Church, kitchen, and nursery") were linked together and treated with scant respect as fit only for women.

Along with the intellectual devaluation of woman's activities came the profound economic and social changes created by the Industrial Revolution. Seventy-five years ago the woman in the home was still the center of a variety of economic enterprises of unquestioned value and importance. But one by one almost all the activities through which a woman served her family, developed herself, and earned the esteem of society, have been lifted out of her hands and transferred to the factory. The sphere in which most women had found their means of dedication was severely curtailed. At the same time, economic necessity forced many women into the labor market to help support their families and thus led them further away from a womanly pattern.

The third influence which has contributed to the loss of a true concept of woman's function is the feminist fallacy. Feminism was born of woman's natural reaction against the depressed condition in which she found herself in a secularized, masculine, industrial culture. The feminists vociferously demanded equality, but unfortunately they conceived equality on a masculine pattern. Their whole struggle for woman's rights has simply helped to destroy the difference between the sexes and has worked to make the woman a slavish imitation of the man. Feminism is an abject surrender to the masculine ideal as the only ideal. The feminist has completely lost faith in herself as a woman. Her effort to prove herself "just as good as a man" betrays her insecurity and is a tacit admission of inferiority.

Woman's struggle for freedom has led her deeper and deeper into a morass of conditions which frustrate her nature and her mission. Chesterton's bon mot is more than a witty pun: "Twenty million women rose to their feet with the cry: 'We will not be dictated to' and proceeded to become stenographers." It is a summary of woman's situation in the modern world. Women rebelled against the confinement of the home; they find themselves now confined to the mechanical routine of the typewriter and the assembly line, rendered all the more monotonous for a woman because of its exceedingly impersonal character. Woman is made for marriage and motherhood; the modern woman in the name of freedom urges easy divorce and artificial sterility. Woman is well adapted to the universal activity of the home; her demand for freedom leads her to a narrowly specialized education and still more narrowly specialized career. Woman is made for love, for the giving of herself in personal, devoted service. In the modern world she has found her way to a position of lonely and selfish independence.

Towards a Solution

The problem of woman's role is fundamental and no simple, facile solution will meet it. It is not surprising that a society which has lost its sense for divine things and for man's own nature should have lost also the true concept of woman. The unnatural position of woman in our society is but one aspect of the disintegration of modern culture. Nothing short of an intensive and all-embracing renewal of the modern world in the Christian spirit will restore woman to her proper functions. What can we do as women to restore a true concept of womanhood?

(1) *Know Thyself*: As women, our first task is to regain our self-respect in the light of a clear concept of our nature and our role. We must grasp the full splendor of the divine idea of woman as it is revealed to us in the sacred writings, climaxing in the figure of Our Lady. If we have the courage to be ourselves and to follow our spiritual mission, then the world will once again recognize and reverence the immeasurable dignity of womanhood.

(2) *Restore the Christian Family*: We must strive in all ways to restore the family to its rightful dignity and full vigor as the basic cell of the social organism. The family must regain the entire range of its functions, the full scope of its gigantic task--religious, educational, cultural, economic. As women it is our particular responsibility to develop a new pattern of integral Christian life in the family, in which common prayer, work, study and recreation will build the bonds of unity and draw the family heavenwards.

(3) *Create Womanly Work*: If woman is to give the full benefit of her special qualities to society, it is of the utmost importance that we create, especially for the unmarried woman, many types of womanly work. We need pioneers of vision and imagination to take the lead in developing occupations which give woman the opportunity to mature and use her distinctive gifts. We must be alert to discover appropriate spheres of activity in which woman may realize her dedication to God in loving service of humankind.

(4) *Become Radiant Examples of the Spirit of Total Dedication*: Most important of all we must fulfill our primary mission to radiate the spirit of dedication in the world. Never has there been a period in the history of the race when the need for woman's spiritual mission was so great. At the root of all the disorders of our sad, sick world lies man's attempt to assert his independence of God. To bring tranquillity and joy into the chaos of modern society, the first necessity is a profound renewal of spirit, a wholehearted surrender of

man to God, a humble and joyful acknowledgment of our complete dependence on Him. To light the way to this surrender is the spiritual mission of the women of the twentieth century, Media Commercialisation and the Women's Market.

FAITH AND FREEDOM

Muslim women around the world see their future in democracy-and in Islam. To veil or not to veil is hardly the question. The fate of women's rights throughout the Islamic world today hinges on matters of far greater substance, from reforms of family and penal codes to new understandings of Islamic law and teaching. In these best and worst of times for Muslim women, it is perhaps not surprising that every promising bit of news seems to come with a disturbing counterpoint.

Take Shirin Ebadi, an Iranian lawyer and former judge, who in mid-October won the Nobel Peace Prize for her unceasing efforts to promote women's rights and democracy in her native land. In response to the jubilant reaction of Iranians throughout the Islamic republic, President Mohammad Khatami--a reformist, no less--dismissed it as "not worth all that fuss!" Several days after the Nobel was announced, Morocco's King Mohammed VI, who claims descent from the prophet Mohammed, proposed reforms in family law that stand to improve the lot of women throughout the North African kingdom. But long before he presented the reforms to the national parliament, Islamists had taken to the streets to denounce them, dwarfing a pro-reform demonstration by roughly 3 to 1. Also in mid-October, in an unusual instance of Bedouin perestroika, authorities in Saudi Arabia announced that the kingdom would permit the holding of municipal elections within a year--though it's still unclear whether women will be able to run for office or even vote. And at the end of September, in one of a dozen Nigerian states that have adopted sharia (Islamic law), a religious appeals court overturned the death sentence of Amina Lawal, 32, a Muslim woman accused of adultery. Yet while Lawal was spared the gruesome fate of death by stoning, at least five other women in Nigeria still face the same sentence.

Women's rights face an uncertain future throughout much of the Islamic world--though nowhere more pointedly than in the constitution-making efforts now underway in both Afghanistan and Iraq. In two nations widely viewed as test cases of the compatibility of Islamic and universal values, it remains to be seen whether and how the principles of sharia, or even the more general spirit of Islamic traditions, will inform their future laws. And behind those uncertainties loom even broader questions facing Muslim women everywhere. In particular, rights activists wonder, are the foundations of Islamic law and theology compatible with international standards of human rights in general and women's right in particular? And if so, what must be done to surmount the practical hurdles--including the crucial matter of who interprets the law--that stand in the way of reconciling Islam with universal principles of women's rights?

Muslim women themselves are already actively engaged with these issues. "When I talk with educated women from Morocco to Pakistan," says Ann Mayer, a professor of legal studies at the University of Pennsylvania's Wharton School and author of Islam and Human Rights: Tradition and Politics, "I find that they are much more inclined to evaluate their condition in relation to international standards of human rights. And they say that international standards only reinforce Islamic standards."

Confidence. That underscores one notable development of the past decade: a new confidence among Muslim feminists and human-rights activists that Islamic teachings and sources can support their efforts. This represents a sea change, says Amina Wadud, professor of Islamic studies at Virginia Commonwealth University and author of Qu'ran and Woman: Rereading the Sacred Text From a Woman's Perspective. As late as 1995, at the Global Women's Conference in Beijing, many feminists from Islamic countries insisted women's equality could be attained only by jettisoning religion, including the outward trappings of the faith, such as the veil.

Since then, though, an expanding reform movement within Islam, driven largely by increased literacy and an explosion of new media outlets, has led more Muslims to explore the sacred writings on their own. While this has often reinforced the patriarchal viewpoint of militant Islamists, it has also supported progressive and feminist interpretations. Wadud insists that it is unnecessary and even constraining to argue only on the basis of historical precedent, but she finds there is more in the sacred texts and traditions to support notions of gender equality than there is to deny them. She notes, for example, that in the period after Mohammed's death, women, including the Prophet's favorite wife, Aisha, played "key roles in preserving traditions, disseminating knowledge, and challenging authority when it went against their understanding of the Koran or the prophetic legacy."

Referring to the decision of Iran's mullahs to remove Nobel winner Ebadi from her judgeship on religious grounds, Wadud notes, "Nowhere is it said that women cannot interpret the law." Ebadi herself, in a recent interview with Iranian emigre author Amir Taheri, makes the same point in her words of advice to Muslim women: "Don't believe that you are decreed to have an inferior position. Study the Koran carefully, so that the oppressors cannot impress you with citations and interpretations. Don't let individuals masquerading as theologians claim they have a monopoly on understanding Islam."

Fine words, but have they yet had any practical consequences? The answer, many activists say, is a qualified yes. In that widely followed adultery case in Nigeria, for example, Amina Lawal's attorney, Hauwa Ibrahim, got her client exonerated, but on several technicalities that may not work for other women. The real problem, says Mayer, is that Nigeria's version of sharia involves a "folkloric version" of Islamic adultery law. First of all, the rules of evidence spelled out in the Koran require either a freely gained confession from the accused or four eyewitnesses to the act of sexual penetration, neither of which was obtained in Nawal's case. Just as important, the maximum punishment for the crime is supposed to be 100 lashes, not stoning.

Illegal. Of course, even if the Nawal case and others did not involve a corrupted use of sharia, the punishments that Nawal faced would be in violation of both the spirit and letter of the U.N. Convention on the Elimination of All Forms of Discrimination Against Women (CEDAW), which Nigeria has signed and ratified. But appeals to international agreements have only limited effectiveness in advancing women's rights in the Islamic world. (Saudi Arabia is one of 50 out of the 57 Organization of Islamic Conference nations to sign and ratify CEDAW, but it explicitly stipulates that it will not observe any terms that contradict "norms of Islamic law.") In some cases, appeals might even backfire. According to Wadud, the defense attorneys involved in another Nigerian adultery case had to send out word that any additional international pressure might actually sway the jurists on a religious appeals court not to overturn the verdict.

In a more general way, says New York University law Prof. Noah Feldman, the former U.S. adviser to the Iraqi Governing Council on constitutional matters, the United States faces a similar challenge in its efforts to guide Afghanistan and Iraq toward becoming democratic and rights-respecting regimes. Feldman points out that as long as America is an occupying power, it can accomplish much "just by suggesting"--though, he promptly adds, the U.S.-led Coalition Provisional Authority had to insist on the appointment of several women to the 25-person Governing Council. "But at a certain point," Feldman cautions, "you cross the line to coercing people on how to run their lives."

Feldman prefers to stop short of that line, having disagreed openly with Sen. Sam Brownback and Rep. Frank Wolf's proposal for requiring explicit religious-freedom language in the Iraqi constitution. "Senator Brownback says if we allow the constitution to mention the word `Islam,' we'll have problems down the road, but I say if we don't, we'll have troubles immediately," Feldman explains. That does not mean that he has little hope for women's rights. To the contrary, says the author of After Jihad, an argument for the future of Islamic democracy, "I am for promoting women's rights by saying they are compatible with Islam."

In Iraq, there are good reasons for thinking that Islam and

women's rights can go together. Before the U.S. invasion, says Khaled Abou el Fadl, a visiting professor at Yale Law School, Iraq was one of the most progressive of Muslim nations in relation to women. Not only were there female jurists and lawyers, but there was a civil code that blended the best of French and Islamic laws. Among the latter, he points out, was a law allowing a woman the right to divorce her husband and sue for alimony and child support if he decided to take another wife.

(A similar expansion of women's prerogatives is one of the reforms that Morocco's king has just proposed.) Like Feldman, Abou el Fadl worries that attempts to expunge Islam from Iraq's laws will only trigger a stronger urge on the part of many Iraqis to put more of Islam in--and that might mean the most sexist and partriarchal versions of Islam.

Which raises the most important issue: How can Muslim feminists and rights activists win the interpretive struggle against those mullahs and muftis who confuse partriarchal codes and customs with the core principles of the faith? That is a major concern for Irshad Manji, a Canadian author and journalist.

Like many other Muslim feminists, she sees the real problem of interpretation as one of overturning Arab traditions of honor that accompanied the spread of Islam and are now being recirculated throughout the world via the Saudi-funded Wahhabi religious establishment. As Manji explains, within the Arab honor code, individual rights are secondary to one's status within the family or tribe. Women are reduced to "communal or tribal property." In Pakistan or Nigeria, she says, a man from one tribe or family may rape a woman from another as an act of communal retribution.

For Manji, who develops her argument in her forthcoming book The Trouble With Islam, one of the best solutions lies in women's growing participation in trade, commerce, and capitalism, all of which have been valued since Islam's founding. (Mohammed's first wife, Khadija, was an astute businessperson.) And the economic empowerment of women in the Islamic world is not merely theoretical. It is already underway even in the most Arab of states,

Saudi Arabia. In Jidda and Riyadh, respectively, women own a quarter and a third of all businesses. And it is no secret among foreigners working in Saudi Arabia that women are the most educated, able, and productive employees in the kingdom.

By consolidating and advancing their economic position, Manji says, and by becoming tax-paying citizens, women can assert their standing as individuals. This emerging reality is hard to ignore, whether in Saudi Arabia or Iran. Already in Malaysia, Amina Wadud notes, women working through Sisters in Islam and other groups have helped reform domestic violence law by promoting what she calls a "nice blend of sharia and civil law."

Still, it is one of the sad ironies of Islam, Manji says, that a religion originally intended to transcend tribalism has, at least in many parts of the world, allowed the tribalist codes to reassert themselves. But Manji refuses to accept that irony as the last word on women's fate within Islam. And she is far from alone.

6

Opportunities for Women Through Reproductive Choice

INTRODUCTION

If music television targets the 'youth demographic' by using highly sexualised male fantasy images of women, the 'female demographic' is itself an increasingly important market in today's commercial media environment. According to Tor Hansson, managing director for Universal Media in Norway, 'the most sought-after demographic group in Norway is women between the ages of 25 and 45-and especially professional and middle management women' (Edmunds 1994, p. 4). With advertisers in Norway and Sweden complaining that this lucrative market was not being delivered to them, the powerful Kinnevik media group launched TV6-Scandinavia's first channel targeted solely to women-in April 1994. Three weeks before its launch, all advertising spots for TV6 had been sold out.

Most of the new channels aimed at women adopt the style and mode of address of women's magazines-the vehicle through which advertisers have traditionally reached the female consumer. Not surprisingly, publishing giants such as Hearst (USA), Hachette (France), D.C. Thompson (United Kingdom) and Bertelsmann (Germany) were among the first to grasp the additional routes into the female market opened by a proliferation of new cable channels. In 1993 three channels aimed at women were launched in the UK alone. The most successful has been UK Living, providing 'practical and entertainment' programmes for women. The output is 'comforting, non-threatening and promises not to over-tax your senses, sensitivities or brain-cells. It smacks of tabloid television-the agony aunts, the special offers,... the game shows, the cult of the minor celebrity as social pundit. There are no documentaries or news' (O'Brien 1993, p. 20). Apolitical and uncontroversial, these channels fit perfectly within the framework of consumerism. To paraphrase the (male) director of Germany's first women's television channel TM3, launched in August 1995, they pursue an ideal viewer who is 'feminine rather than feminist'.

Gems, the first transnational television channel aimed at women, was launched in April 1993 for distribution in the USA and Latin America. The (male) president of International Television which produces the channel's shows, all made in Spanish, describes it as 'programming that's relevant to women, showing musicals, movies and mini-series featuring women's unique roles' (Burnett 1993, p. 25). Particularly revealing of the Gems ideology is an advertisement for the channel, run in the trade magazine 'TV World' in April 1994: 'She's a romantic and a realist.

A caretaker and an emerging power. She's the gatekeeper of more than $260 billion in the U.S. alone. And she has just one international Spanish-language cable television service talking directly to her. GEMS Television.... GEMS is her TV. Because we empower her in a way cable programming never has before. And because we know she is a treasure. GEMS is her TV. That's its brilliance'. Telenovelas feature prominently in the schedule, ensuring-according to marketing director Grace Santana-success against any competition: 'We've programming that's proven-novelas have been around for 40 years'.

That such a channel will 'empower' women seems improbable. What does seem likely, however, is that Gems will indeed open up a new gateway to capital-potentially '$260 billion in the U.S. alone'. With an audience of 600,000 subscribers shortly after its launch, by early 1995 the Miami-based channel was reaching a potential audience of almost five million viewers throughout the Americas.

While male-owned commercial women's channels like these are flourishing, the Canadian Women's Television Network (WTN)-launched in January 1995 as 'a dynamic alternative to mainstream viewing: a channel run by women, for women'-is attempting to succeed in the same market, but on quite different terms. In May 1995 Barbara Barde, WTN's first Vice President of Programming outlined some of the channel's distinctive features: 'WTN has no victims, no violence.... We have women as chief protagonists, women who drive the stories, are in control of their lives.... For us, it is very important that women form part of the creative team of producers, directors and writers... We also have a foundation to which we pledge three-quarters of 1% of our revenues. Its job is two-fold.

The first part is research rojects, looking at issues relating to women in broadcasting. The second is concerned with mentoring, apprenticeships, etc.... not only mentoring women within our own organisation, but also encouraging conventional broadcasters to do the same.... I think we can be a role model'.

The philosophy has little in common with that of the male-controlled channels described earlier and-almost inevitably-WTN has met with hostility from male media establishment. When industry ratings, released in July 1995, showed that WTN was the least-watched of Canada's new cable channels, male critics rushed to the attack. An article by John Haslett Cuff in the Toronto 'Globe and Mail' declared that 'WTN was born with a large chip on its padded shoulders'; in his view, no-one would be surprised by the ratings.

On the other hand, Cuff was surprised and disappointed that Bravo, an arts channel, had tied for second-last place in the ratings since it was 'easily the most stimulating and original of all the new specialty services'. It is instructive to contrast this review with another in 'TV World', by Claire Atkinson. She noted that both WTN and Bravo were 'still finding their audience, although both have won recognition for their programming philosophies.... For WTN.. the problem is that TV viewing is a family affair during primetime, and it isn't until after 22.00 that women will watch channels on their own'.

The gendered nature of these two reviews is illuminating. Cuff's comments display a deep and subjective antagonism to the channel; Atkinson reveals a knowledge of the context in which female viewing takes place, and uses this knowledge to interpret the ratings. For WTN itself the ratings would have come as little surprise.

As Barbara Barde remarked two months before they appeared, 'We always expected that our audience would grow slowly, and that we would have to change habits in a large number of households, because guess who controls the remote controls? Not women' (ibid.). Whether the finances of WTN will allow the channel sufficient time to build up its audience remains to be seen.

Rosalind Coward has argued that during the 1980s, series after series of women's television programmes in the United Kingdom were simply 'allowed to fail', while other genres were protected and preserved until they had established themselves (Coward 1987, p. 100). In the 1990s it is clear that any venture of this kind faces an even more formidable array of obstacles, most of which will never be experienced by channels which treasure women as the gatekeepers of dollar bills.

POLITICAL ECONOMY OF COMMUNICATION

Any consideration of gender portrayal in the media must take account of these wider issues of political economy if existing patterns of representation are to be properly understood and challenged. For as Kamla Bhasin has rightly pointed out: 'We are not just concerned with how women are portrayed in the media or how many women work in the media. We are also concerned about what kinds of lives they lead, what status they have, and what kind of society we have. The answers to these questions will determine our future strategies for communication and networking. Communication alternatives therefore need to emerge from our critique of the present world order and our vision of the future'. Certain trends in the information and communication system of the present world order are set to have a considerable impact on the future of people throughout the world. The media mergers of the past decade have not only consolidated huge power in a decreasing number of corporations with global reach. They have also begun to erode old distinctions between information and entertainment, software and hardware, production and distribution. It is this fusion of communication forms, which constitutes a radical break with the past, that presents such a challenge for the future. For although the influence of a single medium such as television is clearly limited in many ways, it is the 'panoply of cultural means together' (Schiller 1989, p. 151) that is central to the ability of large media conglomerates to present a world-view that bolsters and reinforces their position in the modern economic system and that system itself.

In this context the significance of 'lipstick imperialism' becomes clear. The term puts an intriguing new spin on a concept that dominated much of the debate on international communication during the 1960s and 1970s. 'Cultural imperialism'-the rallying cry of communication scholars and activists who sought to defend indigenous cultural identity and economic independence-now has a rather anachronistic ring. Yet the free-market economic policies adopted by many countries around the world in recent years have opened the doors to new forms of consumerism, driven by increasingly commercial, increasingly transnational communication media. Reflecting on the current situation in Latin America, Gabriel Escobar and Anne Swardson take the example of MTV Latino, whose 'message is powerful and still growing, an influential cultural tool in a market already saturated with images and products from the north.

But what is most striking about this loud invasion is the silence that has greeted it. Three decades after the Latin American left led a call against cultural imperialism... the continent has unabashedly embraced-cultura lite'-a universal, homogenised popular culture in which touches of Latin American rhythm or-Spanglish' accent a dominant North American diet of songs, words and images' (Escobar and Swardson, 1995). To explain the lack of opposition to this contemporary cultural invasion, Uruguayan writer and journalist Eduardo Galeano echoes Schiller's 'panoply' thesis. By stimulating consumption, he argues, the neo-liberal policies which the countries of the North passionately promote simultaneously stifle resistance and creativity. They have helped to develop in Latin Americans a trend towards imitation and what he describes as a 'mentality of resignation' (see Hamelink 1994, p. 132).

Such an analysis is equally applicable outside Latin America. MTV Asia-with 28 million viewers in the region-is said to have triggered a change not just in musical tastes, but 'in social style. In fashions, behaviour, language and morals, more and more youngsters are falling to the thrall of MTV and are drawn into aping the West' (Menon 1993a, p. 29). Again, this cultural invasion is dictated by economics-as MTV's director of international programme sales explains: 'The youth audience is the most sought-after and most lucrative demographic internationally' (Jenkinson 1994, p. 104). Again, the representation of women plays a particular role in the channel's iconography. Sut Jhally, in his educational documentary Dreamworlds, argues that MTV works systematically to deny women subjectivity. Jhally demonstrates how the channel constructs an image of women through a patriarchal discourse of 'nymphomia'-as ever-available objects in an endlessly repetitive male adolescent fantasy world. Other studies agree that, despite the presence of strong female images in some music videos, it is hard to fault the essential truth of this argument.

BENEFITS FROM FAMILY PLANNING EMPLOYMENT

What do women gain by working in family planning? Almost all research has concerned community-based distributors. Studies in seven countries conclude that women working as community-based distributors benefit because they earn money, receive useful training, and gain status in their communities. Of course, other kinds of work, outside family planning, might benefit women similarly or more, while still other kinds of jobs can make life worse.

Income: The salaries, honoraria, or fees for service paid to family planning workers can make a difference to their quality of life. In a survey by the Center for Development and Population Activities

(CEDPA) of 305 field workers employed in 11 family planning projects in Bangladesh, India, Kenya, Mali, Nepal, Pakistan, and Turkey, 76% reported that the income they received from their jobs improved their economic status.

Most of these women use their income to help their families. In the CEDPA study 51% used their earnings largely for general household expenditures; 29%, for their children's education; 10%, for themselves; and 6%, for other miscellaneous, unessential expenses. The remaining 4% gave the money to their husbands.

By earning money, some women improve their position in the household. Most women in the CEDPA study gained more control over their children's education, medical care, and household expenditures. Many also found that relations with husbands and in-laws improved. Just earning money does not guarantee better status at home, however. Some case studies of women earning money in the informal sector (not in family planning) experienced no increase in household influence.

Of course, many programs ask women to work as volunteers. Even if women cannot be paid for their work, programs can make special efforts to recognize their contributions and publicly honor their contribution to their communities.

Competence in new skills: Family planning providers can learn new information and skills. In the CEDPA study community-based distributors' reports suggest that their leadership and communications skills improved, as did their knowledge of family planning methods and service delivery. For many, this is their first paying job. Unlike physical labor such as sewing, farming, or typing, family planning field work teaches women skills that meet the social needs of the community and that enable women to teach others. Community-based family planning providers often help people obtain medical care at clinics. Some are trained to provide directly and/or to teach oral rehydration therapy, immunization, nutrition services, safe delivery practices, and broader maternity care. Professional status and respect. Female family planning workers often win respect for their knowledge.

These women become community authorities in family planning and other health matters. In Matlab, Bangladesh, both field workers and community members report that field workers are important community resources not only for family planning services but also for general medical advice and referral. Community members even seek field workers' advice on financial matters and neighborhood disputes.

Respect is not always easily earned, however. New roles for women sometimes threaten community norms, and those who break the rules may be scorned. For example, in Muslim countries where purdah is practiced, custom prohibits women from moving about alone in public, and yet family planning field workers must visit homes and clinics.

In the face of initial hostility from the community, female workers often find ways to maintain their self-respect. For example, Bangladeshi family planning workers redefined for themselves the traditional norms of purdah and female modesty. They spoke of "inner purdah," shifting emphasis from physical seclusion to an internalized moral code of conduct.

In various cultures and countries, female family planning workers have experienced initial rebuke, then gradual acceptance, and eventual respect. For example, in Bangladesh the field workers initially scorned for violating purdah eventually regained their prestige and at the same time legitimized family planning services. In a few cases female field workers have been unable to win community respect. A study of auxiliary nurse-midwives who provided family planning services in Maharashtra, India, found that many of the women had been abandoned by their husbands or had difficulty finding a husband.

In general, women working as community-based distributors feel strengthened by their work. They reported in the CEDPA study that their achievements and value to the community enhanced their self-esteem and sense of autonomy. Particularly in cultures that generally isolate women, work in family planning is a gateway to new ideas, new information, and new opportunities.

MODELS OF CHANGE

Women working in family planning offer other women more than family planning information and supplies. They often are agents of change and new role-models for their communities.

By persevering and winning respect, women working in family planning set an example for other women. They legitimize women's employment, and family planning workers can serve as examples that young women can aspire to emulate.

Family planning workers can stimulate change in their communities in many ways. Their work can loosen taboos detrimental to women and even help other women assert themselves. For example, after three years of a women-staffed community-based project in Mali, villagers were more willing to discuss such previously taboo topics as family planning and contraceptives.

In Nairobi, Kenya, female volunteers in a family planning project spoke with confidence in public gatherings. In both India and Bangladesh community acceptance has enabled female field workers to intervene in family disputes, rebuking and advising men and providing moral support to women.

Challenges for Family Planning Programs

Through careful selection, training, and support, family planning programs can make special efforts to see that their female employees benefit from their work. Women's employment in family planning needs more study. Other female providers, not just community-based distributors, need to be surveyed. Also, pay scales, working conditions, and potential for training and career advancement should be analyzed with an eye to increasing opportunities for women.

Workers selected with their communities' input may have a better chance of being accepted than workers chosen by outsiders, as a review of community-based programs in Africa suggests. In some cases newly employed family planning workers may displace traditional practitioners, such as traditional birth attendants and midwives, who play a vital social role. Collaboration may be important to win support from traditional practitioners and avoid resistance that could make the task of family planning workers more difficult.

Promoting family planning providers helps women win community respect as qualified, trustworthy professionals. Strengthening both the image and the skills of providers can attract and keep clients. Johns Hopkins Population Communication Services has dubbed this the PRO approach-Promoting Professional Providers. A survey in Kenya showed that people who had heard the radio drama in the Haki Yako ("It's Your Right") PRO approach campaign were less likely to have a negative image of family planning providers than people who had not heard it.

Visible symbols of family planning employment help, too. In Kenya and Zimbabwe, for example, female community-based distributors wear uniforms and have signs outside their homes signifying official endorsement of their work. Recognized as community leaders and authorities, family planning workers are often the only women who sit on the podium at official village events.

SHAPING POLICIES TO MEET CLIENT'S NEEDS

While family planning programs can do much to help women meet their needs, debate continues about how meeting women's needs can be made more central to population policy. Some have criticized population policies as aiming at national goals such as slower population growth, environmental protection, or economic development while neglecting the needs of women as individuals and as a group. Some critics argue that such policies focus on only one aspect of women-their ability to bear children. Ruth Dixon-Mueller has argued that population and development policies must change to reflect "a thoughtful engagement of the difficulties that women face around the world in the struggle to take control over their own fertility and their own lives."

How can population policies better reflect women's interests? Improving the quality of care and protecting women's health have long been concerns of family planning advocates. The United Nations has declared that the goal of family planning should be "the enrichment of human life, not its restriction," pointing out that women in developing countries need a broad range of economic, health, and social rights and services. Many family planning programs are still struggling to meet more modest goals, however. As demand for contraception has risen rapidly in developing countries over the past two decades, programs often have not been able to serve all the people who want family planning.

Recognition is growing that population policies--and development policies in general-must pay attention to their clients' needs and preferences if they are to succeed. J. Brian Atwood, Administrator of the United States Agency for International Development, describes the need in this way:

Attention to gender roles is fundamental to the success of programs we assist. We must support full participation of women at all levels of family planning and-indeed-all health and development programs. We must help women overcome the obstacles they face in obtaining services or using contraceptive methods. We must see that programs are designed to benefit women. And, we must help programs strengthen men's support and participation.

To accomplish this at the program level, family planning program managers are increasing their efforts to learn from clients. At the same time, women's advocates are seeking more opportunities for women to participate in planning services. Thus program managers and women's groups have begun to work together. At the policy level, policy-makers, family planning organizations, women's groups, and other nongovernmental organizations have been building links between population policy-makers and women's advocates. This discussion and debate has grown as world attention has focused on the United Nations International Conference on Population and Development (ICPD) in Cairo in September 1994.

In this discussion diverse policy-makers are recognizing that their various goals can be achieved by the same means-offering services that people want. Policies that serve clients:

- Recognize that reproductive choice is a human right,
- Focus on meeting clients' unmet needs for reproductive health services, and
- Involve clients, especially women, in program design.

REPRODUCTIVE CHOICE IS A BASIC HUMAN RIGHT

Today there is widespread agreement that reproductive choice is a human right. This means that women have the right to control their own fertility and the right to refuse unwanted sexual intercourse, including the right to protect themselves against the violence of men, including husbands, who force intercourse.

Women's advocates have had to struggle to gain recognition of women's reproductive rights. Early in the 20th century women's advocates established the first programs to provide contraceptive information and services so that women could exercise their rights to protect their own health and control their own fertility. Often religious, medical, and government leaders stood in their way. It was not until the 1940s that contraception began to be accepted in developed countries as a medical service and become more widely available.

In recent years international organizations have recognized the right of all individuals and couples to make reproductive choices. In 1968 the International Conference on Human Rights in Teheran affirmed the right of reproductive choice. This right was reaffirmed at the first UN World Population Conference, held in Bucharest in 1974, and again at the second such conference, in Mexico City in 1984. In the words of the report of the Bucharest conference, "All couples and individuals have the basic right to decide freely and responsibly the number and spacing of their children, and to have the information, education, and means to do so."

International institutions consider securing reproductive choice to be an important part of improving women's well-being. For example, the Committee on the Elimination of Discrimination Against Women (CEDAW), established by the United Nations to gauge progress toward ending discrimination against women, monitors access to family planning as an important indication of women's situation.

The declarations of international institutions and global conferences put governments on notice that women should have the right to control their fertility and their own lives-and that family planning programs can help women to achieve these rights. Governments and reproductive health programs face the challenge of turning these broad principles into policies and programs.

Meeting Unmet need for Reproductive Health Care

Over the past decade the percentage of surveyed women who say they do not want to have more children has grown substantially in every region except sub-Saharan Africa. Even in Africa, although most women want large families, there is great interest in spacing births. In nearly all sub-Saharan countries surveyed by the Demographic and Health Surveys (DHS), between one-third and one-half of married women said that they wanted to space their next births by at least two years.

Such statistics imply large potential demand for family planning services. Even though contraceptive use has risen substantially in recent years, in most surveyed countries between 20% and 30% of married women of reproductive age report that they are not using contraception but do not want any more children or else want to delay their next birth at least two years. Rates of abortion, even where abortion is illegal and unsafe, also testify to women's strong desire to control their own fertility.

Demographers describe women who are not using contraception but want to space or limit births as having an unmet need for family planning. Using this definition, Population Reports has estimated, based on DHS data, that 120 million married women of reproductive age in developing countries have an unmet need for contraception. Ruth Dixon-Mueller and Adrienne Germain suggest widening the definition of unmet need to include unmarried women, women who need better or more suitable contraceptive methods, women who need abortion services, and women who need more comprehensive reproductive health services than are currently available. These numbers cannot be easily estimated, but they would surely add substantially to the 120 million figure.

Men also have unmet needs for family planning. In DHS in Burundi, Egypt, Ghana, Kenya, and Pakistan, over half of men approve of family planning, but very few are using a contraceptive method. In smaller, qualitative studies as well, men have asked for more information about reproductive health services including both contraception and treatment for sexually transmitted diseases.

Effectively serving all who want to avoid pregnancy but are not using contraception could help reconcile the dual goals of (1) serving individual clients and (2) slowing global population growth. Steven Sinding has suggested that family planning programs replace demographic objectives with the objective of meeting unmet need. In 9 of 12 countries studied, levels of contraceptive use would be higher if all unmet need were met than if current demographic objectives were reached.

To translate this unmet need to control fertility into utilization of reproductive health services, policy makers must let clients know that these services are a safe and effective way to achieve their personal goals.

Reproductive health programs can identify the obstacles that prevent women from using services and can design services and communication that will help overcome some of those obstacles. Obstacles may range from lack of supplies and services to dissatisfaction with current services to fears of contraceptive side effects, to social limits on women's mobility or decision-making. Beyond the need to control their own fertility, women also need other reproductive health services, and family planning programs may be able to meet these needs, as well.

INVOLVING CLIENTS IN PROGRAM DESIGN

Serving clients' needs requires learning and heeding what clients want. Since most family planning clients are women, women should be involved at all levels in population and reproductive health programs and policy-making. Women can offer valuable insights as policy-makers, program managers, and health professionals. Most importantly, programs should consult with clients about their reproductive health care priorities.

Policy-makers can use various means to learn what clients and the public want. A recent review has identified a range of approaches. Many of these approaches are routinely used in the audience research that is part of designing and monitoring family planning communication programs:

- Observation of client-provider interactions,
- Feedback from "mystery" or "simulated" clients-people who use services and then report on their experience,
- Patient flow studies to determine how long patients spend in such activities as waiting and talking to providers,
- Focus-group discussions with clients and potential clients about their experience and their preferences,
- Exit interviews or other post-service interviews with clients,
- Interviews with service personnel about what they think would constitute a good client visit and what they see as difficulties,
- Involving women directly in program design as program administrators or on advisory groups,
- Working with women's health advocacy groups to benefit from their analyses of women's health needs,
- Open discussion meetings in the community, sometimes specifically for women or for men, and
- Learning from other programs with services that clients like.

In Chile, for example, researchers interviewed women who had come in for clinic services. The clients wanted cleanliness, a reasonable waiting time, accessible services such as pharmacies, enough time with providers to ask questions about such topics as physiology and childrearing, and staff with a positive, respectful attitude toward clients.

Some women's grass-roots organizations have identified their own reproductive needs and responded to them. For example, the Working Women's Forum in India and the Mothers' Clubs in South Korea offer family planning services that complement the economic help and other services that they provide to members.

The seven clinics run by the Bangladesh Women's Health Coalition each have a local advisory committee to ensure that the clinics meets local needs. Some women's organizations have focused on informing other women. In 1991 a collective of Egyptian women wrote a nontechnical book on women's reproductive health. In Peru women in focus groups helped Peru Mujer, a nongovernmental organization, design educational materials for nonliterate women like themselves.

Women in Fiji made videos for women's groups on topics that they wanted discussed, such as sexually transmitted diseases and women's attitudes toward menstruation and family planning. Other family planning organizations can learn from such groups and perhaps collaborate with them.

Involving women more deeply in program design should not mean excluding men. Men and women share responsibility for reproductive health. Policies and programs will work best if they are planned by, and for, both women and men. Ideally, the insight and experiences of both women and men will create better programs that improve the lives of all clients.

Improving the lives of women and men should be a primary goal of population policy. Reproductive health care programs contribute by enabling men and women to live healthier lives and to plan when they will have children.

Women, and men who enjoy better health and more control over their reproductive lives can have more opportunity to fulfill their hopes for their children, themselves, their families, and their communities.

OPPORTUNITIES FOR WOMEN THROUGH REPRODUCTIVE CHOICE

Women around the world hope for the future-for better lives for themselves, education and prosperity for their children, and security for their families. A broad array of social and economic changes is necessary to overcome the poverty, lack of education, and limited control over their own lives that often keep women's hopes from coming true. But women can take an important step forward when they make their own reproductive choices-about marriage, sex, childbearing, and contraception.

The great majority of women want to control their own fertility. Growing contraceptive use in nearly every developing country attests to women's desire to plan their pregnancies. Many other women want to space or limit births but are not using contraception. The continuing high number of abortions, often undertaken illegally at great risk, also testifies to women's desire to control their own fertility.

How can reproductive choice improve a woman's life? Making choices about the course of one's own life asserts a person's fundamental dignity. Thus family planning is a basic human right, although many women are unable to exercise that right. Also, the woman who chooses when she has children, and how many, exerts an important measure of control over her own physical, emotional, and economic well-being. She contributes to her children's well-being too.

Health: More than half a million women die each year from causes related to pregnancy. Many of these deaths follow unwanted pregnancies: 20% to 40% result from unsafe abortions. For women who want to avoid pregnancy, using contraception means avoiding the risks of pregnancy and childbirth or of unsafe abortion.

Planning: By determining when she will have children and how many, a woman takes a step toward deciding how she will spend much of her life-whether to finish school, to give more attention to each child she has, to better manage household duties, possibly to earn income so that she and her family can live more prosperous lives, or even to contribute more to her community and society as a whole. Internationally comparable surveys find that, in countries where levels of contraceptive use are above average, women start childbearing later, end childbearing sooner, have fewer children, and spend fewer years caring for young children. Of course, a woman's decision to control her fertility does not guarantee her new opportunities. It does, however, help enable her to take advantage of opportunities that present themselves and to provide new resources to the family.

How can Family Planning Programs Help?

Family planning programs contribute most by helping women prevent unwanted pregnancies. Well-designed, high-quality programs can do even more by delivering services in ways that help women meet other needs as well. They can:

- Show by example that women should be treated with dignity: their opinions, valued; and their decisions, respected;
- Provide additional contraceptive and other reproductive health services that can meet common and serious needs-possibly care for sexually transmitted diseases and information and services for young people, for example;
- Influence public perceptions of women's roles by depicting in the mass media women who act with courage, take responsibility, and succeed in new roles;
- Encourage men to understand their own and women's reproductive health needs, share reproductive decision making, and take more responsibility for reproductive health, contraceptive use, and their families' welfare; and
- Employ women as family planning professionals, treat them equitably, and offer them opportunities to lead.

With the advice and involvement of the women they serve, well-designed reproductive health programs can help women in a variety of ways to improve their quality of life for themselves, their families, and their communities

RESISTING THE MENTALITY OF RESIGNATION

The immensity, facelessness and apparent impregnability of today's media conglomerates undoubtedly help to foster a 'mentality of resignation', as Galeano puts it. The mentality of resignation is a sign that people are being, or have been, disempowered. But if certain forms of communication and culture can disempower, others can empower. Over the past twenty years women have not been content merely to denounce biases and inequities in the established media.

Women have created and used countless alternative and participatory communication channels to support their struggles, defend their rights, promote reflection, diffuse their own forms of representation. Pilar Rian~o argues that this process has made women the primary subjects of struggle and change in communication systems, by developing oppositional and proactive alternatives that influence language, representations and communication technologies.

Standing outside the mainstream, 'women's movement media' have certainly played a crucial role in women's struggle around the world. Part of a global networking, consciousness-raising and knowledge creation project, they have enabled women to communicate through their own words and images. If print and publishing have been the most widely used formats, in the past two decades other media such as music, radio, video, film and-increasingly the new communication technologies-have also been important.

Over the same period, in most regions there has been a steady growth of women's media associations and networks, and an increase in the number of women working in mainstream media. Yet as Donna Allen points out 'there is still a wide gap between the women who have formed networks outside of the 'mainstream' media and those women who are employed in mass media who hold the key to reaching the larger public'. The closing of this gap, she argues, 'is a crucial step toward the advancement of all women.'

The building of such alliances, and the merging of women's diverse experiences of working with and in the media, is surely one of the most urgent tasks for women struggling for a more diverse and democratic world information and communication system.

GENDER PORTRAYAL IN THE MEDIA

Clearly the debates around gender representation in the media have moved on since the content analyses of 'sex-roles and stereotypes' which typified studies of the 1970s in North America and in countries such as Japan, Korea, the Philippines where quantitative social science methods were favoured. These studies certainly documented women's exclusion from or silencing in many media forms, and helped to show how media images reinforce notions of 'difference'-in behaviour, aspirations, psychological traits and so on-between women and men.

Studies of this kind are of course still carried out, and they remain important in recording some of the basic elements in a very complex situation. In an ambitious global monitoring exercise, women from 71 countries studied their news media for one day in January 1995. More than 15,500 stories were analysed, and the results were dramatic. Only 17% of people interviewed in the news were women. Just 11% of news stories dealt with issues of special concern to women, or foregrounded any gender perspective on the events reported (MediaWatch, 1995).

National monitoring studies, over longer time periods, show similar patterns. The particular power of these studies lies in their potential to document change. In fact, regular media monitoring in Canada and the USA shows surprisingly slow progress towards equal representation of women and men in the media. Studies since 1974 indicate that 'peaks' may be followed by 'troughs', with no sustained pattern of improvement (see CRTC, 1990; Stephens 1994; Women, Men and Media 1995). Indeed, according to one of the longest running studies of trends in gender portrayal on US television (carried out since 1969 by the Cultural Indicators research team at the Annenberg School of Communication, University of Pennsylvania), 'the demography of the world of television is impressive in its repetitiveness and stability:... women comprise one-third or less of the characters in all samples except day-time serials where they are 45.5%, and in game shows where they are 55.3%.

The smallest percentage of women is in news (27.8%) and in children's programmes (23.4%). As major characters, women's role's shrink in children's programmes to 18%... A child growing up with children's major network television will see about 123 characters each Saturday morning but rarely, if ever, a role model of a mature female as leader' (Gerbner 1994, pp. 39, 44). The world depicted by the media 'seems to be frozen in a time-warp of obsolete and damaging representations' (op. cit., p. 43).

INTERPRETING PATTERNS OF PORTRAYAL

Obvious numerical imbalances in media portrayals of women and men tell only a small part of the story-and not necessarily the most important part. Of course most studies go further, investigating gender differentiation in social and occupational roles, psychological and personality traits, physical attributes and so on. The results have been extensively documented for most world regions (see Gallagher and Quindoza-Santiago, 1994) and will not be detailed here. Perhaps the more interesting questions concern the implicit messages which are woven into these media portrayals of women and men. Why is the pattern as it is, and why does it so stubbornly persist despite two decades of research and action aimed at changing it? There are many ways of approaching such questions. For example, I have already argued that discrimination or imbalance in gender portrayal is not an isolated phenomenon which can be studied-or changed-in a compartmentalised way. Media representations of women and men take shape within particular, and changing, socio-economic formations which must themselves be analysed and understood. But there are other issues to consider too.

One is the question of political ideology. In most parts of the world, at different times in history, representations and images of women been used as symbols of political aspirations and social change. An obvious example was the widespread use of particular asexual, 'emancipated' female images in Soviet culture: the confident, sturdy woman on her tractor, on the farm, or in the factory. As various recent commentators have pointed out, images of this kind never reflected existing reality. In the words of Olga Lipovskaya, 'the social realist tradition was intended to create an ideal reality and utilised this model to portray the exemplary woman of the radiant Communist future' (Lipovskaya 1994, p. 124; see also Voronina 1994; Azhgikina 1995). In such a situation female imagery becomes a metaphor for a particular political ideology, rather than a representation of women's lives. In her analysis of the powerful media definitions of womanhood in revolutionary China, Elizabeth Croll maintains that 'imaging' actually became a substitute for living or experience: 'With the gradual exclusion of semantic or visual variations of image and text, the rhetoric of equality and celebration soon became the only language officially tolerated... There were no images of, or words for representing, the inequality of experience' (Croll 1995, p. 80).

In one of the few extensive analyses of female imagery in the Arab States, Sarah Graham-Brown points out that images of women may be used in conflicting ways-as symbols of progress on the one hand, and as symbols of continuity with the cultural past on the other-frequently in reaction to representations of women imposed from outside the society, for instance by the Western media. Major ideological changes obviously affect the use of female imagery to promote national goals. A clear example, cited by Graham-Brown, is the contrast between the way women were portrayed in the media in Iran during the Pahlavi rule and since the revolution. 'In both instances, these images form an important element in the way the regimes promote and legitimize themselves. At the same time, neither kind of image necessarily reflects with accuracy the changes or continuities in the everyday life of women in different classes'. The disjuncture between image and reality becomes profound in situations where governments are attempting to mobilize people for certain kinds of social change.

Graham-Brown gives examples from post-independence Algeria and Nasser's Egypt, where 'modernist' and westernised images of women were used as emblems of progress and enlightenment. Yet 'on the whole, these images of emancipation, while they might promote the idea of the progressive nation, did not challenge basic gender relations in society, particularly male domination of the family structure' (Graham-Brown 1988, p. 245). In contemporary Egypt, according to Lila Abu-Lughod (1993), there is a similar gap between the ideological message of certain 'national interest' television serials and experience of life in particular communities. The interpretation of such images is thus fraught with complications. This does not mean that no indication of changing status, or changing attitudes to women can be gleaned from them. But they cannot be 'read' according to any simple formula whereby changes in imagery are assumed to equate with changes of the same magnitude in women's lives.

DIVERSITY AND CHANGE IN GENDER PORTRAYAL

These examples illustrate the limitations of a framework which sets out to critique 'negative' images and to demand 'positive' media representations of women. Such a juxtasposition assumes that there is a norm against which images can be judged. In reality, things are much more complicated. The same kind of image can embody a variety of different meanings, depending on the context. A more promising route seems to be offered by the search for greater 'diversity' in gender portrayal. But here again, the situation is not completely straightforward. Media representations of women and men in the 1990s may indeed be more diverse than they were twenty years ago. Lawyers, doctors and police officers are no longer inevitably male; and we may even see the occasional male character in the kitchen, weeping into the washing-up bowl. But how important is this change, and what is its significance?

It is true that drama-including popular fiction, soap operas and telenovelas-has to some extent begun to respond to new currents and complexities in gender relations, with occasional portrayals of the 'new man' (gentle, supportive, emotional) and the 'modern woman' (independent, assertive, resourceful). But detailed analyses suggest that such innovations are often simply a modish facade, behind which lurk old-fashioned formulaic assumptions. Longitudinal studies of Italian television drama show that, despite a scattering of 'anti-heroes', output remains overwhelmingly male-centered and success-oriented.

In Germany and the United Kingdom, studies have called into question claims that 'progressive' soap operas have actually introduced radically different points of view (for example, Externbrink 1992; Geraghty 1995). In Latin America most of the independent new heroines of recent telenovelas, on closer examination seem to have been introduced as a means of changing the 'outer wrappings' of the genre rather than its core messages. In the USA several studies of the successful prime-time series thirty something have concluded that despite claims that it articulates a 'new view of manhood', the show's construction of reality is substantially conservative (see Hanke 1992; Heide 1995). Even the trail-blazing 1980s female detective series Cagney and Lacey does not escape criticism. Julie D'Acci's detailed study reveals that although the writers struggled to maintain the show's original feminist orientation, in the face of pressures imposed by commercial network television, the series gradually became more conventional, 'feminine' and exploitative-in the sense of promoting stories that literally 'cashed in' on issues of great complexity for women, such as rape, abortion, marital violence and so on (D'Acci 1994).

Sightings of the 'new man' in media portrayals have been recorded in countries as different as India, Italy and the USA (Shelat 1994; Buonanno 1994; Douglas 1995). Again, this phenomenon can not automatically be taken at face value. Milly Buonanno sounds a note of caution, pointing out that the 'new man' in Italian drama is winning the central position in the family and domestic domain at the expense of women, whose overall share of central roles has fallen over the past four years: 'Even the domestic sphere, the traditional stronghold of the female character in drama, now seems to be increasingly inhabited by males who show themselves more in command of emotional life than the women do' (p. 82). A similar concern is expressed by Susan Douglas. Both she and Manisha Shelat question the extent to which these images actually reflect reality in their societies, though for Shelat they are a 'welcome change' from the role stereotyping that predominates in the majority of Indian media. But Douglas is less sanguine, seeing the development as a 'bizarre twist on the real world, where many women have changed, but too many men have not' (p.81).

This review raises important questions about the extent to which the mainstream media are capable of reflecting diversity and complexity in a way which would properly respond to the current criticisms of women media activists. For this reason, some women remain sceptical of any engagement with the mainstream. But others-like film-maker Michelle Citron-regard it as an essential step forward, providing a possibility of 'subverting' and changing mainstream media content, despite the compromises involved: 'These are risks we need now to take. We will lose a certain amount of control, despite our best intentions and preparedness... But we need new-data' in order to refine our understanding of (the media) and our relationship to it' (Citron 1988, p. 62).

7

Women Development in Information and Communication Technologies

Women, mostly from the developing world, often lack the necessary infrastructure and skills to make the most of the opportunities opened up by ICTs. For example, women constitute only 22 percent of Internet users in Asia, 38 percent of those in Latin America and only 6 percent of Middle East users. The World Development Report 2000/2001 asserts that information and communications technology (ICTs) can enhance poor people's opportunities by improving their access to markets and creating new employment opportunities. The World Bank currently has over a thousand projects with Information Technologies components; however, many of these projects have missed opportunities to address women's and men's different needs.

If gender-sensitive, ICTs have enormous potential to increase women's enterprises and the participation of poor women in the ICT-driven information economy. For example: Women's enterprises: New ICT-enabled businesses and businesses servicing the ICT sector are proving to be particularly fruitful areas for women entrepreneurs. A number of e-business ventures, including provision of Internet services and telecenters, increasingly employ urban and semi-urban women. Case studies also illustrate how e-commerce can be useful for self- employed women in the informal sector. If IT literate, women entrepreneurs working in conventional enterprises such as handcraft or other cottage industries could also benefit from e-research, e-networking, e-marketing, and e-transactions. These facilities might be particularly beneficial to societies where cultural traditions do not encourage women to interact openly with the world outside their immediate vicinity.

Labor force participation: ICTs also have given rise to large IT industries, including software development, manufacturing, and assembling of electronic and computer spare-parts. The increasing trends on outsourcing have resulted in employment opportunities for developing countries in all of these areas.

Cultural and social attitudes can sometimes be unfavorable for women in terms of learning ICT-related skills and taking advantage of ICT-based services and IT-generated economic opportunities. In some societies, Internet cafes and computer training institutes are seen to be male-dominated, which discourages women from obtaining training, accessing information and developing networks. In some settings, women have less control over economic resources such as credit, bank account, or disposable income to purchase mobile phones or pay for information access (e.g., at an Internet cafe).

Literacy levels for women, in some countries, especially in the rural areas, tend to be lower than literacy levels for men. Women's enrollment in professional and technological education are even lower in most parts of the world. Women constituted only 1.6 percent of all engineering students in Kenya and 2.1 percent in Ghana.

Throughout the IT industry in developing countries, women are concentrated in routine jobs at lower levels and lower salaries than men. For example, women constitute a disproportionately high number of employees in call center services, data entry, and programming, but there are very few women at the managerial levels.

Where urban-rural infrastructure gaps are wide, as in many developing countries, men have more mobility and migrate in larger numbers to urban areas where they have better access to ICTs. Women on the other hand often lack such mobility, which further limits their access to ICTs. Emerging projects on gender and ICT: The World Bank is supporting ICT-based social entrepreneurial projects. Good examples of projects on gender and ICTs, by the World Bank and other organizations include: Tianjin Women's Business Incubator: Supported by the Information for Development Program (infoDev), a multi-donor grant facility of the World Bank, the Tianjin Women's Business Incubator is a non-profit organization in Tianjin, China. It provides business start up training for women who are retrenched as a result of China's the industrial modernization, especially in the industries related to textiles and garment manufacturing. In addition to training on income-generating skills, these women receive training on basic ICT skills such as e-mail, Internet, online searches, and e-commerce.

Bank grant award, DDD is a self sustainable co-operative which employs disenfranchised women and youth to provide data outsourcing services to global clients. DDD has created data entry outsourcing centers in the villages around Phnom Penh which only hire those youth who are especially vulnerable, such as orphans, the physically disabled, landmine victims, and trafficked women.

A new social group that is currently being brought under the umbrella of DDD is the female labor force that has been retrenched by the shrinking garment industry of Cambodia. A second outsourcing center is being established in Batambang, the second largest city of Cambodia, which houses a large garment industry. The social enterprise has already proven a success in terms of financial self-sufficiency. Tortas Peru is a women-owned enterprise that uses the Internet to reach a wider market, selling cakes and desserts through their website, mainly targeting the two million Peruvians living outside the country, who send orders by e-mail. With just three hours of instructions, the housewives of the network learn to use e-mail, find the website, and interact with clients through public computer booths.

Mongolia Telecom (MT) is a recently privatized public sector enterprise, which offers various services in the telecommunications sector. More than half of its 4,500 employees are women. To enable professional development of women, MT adopted strategies that included participatory training, and incentives for women workers.

Supportive organizational policies helped women to acquire skills that put them on an equal footing with their male counterparts and gave them the opportunity to move up the organizational ladder.

The flexibility of time and space that the ICTs offer might open new avenues for women especially in economies where women's opportunities are constrained by social and cultural bias. NEC Corporation, the leading IT firm in Japan, introduced women-friendly company policies such as training and mentoring systems to help women move into managerial positions. Global IT businesses such as DELL, AT&T, Xerox, Cisco Systems and HP are also changing their recruitment policies to include women at all levels of production and maintenance. This has shown very positive results, and could be replicated elsewhere.

Globalization has changed the world. Commodities are bought and sold across national borders and continents with unprecedented frequency. Unfortunately, one of the hottest commodities in this new world order is young women.

The profits gained from trafficking women exceed $8 billion annually. This is comparable to the lucrative trade in guns and drugs. In addition to the considerable financial gains, there are also fewer risks in trafficking women than in trafficking other illegal goods such as arms, drugs, and endangered species of animals and plants. These factors combined draw many people into the business, including well-established crime syndicates such as the Japanese Yakuza and the Hong Kong Triad.

Law enforcement has generally proved inadequate in combating this problem, both nationally and internationally. This is because of a general perception that trafficked women migrate willingly and allow themselves to be sold. According to Lois Chiang, Assistant Dean at U of T's Faculty of Law, "The impediments [to combating trafficking] are first a lack of understanding of what trafficking is--and this in not purely a legal issue. We need a better understanding of this phenomenon, and this gets intimately tied up with issues around women's agency and women's sexuality."

The causes of trafficking are complex and multifaceted. The intensification of international trade and foreign direct investment was intended to improve the economies of developing countries. Unfortunately, it appears that the opposite has occurred and poverty is rising in many developing countries. Large numbers of women are now leaving their home countries in the hope of finding better wages in developed countries.

In addition, the sexual division of labour has also intensified the vulnerability of young women (aged 15-25) to trafficking rings. Girls are often educated to lower levels than boys and have fewer work opportunities in skilled professions. The jobs available to them are often limited to domestic service and factory work.

The merchandizing of women takes a variety of forms including forced labour, mail-order brides, arranged marriages and slavery-like practices in prostitution. As such, trafficking may be defined as the exploitation of women for their labour, with or without pay and with or without their consent.

Surprisingly, many of the manifestations of trafficking can be found in our own backyard. According to Chiang, "There are many instances of trafficking in women in Canada-both as a domestic issue and a cross-border issue. As a domestic issue, we have seen in the press stories of young girls being deceived or coerced and kept forcibly confined and then raped by either the abductors or others and forced into prostitution. We see similar stories about women being brought over to Canada by traffickers and also forced into prostitution."

EQUALITY OF MEN WOMEN: A NEW REALITY

Over a century ago, and for the first time in the history of revealed religion, Bahaullah, Prophet-Founder of the Bahai Faith, proclaimed the equality of man and woman. He did not leave this pronouncement as an ideal or pious hope but wove it, as a basic factor, into the fabric of His social order. He supported it by laws requiring the same standard of education for women as for men, and equality of rights in society.

Equality of the sexes is, for Bahais, a spiritual and moral standard essential for the unification of the planet and the unfoldment of world order. Without the qualities, talents, and skills of both women and men, full economic and social development of the planet becomes impossible. The world of humanity is possessed of two wings the male and the female. So long as these two wings are not equivalent in strength the bird will not fly. Until womankind reaches the same degree as man, until she enjoys the same arena of activity, extraordinary attainment for humanity will not be realized; humanity cannot wing its way to heights of real attainment.

In the present transition of humanity from adolescence to maturity, signs of this evolving equality can be observed everywhere. In the Bahai view this is hardly surprising, for "As long as women are prevented from attaining their highest possibilities, so long will men be unable to achieve the greatness which might be theirs."

The character of this unique age we are entering is further brought into focus in the following statement from the Bahai BIC Document #93-0405 Writings:

The world in the past has been ruled by force and man has dominated over woman by reason of his more forceful and aggressive qualities both of body and mind. But the scales are already shifting, force is losing its weight, and mental alertness, intuition, and the spiritual qualities of love and service, in which woman is strong, are gaining ascendancy. Hence the new age will be an age less masculine and more permeated with the feminine ideals, or, to speak more exactly, will be an age in which the masculine and feminine elements of civilization will be more properly balanced.

UNITY AND EQUALITY IN THE FAMILY

The Bahai world community has, for more than one hundred years, accepted as truth the principle of equality of the sexes and has understood the importance of implementing this standard in individual, family, and community life. The institution of marriage, the basis of the family in the Bahai community, is part of this process. Before a Bahai marriage can take place the couple, who have freely chosen each other, must obtain the consents of all parents and transmit them to the communitys governing body.

The couple then weds in an atmosphere of loving parental approval and acceptance by the community. With the exchange of vows, in which each partner repeats, "We will all, verily, abide by the Will of God," the newly wedded begin their lives together on a basis of true spiritual unity and equality.

This unity and equality, rooted in the rights and responsibilities of every person before God, unfolds in the family. Here, values and attitudes essential for the development of the individual, the community, the nation, and humanity must be taught from early life. In the Bahai view the family being a human unit must be educated according to the rules of sanctity. All the virtues must be taught the family. The integrity of the family bond must be constantly considered and the rights of the individual members must not be transgressed.... All these rights and prerogatives must be conserved, yet the unity of the family must be sustained. The injury of one shall be considered the injury of all; the comfort of each the comfort of all; the honor of one the honor of all.

Equality in Education and Training

Although both parents share in the overall responsibility of educating the children, the mother is given recognition as the first educator of humanity, and she must be carefully prepared for this task. Her education, in fact, from the Bahai point of view, is more necessary and important than that of man, for woman is the trainer of the child from its infancy. If she be defective and imperfect herself the child will necessarily be deficient; therefore imperfection of woman implies a condition of imperfection in all mankind, for it is the mother who rears, nurtures and guides the growth of the child.

Since Bahais do not separate life into religious and secular compartments, and since faith must be expressed in social action, education for men and women, in all its facts, "holds an important place in the new order of things." For this reason, the education of each child is compulsory. If there is not money enough in a family to educate both the girl and the boy the money must be dedicated to the girls education, for she is the potential mother. If there are no parents the community must educate the child. In addition to this widespread education each child must be taught a profession, art, or trade, so that every member of the community will be enabled to earn his own livelihood. It is also significant that, in the spirit of this new era of human evolution, Bahaullah has "promulgated the adoption of the same course of education for man and woman," making clear that "daughters and sons must follow the same curriculum of study, thereby promoting unity of the sexes."

Contribution of Women to Peace

The Bahai Writings promise that "the entrance of women into all human departments is an irrefutable and incontrovertible question. No soul can retard or prevent it"; that in "no movement" will women "be left behind; that they "will attain in all such a degree as will be considered the very highest station of the world of humanity and will take part in all affairs"; that "when women participate fully and equally in the affairs of the world...war will cease." This contribution of women to the establishment of world unity and peace will inevitably be recognized and developed.

In past ages humanity has been defective and inefficient because incomplete. War and its ravages have blighted the world. The education of woman will be a mighty step toward its abolition and ending for she will use her whole influence against war.... In truth she will be the greatest factor in establishing Universal Peace and international arbitration. Assuredly woman will abolish warfare among mankind.

An Equal Voice

A great responsibility is, however, placed on woman to develop her potentialities fully.

She must make every effort to attain greater perfection, to be mans equal in every respect, to make progress in all in which she has been backward, so that man will be compelled to acknowledge her equality of capacity and attainment.

Certainly the well-being of mankind depends on the development of the potential virtues and abilities of every individual, regardless of race, nationality, class, religion, or sex. For this reason prejudices, which cause division and oppression, are systematically abolished in Bahai community life. A unique administrative system, rooted in the concept of unity in diversity, both insists on education for all members of the community and allows for the immediate assimilation of all those who in the past have been deprived of their rights. The Bahai electoral system, operating by secret ballot, with no nominations or electioneering, encourages universal participation: every adult Bahai is eligible for election to local and national administrative bodies responsible for decision in the conduct of Bahai affairs. The ease with which women, long deprived of equal opportunities, can now be integrated into the life of society, is vividly evidenced by the participation of women in all areas of Bahai community life.

Today, in the Bahai world community, in over 200 nations and territories, women are joining with men in building a global society. Their full contribution toward the establishment of a world civilization is possible, Bahais believe, because of the all-pervasive spiritual power released in this age by Bahaullah, Who has erased all limitations preventing the fulfillment of human potentialities. For in the Bahai view, since this is the century of light, it is evident that the Sun of Reality, the Word has revealed itself to all humankind. One of the potentialities hidden in the realm of humanity was the capability or capacity of womanhood. Through the effulgent rays of divine illumination, the capacity of woman has become so awakened and manifest in this age that equality of man and woman is an established fact.

THE MEDIA AND VIOLENCE AGAINST WOMEN

In a detailed analysis of how the press covered four prominent sex crimes in the USA over the period 1978 to 1990, Helen Benedict concludes: 'During the 1980s and 1990s, the quality of sex-crime coverage has been steadily declining... Rape as a societal problem has lost interest for the public and the press, and the press is reverting to its pre-1970s focus on sex crimes as individual, bizarre, or sensationalist case histories' (Benedict 1992, p. 251). Benedict offers a useful set of suggestions to improve the reporting of sex crimes-covering language, balance, context, focus on attacker rather than victim, and so on. On the specific question of language Ann Jones, author of Next Time, She'll Be Dead: Battering and How to Stop It, gives numerous examples of crime reporting in which women are victims but their attackers' violence is masked in the language of love. Says Jones, 'this slipshod reporting has real consequences in the real lives of real men and women.

It affirms a batterer's most common excuse for assault: "I did it because I love you so much" (quoted in Media Report to Women 1994). It does seem justifiable to suppose that what we see and hear in the media has real consequences in our lives. However the issue of 'media effects' raises many complicated questions which I will not attempt to take up in this short paper. Instead I will approach the question of violence primarily from the perspective of the female consumer. How do women react to the portrayal of violence? It seems fair to conclude that if women are made uncomfortable, anxious or frightened by depictions of violence, then their views deserve to be heard.

In fact, the presentation of violence in the media is an issue which provokes quite divergent reactions between women and men. Women are less likely than men to watch violent programmes and films. And even if they do watch, women may not actually enjoy what they see. In the words of one woman interviewed in a recent British study, 'women don't enjoy watching violence in the way that men do, judging by the popularity of violent films. I don't know any women who get a kick out of watching the after-effects of violence' (Hargrave 1994, p. 20). Research in the USA shows that women (47%) are much more likely than men (24%) to object to the level of violence on television (see 'Marketing to Women' 1993, p. 6). A survey of women viewers in Canada found that violence was what concerned women most about television: 34% selected this from a list of seven items of concern, and 36% said they avoid violent programmes on television (MediaWatch 1994).

In India women were found to have a 'strong dislike for (television) films which show violence, and admit to just waiting for the violent scenes to be over so that they could enjoy the next violent-free scene' (Media Advocacy Group, 1994). Women are also more concerned than men about the possible impact of violent messages. Research in the United Kingdom has shown that 59% of women-compared with 45% of men-would be prepared to give up their freedom to watch violent programmes if it was widely believed that these caused some people to be violent (Docherty, 1990). Of the Canadian women questioned in MediaWatch's 1994 survey, 82% said they believed that violence in the media contributes to violence in society. More informal reports have found that women in many countries around the world express high levels of anxiety about media violence, and groups such as the Tanzania Media Women's Association (TAMWA) and Women's Media Watch in Jamaica have launched campaigns and activities to address the problem (see Davies 1994).

For women who have actually experienced violence, subsequent exposure to scenes of media violence against women-particularly when portrayed as 'entertainment' may be especially painful: 'There are things that bring it back... I can't watch extremely violent things, I just want to turn off because the thoughts start and I just don't want to know' (see Kelly 1988, p. 193). But even if they have not been victims themselves, seeing violence on television is an extremely disturbing experience for many women. Recent audience research in Germany found that more than half of all female viewers are frightened and feel threatened by the kind of violence presented on television (Roser and Kroll, 1995).

Similar findings emerged clearly from an in-depth study in the United Kingdom (Schlesinger et al., 1992) in which women were shown various kinds of violent material, including an episode from Crimewatch UK (a series which reconstructs crimes: the reconstruction used was of a young woman's rape and murder), and the Hollywood film The Accused (which includes a graphic portrayal of gang rape). One of the most striking findings was 'the fear of male violence, particularly of rape. This was generally found across all of the viewers, despite class or ethnicity, as was the concern about the possible impact upon children of viewing violence against women on television. In relation to the rape/murder in Crimewatch and the gang rape in The Accused, group discussions revealed a profound anxiety about personal safety' (op. cit., 166). In the case of The Accused, 'there was considerable concern about the appropriateness of a Hollywood film-essentially premised on entertainment values-as the most suitable vehicle for dealing with this troubling subject... and worries (which) centred upon what-men' were likely to make of this film' (op. cit., 163).

The Center for Media and Public Affairs in the United States analysed the incidence of violence on television over a twenty-four hour day in April 1994.

The number of violent scenes ranged from a low of 71 in the hour between 2 p.m. and 3 p.m., to a high of 295 scenes of violence in the hour from 6 a.m. to 7 a.m. (Kolbert 1994). An eight-country study of television violence in Asia conducted by the Asian Mass Communication Research and Information Centre classified 59% of all the programmes studied as 'violent', with particularly high levels of violence in India, Thailand and the Philippines (Menon 1993b).

George Gerbner, who has studied television violence for the past twenty years, maintains that 'Constant displays of violent power and victimization cultivate an exaggerated sense of danger and insecurity among heavy viewers of television.' Clearly, many of the women in the studies mentioned earlier experience this sense of danger and insecurity. Strong sentiments were also expressed by these women about the extent to which it is acceptable to show representations of violence against women to the general public without adding special safeguards.

Such ideas deserve to be taken seriously, and to enter the public domain so that they become part of the debate on regulation and self-regulation. Satellite communication, by weakening the control of national governments over a growing proportion of media messages and images beamed into their territories from elsewhere, has given this debate a new urgency. But proposals for a global code of practice have been met with general scepticism by the media community (see Shaw 1993). At the national level only a few countries-for example, Australia, Canada and New Zealand-have so far taken a new, tougher stand on television portrayal of violence against women (see Racine 1995; Mills 1995).

The United Nations Declaration on the Elimination of Violence Against Women-which defines the term 'violence against women' as 'any act of gender-based violence that results in, or is likely to result in, physical, sexual, or psychological harm or suffering to women'-certainly provides scope for actions aimed at reducing or eliminating media violence in general, and scenes of violence against women in particular. Here it is important to bear in mind that media depictions of dramatic aggression against women are at one end of a continuum of media images of women which build up from an apparently benign starting point. For instance the educational video Dreamworlds, mentioned earlier, demonstrates how an accumulation of images in which women are presented as submissive objects of male fantasy in music television may contribute to a perception of the ultimate act of sexual violence-rape-as justifiable and 'natural'. At the very least, the development of further materials of this sort should be undertaken with a view to documenting how patterns of media violence against women are constructed, and what their implications may be for the lives of women everywhere.

PORNOGRAPHY AND FREEDOM OF EXPRESSION

Pornography has for many years been a multi-billion dollar international industry. In the United Kingdom alone, œ52 million was earned from the sale of pornographic magazines in 1993 (Davies 1994). Recent developments in the information and communication system have made pornography more widely available than ever before.

For instance television deregulation, combined with transborder satellite channels, has resulted in a tenfold increase in televised pornography over the past decade in Europe, and the demand is escalating (Papathanassopoulos 1994). New information technologies have introduced various forms of 'on-line' pornography. Interactive computer porn is a particularly menacing development. This is quite different from earlier forms, in that the user becomes a participant-a 'doer' of pornography rather than merely an observer. Male fantasy myths about women's sexual availability feature strongly in these products.

In cyberspace and elsewhere, pornographers routinely use 'freedom of speech' arguments to defend their right to distribute material which is nothing other than a violation of women's human right to safety and dignity. In 1986 British Member of Parliament Clare Short tried to introduce a Bill to make illegal the display of naked or partially naked women in sexually provocative poses in newspapers (known in the UK as 'Page 3 girls'). 'Killjoy Clare', as she was dubbed by the Sun newspaper, was accused of 'authoritarianism', of wishing to deprive people of one of their few 'pleasures', of wanting British newspapers to resemble Pravda. Compared with the displays used in hard-core pornography, Page 3 may seem relatively innocuous. But Clare Short received 5000 letters of support for her proposal, the overwhelming majority from women. Twelve women who had been raped wrote that their attackers said they reminded them of a woman on Page 3, or said they ought to be on Page 3 (see Short 1991, p.xxi). Since 1986 one major British tabloid newspaper has abandoned its 'Page 3 girls', but others maintain the practice.

Pornography is a central issue for the women's movement, especially in relation to violence against women. It is regarded by many as the key site of women's oppression. Yet disputes over the regulation of pornography have split women's groups, raising the spectre of censorship-a weapon which could be used against minority groups and against women themselves. In this respect, recent developments in Canada are of note. In February 1992, in a milestone decision, the Canadian Supreme Court upheld a conviction against a pornography dealer and, in so doing, recognised a new definition of obscenity. The Court 'recognised the harms to women, children and society arising from pornography as justifying constraint on the free speech rights of pornographers. The expression found in obscene material, the Court concluded, lies far from the core of the guarantee of free expression' (Easton 1994, p. 178). The Butler decision, as it became known, has had important and not entirely predictable consequences. Women saw it as a huge step forward, opening up the possibility of convictions in other areas of media content which could also be proven to degrade or dehumanise women. But the unforeseen consequence was a crackdown on works by prominent homosexual and lesbian authors and, for a time, Andrea Dworkin-one of America's fiercest opponents of pornography, whose book Pornography: Men Possessing Women was temporarily seized by the Canadian customs.

The regulation of pornography is also a contentious issue for women partly because the term 'pornography' has been confused-even in legal instruments-with the concept of 'obscenity'. The definition of obscenity-filthy, disgusting, indecent-implies a moral judgement with which women may feel uncomfortable. The definition of pornography in most feminist literature follows that of Catharine MacKinnon and Andrea Dworkin: 'the graphic sexually explicit subordination of women through pictures or words' (MacKinnon 1987, p. 176). This perspective shifts the arguments against pornography away from the terrain of morality, towards an interpretation of pornography as a violation of women's rights. Yet even here there are problems. One criticism of the civil rights Ordinances of Minneapolis and Indianapolis, drafted by MacKinnon and Dworkin in the 1980s as a means of regulating pornography, was that terms such as 'sexual objectification', 'degradation', 'subordination'-on which appeal to the Ordinances depended-left too much scope for judicial interpretation and could be used against women. As Carol Smart (1989) argues, traditional judicial attitudes reflect a legal framework which is essentially incompatible with the definitions of feminism, and which cannot accommodate the complexity of feminist arguments. However, Susan Easton (1994) takes the view that-rather like the mainstream media-this is an area of challenge for feminists, who must work to infuse new ideas into established legal frameworks. As one of a number of strategies to deal with pornography, she advocates the enactment of a law to prohibit 'incitement to sexual hatred'.

Of course the polarisation of the pornography debate in terms of 'free speech' versus 'censorship' fails to take account of the fact that freedom of expression is limited in all sorts of ways for most people, most of the time. As A.J. Liebling remarked many years ago, 'Freedom of the press belongs to those who own one'. In today's media context, the aphorism rings particularly true. Eastman points out that the feminist argument against pornography 'is not an isolated assault on free speech rights, but could be seen as a recognition of the difficulty and undesirability of an absolutist position on free speech in a pluralist society' (1994, p. 174). Since they have relatively restricted access to the channels of communication, it is hardly surprising that women's attitudes towards 'free speech' differ from those of men.

For example, a study of attitudes among journalism students in the USA found that the women see the free speech issue from a dual perspective. While they value the operation of a 'free press', they also believe that absolute freedom of expression can be harmful to them and to others. The authors conclude optimistically that if the female students carry their attitudes towards free expression with them into the journalistic work force, 'society may see a somewhat different set of professional values in the future.'

WOMEN AS USERS OF MEDIA AND NEW TECHNOLOGIES

Gender differences in media access are linked with patterns of discrimination in society at large, and with patterns of power relations within the home. In many parts of the world, high female illiteracy rates mean that women have little access to the print media. As for television and radio, women may not always be able to watch or listen to their preferred programmes. Research in countries as different as Mozambique, Zambia, India, the USA and the United Kingdom shows that, in family viewing and listening situations, the decisions of the adult male in the household tend to prevail. Nevertheless, these and other studies show that women are enthusiastic media users. In Egypt certain groups of women are particularly avid television viewers: one study found that 21% of women-compared with 11% of men-spent on average more than four hours a day in front of the small screen (El-Fawal 1991). In a study of relatively low-income, poorly educated women in Nigeria, 96% had access to radio within the household or compound and television was available to 89%. More than two-thirds of the women listened to the radio every day, and just under one-third watched television daily (Imam 1992). In Ecuador, Rodriguez (1990) found th 94% of the working-class women she surveyed had radio in their homes, and over half listened at least three hours a day. In Brazil almost every woman in three low-income areas studied by Tufte (1992) had television in her house, and the women watched an average of three to four telenovelas a day, six days a week.

These Brazilian women's heavy viewing of telenovelas reflects a universal, gendered pattern of media preferences. All over the world men prefer sports, action-oriented programmes and information (especially news); women prefer popular drama, music/dance and other entertainment programmes (see Cooper-Chen 1994; Lull 1988; Sepstrup and Goonasekera 1994). These programme choices are most easily explained in terms of the extent to which women and men are able to identify with various types of media content. One of the most obvious reasons for women's preference for serialised drama, soap opera and telenovelas is the exceptionally high proportion of female characters in such programmes. Nor is it surprising that men favour genres such as action drama which feature powerful, dynamic male characters, or sports and news which revolve almost exclusively around male figures. It is reasonable to wonder what impact these repetitive patterns of gender representation have on the female-and the male-audience. During the 1980s there was a vogue for research into 'women's genres'-soap opera, melodrama, magazines-leading to the conclusion that these could 'empower' women. Recent studies have criticised such claims as being wildly exaggerated, and have focused on the fundamentally conservative and patriarchal frameworks within which these genres operate.

The problem is that in most other types of media content women simply do not see or hear any reflection of themselves, or of their experience of life. Television sports coverage in Europe provides a good example of the ways in which women's media choices are limited. Audience data for six countries in 1992 showed that, in all six, the sporting events most watched by men were football matches (Akyuz 1993). But women watched other sports. In France, the event which got the top female audience-over 8 million viewers, which was higher than the male audience for any sporting event-was women's figure skating at the Winter Olympics. According to the same data, the event which attracted the largest female audience in the United Kingdom was the women's 10,000 meters final in the Summer Olympics, though this reached only 8th place among male audiences. So it is not that women don't like watching sport, but that they like watching different sport. In particular, they like 'women's sport'. Unfortunately for women, the television sports schedules are built around male and not female preferences.

Similarly, news and current affairs programmes reflect a hierarchy of values in which the issues that concern women are given low priority, if covered at all. Recent research with British viewers shows that although women feel ambivalent about the concept of 'women's issues'-believing that once an issue becomes labelled as being of exclusive concern to women, it is in danger of being marginalised-there is also a shared understanding among women about issues that do concern them, and a feeling that these are not given priority in the news media. As one woman put it: 'Women's issues don't always get enough airtime on the so-called serious programmes. They don't have the same weight as world politics-which they should do, because they are about changing society in fundamental ways' (Sreberny-Mohammadi 1994, p. 69).

When asked directly, many women are clear that their preferences are not catered for by the media. In common with women recently surveyed in Canada and Germany (MediaWatch 1994; Roser and Krull 1995), most of those interviewed in Annabelle Sreberny-Mohammadi's research said that women should have more visibility on television, that there should be stronger female characters in drama and entertainment, and that there should be more women of authority in news and current affairs output. The participants felt that more women journalists and more female experts voicing opinions across a variety of issues would act as significant role models for other women, stimulate female interest in public issues, and-perhaps-sometimes speak in the interests of and for women.

The potential of the new information and communication technologies for the advancement of women is considerable. Networking, research, training, sharing of ideas and information-all these could be made infinitely easier through relatively affordable computer-mediated communications such as E-mail, Internet, hypertext and hypermedia (Steffen 1995). However, the obstacles are formidable. Unequal access to computers at school and in the home; highly male-dominated computer languages and operating systems; a hostile environment in which sexual harassment, sexual abuse and pornography flourish; these are just some of the factors which deter women from entering cyberspace. Gender-differentiated data on access to the new technologies are scarce, but those available do indicate that women are more reluctant users than men. In the United Kingdom in 1992 27% of women (compared to 37% of men) owned a home computer. Almost identical figures were reported in 1994 for the USA, where just 9% of women (and 15% of men) also had a computer modem-essential for use of E-mail and Internet. However 46% of women in this survey were dissatisfied with their level of technical know-how, suggesting that women may be frustrated users rather than completely uninterested in the new technologies.

Women comprise only about 10% of the Internet population in the USA. On the other hand Women's Wire-a commercial on-line service-has 90% to 95% female subscribers. Aliza Sherman recommends this kind of service-'providing women-specific information on topics such as women's health, politics, news, technology, business, finance, and family'-as a good starting point for women wary of cyberspace (Sherman 1995, p 26). Dale Spender claims that there are literally thousands of women's groups now on-line, though it seems that most of them are located in-and relatively limited to-North America. An exception is Virtual Sisterhood, described as a 'network for women around the world to share information, advice and experiences' which claims to have links with women's networks in a wide range of countries in Asia and Latin America (op. cit., p. 238). At the international level, the Association for Progressive Communications (APC) is among the most actively involved in supporting women through electronic communication. Women in Latin America as well as Canada and the USA have been using the APC networks for information exchange, and the APC Women's Networking Support Program has provided training workshops for women in Africa and Asia. The presence of a 40-strong all-women APC team at the United Nations Fourth World Conference on Women in 1995 introduced countless women to the possibilities of electronic communication, creating connections-technological and human-which will doubtless flourish in the years ahead.

But despite the hyperbole, it is important to remember that these new technologies are inherently no 'better' than the old ones-print, radio, television etc. For example, to claim-as British scholar Sadie Plant does-that the Internet is an inherently equalizing, non-hierarchical, even liberating communication system seems somewhat overstretched. Already, as Herman Steffen points out, 'large corporations are trying to turn cyberspace into a televised shopping mall where communications is one-way (entertainment) unless the consumer wishes to buy something; if so, he is welcome to communicate by punching in his credit-card number'. In that sense, cyberspace merely provides women with a new terrain on which to wage old struggles.

Bibliography

Azmi, Majaz : *Muslim Wife*, Idara Ishaat-e-Diniyat Pvt. Ltd, New Delhi, 1991.

Benjamin, J.: *Socio-religious Status of Girl Child in India*, New Delhi, Ashish Publishing, 1991.

Bhai, N.: *Harijan Women in Independent India*, Delhi, BR Publishing, 1986.

Bronstein, P. A.: *Teaching a Psychology of People*, Washington, American Psychological Association, 1988.

Bruce, J.: *User's Perspectives on Family Planning: Some Operational and Research Issues*, New York, Population Council, 1983.

Calman, J.: *Toward Empowerment: Women and Politics in India*, Colorado, Westview Press, 1992.

Erikson, E. H.: *Childhood and Society*, New York, W. W. Norton, 1993.

Fine, M.: *Women with Disabilities: Essays in Psychology, Culture, and Politics*, Philadelphia, Temple University Press, 1988.

Forbes, Anna: *Kids with AIDS*, New York, Rosen Pub. Group's Powerkids Press, 1996.

Gandy, O.H., Jr.: *Beyond Agenda Setting: Information Subsidies and Public Policy*, Norwood, New Jersey, Ablex, 1982.

Gilligan, C.: *In a Different Voice: Psychological Theory and Women's Development*, Cambridge, Harvard University Press, 1993.

Jordan, J. V.: *Women's Growth in Diversity*, New York, Guilford Press, 1997.

Kegan, R.: *In Over our Heads: The Mental Demands of Modern Life*, Cambridge, Harvard University Press, 1994.

Leslie, J.: *Toward Empowerment: Women and Politics in India*, Colorado, Westview Press, 1992.

Mahler, Margaret: *The Psychological Birth of the Human Infant,* New York, Basic, 1975.

Medawar, J.: *The History of Family Planning in Britain*, England, Penguin, 1971.

Nariman, H.N.: *Soap Operas for Social Change: Toward a Methodology for Entertainment-education Television*, Westport, Connecticut, Praeger, 1993.

Otsea, K.: *Progress and Prospects: The Safe Motherhood Initiative 1987-1992,* Washington, D.C., World Bank, 1992.

Parker, A.R.: *Another Point of View: A Manual on Gender Analysis Training for Grassroots Workers*, New York, United Nations Development Fund for Women, 1993.

Ross, J.A.: *Family Planning and Child Survival Programs as Assessed in 1991*, New York, Population Council, 1992.

Index

□□□